the Complete Guide to

WRITING
FICTION

the Complete Guide to

WRITING
FICTION

by Barnaby Conrad
and the staff of
the Santa Barbara Writers' Conference

Cincinnati, Ohio

The Complete Guide to Writing Fiction. Copyright © 1990 by Barnaby Conrad. Printed and bound in the United States of America. All rights reserved. No part of this book may be reproduced in any form or by any electronic or mechanical means including information storage and retrieval systems without permission in writing from the publisher, except by a reviewer, who may quote brief passages in a review. Published by Writer's Digest Books, an imprint of F&W Publications, Inc., 1507 Dana Ave., Cincinnati, Ohio 45207. First edition.

94 93 92   5 4 3

Library of Congress Cataloging-in-Publication Data

Conrad, Barnaby
  The complete guide to writing fiction / Barnaby Conrad.
    p.   cm.
  ISBN 0-89879-395-5
  1. Fiction—Authorship.   I. Title.
PN3355.C59   1990
808.3—dc20   90-12287
                                                                  CIP

P E R M I S S I O N S / A C K N O W L E D G M E N T S

The excerpt from *The Secret Life of Walter Mitty* is reprinted by permission. Copyright © 1942 by James Thurber. Copyright © 1970 by Helen Thurber and Rosemary A. Thurber. From *My World—and Welcome to It*, published by Harcourt Brace Jovanovich, Inc.

Excerpt from *How to Write Romance Novels That Sell*, by Marilyn M. Lowery, is reprinted with permission of Rawson Associates, an imprint of Macmillan Publishing Company. Copyright © 1983 by Marilyn M. Lowery.

Excerpt from *The Lake*, copyright © 1947 by Ray Bradbury, copyright renewed 1980, is used with permission of Ray Bradbury.

Excerpts from the "The Short, Happy Life of Francis Macomber," by Ernest Hemingway, is reprinted with permission of Charles Scribner's Sons, an imprint of Macmillan Publishing Company. Copyright © 1936 by Ernest Hemingway; copyright renewed © 1964 by Mary Hemingway.

Excerpt from *The Silence of the Lambs*, by Tom Harris, copyright © 1988. St. Martin's Press, Inc., New York. Used with permission.

The improvised ending for the John Cheever story, written by Tony Haskett, is used with permission of Tony Haskett.

The short story "Larry," by Selden Edwards, is reprinted with permission of Selden Edwards.

Excerpt from *Moving On*, by Larry McMurtry, copyright © 1970 by Larry McMurtry, published by Simon & Schuster, is used with permission of Larry McMurtry.

Excerpt from introduction, *The Writer's Craft*, (Knopf, 1975), copyright © 1975 by John Hersey.

Excerpt from *Storytelling* by John Leggett, copyright © 1988. All rights reserved.

Portions of the article by Marilee Zdenek in Chapter 21 were previously published in *The Right-Brain Experience*, by Marilee Zdenek, McGraw-Hill Book Co., New York, 1983; *Inventing the Future*, by Marilee Zdenek, McGraw-Hill Book Co., New York, 1987; "Right-Brain Techniques: A Catalyst for Creative Thinking and Internal Focusing." *Psychiatric Clinics of North America*, Vo. II, No. 3, September 1988.

Grateful acknowledgment is herewith made to these staff members of the Santa Barbara Writers' Conference who contributed to this book: Ted Berkman, Bill Downey, Phyllis Gebauer, Frances Halpern, Anita Clay Kornfeld, John Leggett, Shelly Lowenkopf, Niels Mortensen, Joan Oppenheimer, S. L. Stebel, Leonard Tourney, Marilee Zdenek.

CONTENTS

"Know something?" Sinclair Lewis said one afternoon in 1947. "We writers have a power not given to anyone else."

As his young secretary, I dutifully responded:

"What's that, sir?"

"We have the power to bore people long after we are dead."

This book is dedicated to helping writers learn how to *not* bore people through the printed word. This is what we've been trying to teach at the Santa Barbara Writers' Conference (SBWC) since its inception so many years ago. Not everyone is able to attend our Conference, or any writers' conference, so this book is meant to help fill a void.

What is a writers' conference anyway?

There are hundreds of conferences throughout the United States, but I can only speak for our own. The SBWC is held during a hectic week in June when 300 aspiring writers (not screened for talent, simply the first to apply) bring work and write assignments for the workshops, exposing their efforts to their peers and expert writers, agents, and publishers for criticism, help, and encouragement. The workshops start at 9:00 A.M. and end at 3:30 P.M. There are lectures at 4:00 P.M. and at 8:00 P.M., and then more workshops, for the sturdy and dedicated, from 10:00 P.M. till 2:00 A.M. after the evening lecture. The afternoon lectures tend to be more on the practical side (Getting an Agent, Self-Publishing, How to Write a Cookbook, Writing the Western, a panel on TV writing, etc.). The evening lectures have featured renowned speakers on various aspects of writing; for example, Stirling Silliphant on screenplays, Irving Stone on biography, Dominick Dunne on novels, Judith Krantz on writing sensual stories, James Michener on research, Alex Haley on autobiography, Thomas Mc-Guane on short stories, Joseph Wambaugh on stories with a crime setting, and so forth. Over the years, we have had an amazing procession of talented authors who have given generously of themselves, told of their struggle to get published, and offered valuable advice to the would-be authors at the Conference. In the following pages, you will find a good sampling from the sessions by some of the famous speakers who have come to our clambake.

But what the students really take away with them and value most at the end of the Conference is what happens in the workshops. These workshops are conducted by twenty-four professionals in their fields, and the aspirants are astonished by the caring, individual attention dealt out by these enthusiastic teachers.

In this book we have barely enough space to address the fiction aspects that are discussed during the week, but the Conference also offers workshops in writing poetry, magazine and travel articles, biography, autobiography, romance, and humor, as well as scripts for the screen, TV, and theater.

Can someone actually learn to write in the space of one frantic week? Of course not. Last year in the middle of the Conference I saw an elderly student leaving in a huff with her suitcase. "Been here four days," she grumbled. "Still not published."

One of our workshop leaders, Entertainment Editor of the *Los Angeles Times*, Charles Champlin, has said: "You can't teach everyone to write; some people are born word deaf the way some people are born tone deaf to music. But I think anyone who has any sensitivity to words can be helped to write better, to get over some of the hurdles, to avoid some of the traps that other people have got into before them."

Many, many writers have found their focus here and some seventy-five books and countless short stories have emerged as a direct result of our Conference. For example, we have little contests during the week which one may enter; Fanny Flagg, an actress, had never written much before, but her three-page entry on "youth" won and was read the final day. An agent encouraged her to enlarge it into a book, and the following year it was the successful novel *Coming Attractions*. She is now finishing her third book.

Though there is no guarantee, good books and stories are born year after year at the Conference. More intangible are the enormous benefits students receive from the feedback from peers and workshop leaders who hammer home the basic principles of fiction that we will delve into in this book.

"There are three rules for writing fiction," Somerset Maugham said. "Unfortunately, no one can agree on what they are."

Begging Mr. Maugham's pardon, there *are* some rules that all writers agree on; you *can* learn to tell a story, and you can pick up a great many shortcuts from other writers whether at a conference or from the written page.

There were no writers' conferences around in my teens when I was starting to apply words to paper. But I had gentle feedback from an elderly neighbor in Hillsborough, California—Stewart Edward White, one of the most successful adventurers and writers of his day (a great influence on the young Hemingway, I've recently learned). And I met the flamboyant William Saroyan who took an interest in me (and named a character in one of his plays Barnaby!) I also subsequently learned a lot from a book called *Characters Make Your Story* by Maren Elwood which is amazingly still around and now out in paperback (published by The Writer). I even studied with Miss Elwood for a few months.

But unquestionably I learned the most from Sinclair Lewis, the first American Nobel Prize-winner in Literature, for whom I worked in Massachusetts as secretary/protégé/companion for six months. With his tutelage and encouragement I finished my first novel, *The Innocent Villa*, and saw it published by Random House. I have since written twenty-two books, a Broadway play, many short stories, and hundreds of magazine articles. I owe a lot to Sinclair Lewis and other writers along the way; not many young writers are as fortunate as I was in finding good professional advice and qualified ears to read their work to. That's why we started the Conference. That's why this compilation was put together for the many dedicated aspirants out there.

This book cannot automatically make you into a Welty or a Steinbeck or a Fitzgerald, but it may contain the helpful advice, mechanics, and tips to help you extract the stories that *are* within you. The stardust, the love of words, the heart and the passion and the compassion must come from you. But we hope this book jogs you and helps you achieve your goals in the skills of Scheherazade—the ancient and eternal and invaluable art of storytelling.

Valuable tips from some of the Conference's guest speakers
Over the years we've had some of America's top writers come to the Conference to speak to the would-be writers.

Why do they do it?

I suppose it's the desire to give something back. They've made it big, but they can remember when they too were unpublished, when they rushed to the mail box every day hoping to find a check and a warm letter, and instead were smacked in the face with one cold rejection after another.

Following each chapter are excerpts from some of the speakers' talks or answers to questions from the audience, ranging from work habits to their favorite books. The fact that they sometimes contradict each other or the material put forth in this book by me or a member of the staff only reinforces the fact that each and every writer is different and that the rules are there to be broken.

How Do You Become a Writer?

A suspect statistic from an unreliable source declares that only one American out of 50,000 reads a book a year, but that two Americans out of 50,000 are writing books.

Why someone becomes a writer could fill several books the size of this one and doesn't concern us here.

How is another matter. Let's go straight to an expert of many decades for some answers.

Ray Bradbury was the first person I invited when we decided to start a writers' conference in Santa Barbara back in 1972, and he has returned every year since to share his joy of living and his love affair with writing.

While most people think of Ray as Mr. Science Fiction because of his landmark books like *The Martian Chronicles* and *Illustrated Man*, he has written in virtually every genre and medium from detective novels to plays to screenplays to teleplays. And always the short stories— hundreds of them—many "normal," many science fiction, but dozens defying categorizing.

Here he addresses the subject of writing in general, the way he does when he visits the different workshops at the Conference:

How does one go about becoming a writer?

Well, you might as well ask, how do you go about becoming a human, whatever *that* is! You go about being a sci-fi writer or historical fiction writer or romance writer or mystery writer pretty much the same way you go about being a "normal" writer. We are all, first and last, tellers of stories.

You fall in love, early, with all kinds of things.

I fell in love with books when I was five or six, especially the way books looked and smelled.

I have been a library jackdaw all of my life, which means I have never gone into that lovely holy place with a book list, but only my beady bright eyes and my curious paws, monkey-climbing the stacks over among the children's, and then again where I was not allowed, burrowing among the adults' mysterious books.

I would take home, at the age of ten, eight books at a time, from eight different categories, and rub my nose in them and all but lie down and roll on them like a frolicsome springtime dog. *Popular Mechanics* and *The Boy Mechanic* were my bibles. The encyclopedia was my open meadow-field where I rambled and muttered: "Curiouser and curiouser!" and lay down with Jules Verne's robot pups only to arise with Edgar Rice Burroughs's Martian fleas.

I have run amuck ever since in libraries and bookstores, with fevers and deliriums.

Hysteria must be your way of life, then, if you wish, any of you, to become writers. Or, for that matter, painters or actors or any other crazy lovely things!

If I emphasize libraries it is because school itself is only a beginning, and writing itself is a continuation. But the meat must be found and fed on in every library you can jump into and every bookstore you can pole-vault through.

Even as I did not prowl there with preconceived lists, so I do not send you there with nice, dry, tame, small indexes of my taste, crushing you with an iron-anvil dropped from a building.

Once you start, the library is the biggest blasted Cracker Jack Factory in the world.

The more you eat, the more you want!

And the more you read, the more the ideas begin to explode around inside your head, run riot, meet head-on in beautiful collisions so that when you go to bed at night the damned visions color the ceiling and light the walls with huge exploits and wonderful discoveries.

I still use libraries and bookstores in the same fashion forty years later. I spend as much time in child's country as I do over the corseted adults'.

And what I take home and browse and munch through each evening should give you a relaxing view of a writer tumultuous just this side of madness.

I may start a night's read with a James Bond novel, move on to Shakespeare for half an hour, dip into Dylan Thomas for five minutes, make a fast turnabout and fasten on Fu Manchu, that great and evil

Oriental doctor, ancestor of Dr. No, then pick up Emily Dickinson, and end my evening with Ross Macdonald, the detective novelist, or Robert Frost, that crusty poet of the American rural spirit.

The fact should be plain now: I am an amiable compost heap. For I learned, early on, that in order to grow myself excellent I had to start myself in the plain old farmyard blood manure. From such heaps of mediocre or angelic words I fever myself up to grow fine stories, or roses, if you prefer.

I am a junkyard, then, of all the libraries and bookshops I ever fell into or leaned upon, and am proud and happy that I never developed such a rare taste that I could not go back and jog with Tarzan or hit the Yellow Brick Road with Dorothy, both characters and their books banned for fifty years by all librarians and most educators. I have had my own loves, and gone my own way to become my own self.

I highly recommend you do the same. However crazy your desire, however wild your need, however dumb your taste may seem to others . . . follow it!

When I was nine I collected Buck Rogers comic strips. People made fun. I tore them up. Two months later, I said to myself: "Hold on! What's this all about? These people are trying to starve me. They have cut me off from my vitamins! And the greatest food in my life, right now, is Buck Rogers! Everyone, outa the way! Git! Runty Ray is going to start collecting comic strips again!"

And I did. For I had the great secret!

Everyone else was wrong. I was right. For me, anyway.

What if I hadn't done as I have done?

Would I ever have grown up to become a writer of science fiction or, for that matter, any kind of writer at all?

No. Never.

If I had listened to all tastemongers and fools and critics I would have played a safe game, never jumped the fence, and become a nonentity whose name would not be known to you now.

So it was I learned to run and leap into an empty swimming pool, hoping to sweat enough liquid into it on the way down to make a soft landing.

Or, to change metaphors, I dropped myself off the edges of cliffs, daring to build myself wings while falling, so as not to break myself on the rocks below.

To sum it all up, if you want to write, if you want to create, you must be the most sublime fool that God ever turned out and sent rambling.

You must write every single day of your life.

You must read dreadful dumb books and glorious books, and let them wrestle in beautiful fights inside your head, vulgar one moment, brilliant the next.

You must lurk in libraries and climb the stacks like ladders to sniff books like perfumes and wear books like hats upon your crazy heads.

I wish for you a wrestling match with your Creative Muse that will last a lifetime. I wish craziness and foolishness and madness upon you. May you live with hysteria, and out of it make fine stories—science fiction or otherwise. Finally, may you be in love every day for the next 20,000 days. And out of that love, remake a world.

Thank you, Ray Bradbury. Now:

Niels Mortensen has been a valuable workshop leader with the Conference since its beginning. A novelist and short story writer, he has been a newspaperman, an advertising executive, has written for radio and TV as well as fiction and nonfiction for many national magazines. He generally devotes his first sessions at the Conference to the basics of writing, such as the following. The fundamentals touched on here will be reiterated and expanded upon and hopefully hammered home throughout this book. Here is, in a sense, a glossary, a brief guideline and a set of definitions by Mortensen for the various ingredients that apply to most all story forms:

Any such outline must, by definition, be simplistic but all of us here—and all knowledgeable writers—will be concerned with these same elements. Each of us may use slightly different terms to define these ingredients and we'll probably think of them in somewhat different ways, but we'll still be talking about the same things.

Some of the ingredients or rules may appear confusing or contradictory—especially when compared with great stories by great writers who break these rules.

But rules are *only* guidelines. Rules are made to be broken, especially by great writers. But the reason we refer to rules and guidelines is because this kind of information (rules and guidelines) can be taught. Great writing cannot be taught. We can all learn to play the piano, but there was only one Horowitz.

Nevertheless, you'll find most great writers apply most of these "rules"—either intuitively, or because they've learned what works.

1. The most important ingredients: ideas — thoughts — concepts
The rest is technique and can be, more or less, learned. Nobody can learn to think like a genius through study. (Shakespeare, Dante, Goethe, Tolstoy, Cervantes, etc.) But it is possible for mortals with ordinary intelligence to *learn* to write creatively and express them-

selves successfully. And to learn to improve those skills through study and by the application of such rules and guidelines as can be taught.

2. Story

A powerful story will carry in spite of weaknesses in all other areas . . . a weak story can be successful, but it must be bolstered by brilliant techniques of characterization, dialogue, description, action, etc.

Therefore, it is best to learn what makes a powerful story and then apply the best techniques available. (The *same ones* you might have applied to bolster a weak story.)

I know of no good, absolute definition of what exactly constitutes a story—it is something that each writer must learn to recognize for himself.

And, like beauty, much has to do with the eye of the beholder. Capote will see a story where Hemingway would not; Eudora Welty will find marvelous stories where neither man would notice material for a postcard, while Salinger wraps the whole thing up in a Banana Fish.

Yet there are certain rules of thumb which can be used to determine whether or not a story is a good one.

The prime ingredient for a good story is conflict.

Whatever the conflict, it must be important to the protagonist. Often a story fails because the conflict is too unimportant—not in a global sense but to the hero or heroine. One pitfall to avoid is the confusion between conflict and bickering. For example, if a husband and wife are having a discussion about how to spend the evening, she might well want to go to a party and he to a movie. They argue back and forth, citing reasons pro and con why one diversion is preferable to the other, but it is a foregone conclusion that they both want to go out somewhere. He might finally agree to the party, but suggest that she take the car and he follow in a short time. This is bickering; the reader recognizes it as trivial, and is bored.

NOW—suppose the reason he wants her to take the car is because he has planted a bomb in it, which will detonate when the ignition is switched on. There, to put it mildly, you have conflict. And the immediate interest of the reader.

3. Characters

Many authorities like Maren Elwood claim that characters make your story. I do not disagree with this point of view, but I suspect there may be a confusion of definitions.

Characters do, indeed, make the story—take TV's "L.A. Law" or the "Bill Cosby Show," for example. But good, strong characters, vitally alive and realized, can yet be set adrift and lost in a weak story.

A powerful story, on the other hand, will sustain weak — even card-board-like characters. This has been abundantly demonstrated by such writers as Louis L'Amour, Zane Grey, Mickey Spillane, stock westerns, mysteries, science fiction, soap opera romances, and so forth.

4. Plot

It is easy to confuse Plot with Story — but they are not at all the same. The Plot is simply the mechanical structure that arranges the Story and gives it a particular form.

This is a very important distinction to be able to recognize.

The Plot of a Story can be tinkered with, turned around, inverted and handled in countless different ways . . . while still telling the same story.

Because the subject of Plot could take up several weeks all by itself, let's use a kind of shorthand by way of explanation.

In order to do this, I'm going to introduce the matter of THEME which is merely a simple way of defining what you are writing about. Themes may be simple or complex — they may define the heart of your Story — they are tools of concept.

SO: The theme chosen might be "good will triumph over evil" . . . "Murder will out" . . . "Incestuous love can be hazardous to your health."

Take the incest theme, for example:

Sophocles told the story of Oedipus using that Theme
O'Neill — *Desire Under the Elms, Mourning Becomes Electra*
Shakespeare — *Hamlet*
James Cain — *The Butterfly*

The Plot of each of these has to do with how these various stories worked out.

For example, in *Hamlet* (I choose it because it is probably the best-known Story, not because it is the best example of the incest Theme — indeed it is only one of several Themes in *Hamlet* and somewhat secondary.) Hamlet learns his uncle murdered his father and married his mother to usurp the throne of Denmark. Hamlet learns of this murder from the ghost of his father.

This is a Plot device. The ghost is a Plot device.

Hamlet might have gotten this information from his mother,

Ophelia, Laertes, or a fly on the wall. None of that would have changed the Story. The ghost was simply a device (and a highly dramatic one, playing on the superstitious, thrilling fears of Shakespeare's audience) to move the Story along.

The Story of *Hamlet* could, by switching the Plot around, have been made into a mystery by having Hamlet and friends put the pieces together à la Perry Mason — and still wind up with the dueling scene . . . instead of the court scenes against the District Attorney. The Story would have remained exactly the same.

5. Action

A story should be told in terms of Action as much as possible. Action is far more powerful than narration or internal dialogue because the reader will tend to *react on an emotional level* to an act — whereas he will tend only to observe and keep a *mental record* of information from which action has been abstracted. Action, and reaction to action, not only advances the plot, it reveals your protagonists' character, their strength and their weakness.

And it is very important to realize that it does not have to be *large* action or *violent* action. But *Show* rather than *Tell.*

A. David sat there, bored, barely listening to his mother.

B. David was a busy man and his mother was old and belonged in a home. And God, how he hated when she pleaded like this.

C. God, he thought, she's old; she's an ugly old woman and why the hell do I have to sit and listen to her senile babbling.

D. Her hair was not yet white, but it was thin on top, like a man's, so she always wore her bedcap. Her voice was a whispering rustle reminding David of mice in dry grass.

E. "David, I'm your mother — not just any old woman. David, at the home they tie me in a chair so I don't fall out. David, I don't fall out — I never fall out. David, they forget about me. They forget about the bathroom, David."

F. And David picked his nose, thoroughly, carefully. Then he rolled the results slowly between his thumb and forefinger until it became a hard little ball he could flick away, before he explored the other nostril.

Not a pretty scene — but the reader was *shown,* not *told,* and one sees the scene and reacts to it.

One of the prime reasons for *plotting* is to arrange the story in ways that allow the writer the best and most logical opportunities of *showing* rather than *telling* his stories.

One more small thing: people sometimes confuse the terms "hook" and "lead." Here, for example is the lead of Alice Munro's moving story *Pictures of the Ice* in the January 1990 *The Atlantic Monthly:*

> Three weeks before he died—drowned in a boating accident in a lake whose name nobody had heard him mention—Austin Cobett stood deep in the clasp of a three-way mirror in Crawford's Men's Wear, in Logan, Ontario, looking at himself in a burgundy sports shirt and a pair of cream, brown, and burgundy plaid pants.

The "hook" is the mysterious drowning, the "lead" is the whole sentence—which leads us nicely into the subject of how to begin your novel or story!

K E Y N O T E R

JAMES MICHENER

Michener was invited to come to the Conference in 1974, but we didn't hear from him. Then a week before the Conference he telephoned from Frankfurt, Germany:

"Is it too late to accept?" he asked. And added: "I can only stay for an hour."

He spoke for three hours—the audience wouldn't let him go—and he stayed at the Conference for four days.

"Writers are divided into several groups," Michener said. "There are those with terribly imaginative minds and others who only have one or two books in them. I myself could probably generate three good books to write any week of my life. So it becomes for me a four-year project of focusing on a long book. When I have finished a job, I have eight or nine possible topics and I think about them every day. Then I begin to thin them down to three or four.

"When I do decide on the book, I spend about two years reading almost casually, feeling the area out. I read very widely and I seldom take notes," he continued, explaining the procedure followed in producing such lengthy books as *Hawaii*, *The Source*, and *Iberia*.

"The second two-year period then begins and I become a tremendously oriented man. I get up early, wash my face, and in three minutes I'm at the typewriter. I stop at noon every day; I try to stop at a point where I'm excited about the book.

"This is an exploratory time, when I do an enormous amount of research on various points.

"I work in large units and I start and work right to the end of it. When I'm through I go back and rewrite it.

"I get in trouble with my typist," he continued, "as I'll change the name of my characters four or five times sometimes. I write on an 'as if' basis, never checking a date, time or anything. I don't want to stop. I'm not doing trivial research at that time.

"When I'm finished I fill in the 'as if' situations. Sometimes I carry them eight months before I get back to checking. I just don't want to be stopped at this period. Sometimes as late as the first typesetting I'm still carrying the as ifs. I know I can find the information. If not, I can rewrite the sentence!"

And then much to the audience's amazement we heard that those millions of words have all been typed with two fingers, and all the corrections on what can be an 800,000-word manuscript are printed in capital letters.

"My typist can't read my handwriting. And sometimes neither can I!"

Then he told the audience that he takes very good care of himself when he is working on a book. He plays a lot of tennis and takes long walks. And he lets absolutely nothing interfere with his seven-day-a-week work schedule.

"During *Hawaii* I did break into my schedule for dental appointments. My dentist didn't work in the afternoons either!"

He admitted that when he hits a snag on the book he's always tempted to take a canoe trip, or go to the Virgin Islands or Hawaii with his wife.

But he doesn't give in. He stays there and slugs it out. He may switch over and work on other parts of the book that interest him.

"All I need is a little room with no diversions. Then I get a good door and set it on bricks. It makes the best desk in the world — all that room to spread papers and books out. I've used up at least six doors so far."

One of the questions asked was, "Do you have a favorite book you have written?" The answer was, "I think the best I've written is *Bridges at Toko-ri*. I like it because in it I came closer to achieving what I wanted than I ever did before or after."

Then he added, "Probably the best I've written are the books nobody here has ever heard about — my books on Asian art."

And about his beginnings as a writer, "I never wrote anything until I was forty years old. I start everything slowly. I was the last boy on our block to discover girls!"

Asked what he would recommend for a summer reading program he replied, "If I were a young person and had a summer ahead of me with not too much time to read, the two books I would read would be *Vanity Fair* and *The Old Wives' Tale.*"

The Way of All Flesh and works of Balzac were the other recommendations.

Beginning

E arly one June morning in 1872 I murdered my father—an act which made a deep impression on me at the time."

Could you read that sentence and not want to read the rest of whatever it might be: story, article, novella, or novel?

Ambrose Bierce wanted to get your attention right away when he began his short story "An Imperfect Conflagration"—and he did!

Your beginning—whether a short story, novel, or even a travel article—is *very* important. That first page may make the difference between whether the editor reads on or not. No matter how great the rest of the piece is, the reader may never get to it. Even famous writers are sometimes guilty of slow beginnings. (Much as I ultimately loved the best sellers *Lonesome Dove* and *Presumed Innocent*, I nearly gave up on both of those novels several times during the first slow 100 pages.) The beginning writer, or at least the unknown writer, cannot afford the luxury of a leisurely start. I believe the first page—maybe even the first paragraph—of a story or a novel should either introduce conflict or hint strongly of conflict to come. A word or two can sometimes be enough to whet the reader's interest.

Which story, for example, would you be most interested in reading? One that began like this:

Their annual picnic was always a peaceful, joyous outing where everyone got along.

or

Usually, their annual picnic had been a peaceful, joyous outing where everyone got along. And, at first, that's the way it was this July 4, 1990.

Implicit in the second example is that the picnic we are reading about was not so peaceful, not so joyous, and everyone didn't get along. Why? We want to read further to find out what went wrong, what the trouble was, what happened.

Trouble!

Stories are about people in trouble. Face it; we don't like trouble in real life, we don't like problems, we don't like conflict, yet we love to *read* about how people cope with trouble: marital trouble, martial trouble, parental trouble, trouble with cops, trouble with crops, people with addictions, people with afflictions, and so forth. We are not necessarily sick these days; that has been true throughout all literature. Who has had more problems than Ulysses in his harrowing ten-year attempt to get home to his wife? Hamlet has trouble, his main problem being that he is required to do the one thing in the world he is incapable of doing: killing a man, his uncle, in cold blood. Huck Finn is beset with one trouble after another, starting with his mean, alcoholic father. Scarlett has trouble from the first of the book till the last, her main problem being how to hang on to her only true love—Tara.

So let your reader know as soon as possible that not only does your hero or heroine have trouble but that the problem is an interesting one. Seasickness, a sore throat, or a hangover are not interesting or serious problems (unless, of course, your protagonist is Captain Ahab, Pavarotti, or Betty Ford).

Stanley Elkin once said that he would never write about someone "who is not at the end of his rope."

And you should suggest that idea as soon as possible in the story.

Beginnings do not *necessarily* have to deal directly with the protagonist's problem.

When Jane awoke that morning, it hit her with a sickening rush—*today is the day I get the results back from my cancer tests!*

That is not a bad beginning, but, as they say in the theater, a little "too much on the nose."

A more indirect or oblique way might be better. Such as:

At breakfast both of them pretended it was just a day like any other. "Coffee, dear?" she asked, and the cup trembled only slightly as she passed it to him.

Sometimes an interesting generality will serve to get the reader's attention, like one of the greatest, Tolstoy's opening of *Anna Karenina:*

Happy families are all alike; every unhappy family is unhappy in its own way.

That is such an arresting thought that we wish to hear more from the person who voiced it, so we read on. As with the opening of Michael Chabon's recent story "Ocean Avenues" in *The New Yorker*:

If you can still see how you could once have loved a person, you are still in love; an extinct love is always wholly incredible. One day not too long ago, in Laguna Beach, . . .

The same with the astute observation by Maugham in the first sentence of *Cakes and Ale*:

I have noticed that when someone asks for you on the telephone and, finding you out, leaves a message begging you to call him up the moment you come in, as it's important, the matter is more often important to him than to you.

And the opening sentences of Maugham's *Painted Veil:*

She gave a startled cry. "What's the matter?" he asked. Notwithstanding the darkness of the shuttered room he saw her face on a sudden distraught with terror. "Someone just tried the door."

There is simply no set or standard way to begin a short story or a novel except for the feeble, generalizing enjoinder: "Start interestingly!"

We're always being advised not to start any tale with static, physical, geographical description, yet F. Scott Fitzgerald does in *Tender Is the Night* and his writing is so beautiful that we are hooked and crave more; we *know* we are in good hands. As we are when we read Thomas Wolfe's lyrical beginning to *Look Homeward, Angel*:

. . . a stone, a leaf, an unfound door; of a stone, a leaf, a door. And of all the forgotten faces.

What does that mean, what is the story going to be about? We haven't the foggiest notion—only that it is *writerly* and that we should continue reading. The same goes for George Orwell's sentence in *Down and Out in Paris and London*:

(A wasp) was sucking jam on my plate and I cut him in half. He paid no attention, merely went on with his meal, while a tiny stream of jam trickled out of his severed esophagus. Only when he tried to fly away did he grasp the dreadful thing that had happened to him . . .

Bizarre, but compelling. We will read on in that story. We need not begin, necessarily, in a bizarre or flashy way (as Robert Coover did in a short story: "In order to get started, he went to live alone on an island and shot himself."):

Here is a somewhat calmer beginning, one that hasn't much to do with the story but which foreshadows events and sets a mood. This is how John Mortimer begins his little novel *Summer's Lease*:

The woman walked round the corner of the house and saw a snake consuming a large Tuscan toad.

The victim was motionless, looking about it only slightly puzzled, blinking, whilst the snake attacked its leg. The toad had the appearance of a fat businessman being done some sexual service by a hard-faced girl on the make and doing his best not to notice. The snake, with its sleek, shiny head and curled body, was long and smartly patterned in grey and black.

The woman, wishing to put an end to this outrage and feeling involved on the side of the toad, picked up a stick. But as she straightened, armed, the nervous snake abandoned its prey and slithered away into the shadows under a fig tree. There it was lost among the wild flowers and in the spring grass. The toad sat on, unafraid, bleeding slightly and blinking into the sun. The woman dropped her stick and stood looking at it, bewildered.

"Mrs. Pargeter." A man came up behind her and she turned towards him. He was dressed in a blue blazer and white trousers as though for some pre-war cruise. The sunlight behind him penetrated the thinness of his ginger hair and polished his scalp.

What is happening?
We don't know.
Who are these people?
We don't know.
Where are they?
We don't know.
All we know is that we see the scene very clearly and — all importantly — we want more. For some reason we are intrigued. We don't have a picture yet of the woman, but we have a small glimpse of her character; not every woman would go to the defense of a toad. Who is the man? We must read on to find out.

And that is the name of the game.

Another way to begin is the sort of low-key, artfully disarming one that Maugham uses in *Moon and Sixpence*.

I confess that when I first made acquaintance with Charles Strickland, I never for a moment discerned that there was anything in him out of the ordinary. Yet now few will be found to deny his greatness.

Hemingway's beginnings are usually good ones, and deceptively simple in the way they engage and hook the reader. Here is the first page of *To Have and Have Not* and it is a model of how to blend setting and conflict. We start *in medias res*, in the middle of things, so we really don't know what is going on, but we are intrigued. Whenever you have characters wanting other characters to do something they don't want to do, you have — *conflict!*

You know how it is there early in the morning in Havana with the bums still asleep against the walls of the buildings; before even the ice wagons come by with ice for the bars? Well, we came across the square from the dock to the Pearl of San Francisco Cafe to get coffee and there was only one beggar awake in the square and he was getting a drink out of the fountain. But when we got inside the cafe and sat down, there were the three of them waiting for us.

We sat down and one of them came over.

"Well," he said.

"I can't do it," I told him. "I'd like to do it as a favor. But I told you last night I couldn't."

"You can name your own price."

"It isn't that. I can't do it. That's all."

The two others had come over and they stood there looking sad. They were nice-looking fellows all right and I would have liked to have done them the favor.

"A thousand apiece," said the one who spoke good English.

"Don't make me feel bad," I told him. "I tell you true I can't do it."

The beginning of your story or novel should be an invitation, a beckoning: "Hey, you're going to like it, you're going to like it, I promise! Come into my parlor and I'll tell you a swell tale!"

The beginning should tease the reader into reading further, as Joyce Carol Oates does in this 1989 story "The Swimmers" from *Playboy* magazine.

There are stories that go unaccountably wrong and become imper-
meable to the imagination. They lodge in the memory like an old
wound never entirely healed. This story of my father's younger
brother Clyde Farrell, my uncle, and a woman named Joan Lunt,
with whom he fell in love, years ago, in 1959, is one of those stories.
    Some of it I was a part of, aged 13. But much of it I have to imag-
ine.

I can't remember the name of Eileen Jensen's story but I shall
never forget her opening line:

She had slept naked all her life, and no one knew it.

Larry McMurtry likes to begin *in medias res*, as in this opening of
his 1989 novel *Some Can Whistle* about a writer's long lost daughter
suddenly entering his life:

"Mister Deck, are you my stinkin' Daddy?" a youthful, female,
furious voice said into the phone.
    I could not have been more startled if I had looked up into
the blue Texas sky and seen a nuclear bomb on its way down. I
was on my south patio, having breakfast with Godwin, watching
the fine peachy light of an early summer morning spread over the
prairies; I had assumed the call was from my agent, who was in
Paris and would soon be swimming up the time zones, hoping to
spawn a few deals.
    "I don't think I stink," I said politely.

It is hard to conceive of a better beginning for a tale of horror and
suspense than Poe's *The Tell-Tale Heart*:

True!—nervous—very, very dreadfully nervous I had been and
am! But why will you say that I am mad? The disease had sharpened my senses—not destroyed—not dulled them. Above all was
the sense of hearing acute. I heard all things in the heaven and
in the earth. I heard many things in hell. How, then am I mad?
Hearken! and above how healthily—how calmly I can tell you the
whole story.

Look how much setting, information, and action E. L. Doctorow
crams into the marathon opening sentence of his 1989 best seller *Billy
Bathgate*:

He had to have planned it because when we drove onto the dock the boat was there and the engine was running and you could see the water churning up phosphorescence in the river, which was the only light there was because there was no moon, nor no electric light either in the shack where the dockmaster should have been sitting, nor on the boat itself, and certainly not from the car, yet everyone knew where everything was, and when the big Packard came down the ramp Mickey the driver braked it so that the wheels hardly rattled the boards, and when he pulled up alongside the gangway the doors were already open and they hustled Bo and the girl upside before they even made a shadow in all that darkness.

You might want to start a collection of your own favorite beginnings. Here are some of mine, some from classics, others just good in themselves. Let's start with Florence Aadland's story of the famous romance between her fifteen-year-old daughter, Beverly, and the womanizing Errol Flynn:

There's one thing I want to make clear right off: my baby was a virgin the day she met Errol Flynn.
> Florence Aadland
> *The Big Love*

There once was a boy by the name of Eustace Clarence Scrubb, and he almost deserved it.
> C.S. Lewis
> *The Voyage of the Dawn Treader*

Cigars had burned low, and we were beginning to sample the disillusionment that usually afflicts old school friends who have met again as men and found themselves with less in common than they had believed they had.
> James Hilton
> *Lost Horizon*

They threw me off the hay truck about noon.
> James M. Cain
> *The Postman Always Rings Twice*

He was born with a gift of laughter and a sense that the world was mad.
> Rafael Sabatini
> *Scaramouche*

They met — Colin and Julie — not very long before they were born.
> Mildred Cram
> *Forever*

You can imagine how this one caught people's attention — one just didn't start novels this way in 1927!

Elmer Gantry was drunk.
> Sinclair Lewis
> *Elmer Gantry*

Last night I dreamt I went to Manderley again.
> Daphne Du Maurier
> *Rebecca*

Helen Brent had the best-looking legs at the inquest.
> James Gunn
> *Deadlier Than the Male*

It was the best of times, it was the worst of times.
> Charles Dickens
> *A Tale of Two Cities*

As Gregor Samsa awoke one morning from uneasy dreams he found himself transformed in his bed into a gigantic insect.
> Franz Kafka
> "Metamorphosis"

None of them knew the colour of the sky.
> Stephen Crane
> "The Open Boat"

This must be the shortest one:

"Tom!"
> Mark Twain
> *Adventures of Tom Sawyer*

It is a truth universally acknowledged that a single man in possession of a good fortune must be in want of a wife.
> Jane Austen
> *Pride and Prejudice*

Now at last the slowly gathered, long-pent-up fury of the storm broke upon us.
Winston Churchill
Their Finest Hour

It was the afternoon of my eighty-first birthday, and I was in bed with my catamite when Ali announced that the archbishop had come to see me.
Anthony Burgess
Earthly Powers

This is one of the most famous openings of one of the most famous stories ever written. (But try counting it out—it is numerically impossible!)

One dollar and eighty-seven cents. That was all. And sixty cents of it was in pennies.
O. Henry
"The Gift of the Magi"

And how could anyone resist reading on after this?

I had this story from one who had no business to tell it to me, or to any other . . .
Edgar Rice Burroughs
Tarzan of the Apes

Lolita, light of my life, fire of my loins. My sin, my soul. Lo-lee-ta: the tip of the tongue taking a trip of three steps down the palate to tap, at three, on the teeth. Lo. Lee. Ta.
Vladimir Nabokov
Lolita

Here is the first sentence of the first novel ever written—*Don Quixote* by Miguel de Cervantes—still perhaps the most read novel in the world:

In a village of La Mancha the name of which I don't care to recall, there lived not so long ago one of those gentlemen who always have a lance in the rack, an ancient buckler, a skinny nag, and a greyhound for the chase.

And this, for exquisite brevity, is from M. F. K. Fisher's *Consider*

the Oyster: "The oyster leads a dreadful but exciting life."
Start your own list. And speaking of beginning, here's a question that's often asked at the Conference as people begin to write novels:
Once you begin, how long should it take to write a novel? It took me five months with revisions to write my best seller *Matador*.

Sinclair Lewis used to take a year. Michener told the conference that he'd spend a year or two on research and a year writing the novel. C.S. Forester (*African Queen*, etc.) never spent more than three months on a novel. Evelyn Waugh was asked by *The Paris Review*:

INTERVIEWER: Did you write those early novels with ease or—
WAUGH: Six weeks' work.
INTERVIEWER: Including revisions?
WAUGH: Yes.

I like the great sportswriter Red Smith's reply when asked how long it took him to write:
"As long as I have."
Figure it this way:
If you write a page a day, you'll have a novel, a short one, in a year. Write 1,000 words a day and you'll have a novel in three months.

Most writers think they're doing well to write 750 good words a day, about three pages. You will have to find your own optimum output. But try to write every day—even if only for a short time—rather than waiting for that big chunk of time that never seems to come.

It's astonishing how the pages mount up if you do one a day.

WILLIAM STYRON

He has come twice to speak at the Conference, the first time shortly after his blockbuster novel *Sophie's Choice* was published.

"In the early seventies I fell into that moment of creative impotence in which something goes haywire with the creative process, and one struggles and struggles with the obdurate word, with the intransigent paragraphs, with the hopelessly unyielding sentence, word, comma—and one wants to give it all up and go to Peru and fish sardines or something like that—anything but write."

These words from the Pulitzer prize winner, William Styron, were readily understood by all the writers in the large audience.

"I'm quite proud to say I've never consulted any therapist of the brain," he continued, speaking of the writer's block that had hit him hard. "But I was on the verge of doing it, so hopeless had my writing situation become. I was desperate. And then one morning in the spring of 1974, I had awakened with something that lies between dream and reverie, or fantasy, and it hadn't happened to me in many years. I don't believe in the metaphysical or spooky. But I saw as vividly as I see your faces out there, on the wall of my Connecticut bedroom, the face of the girl Sophie."

Styron had explained earlier about his very brief encounter with a Polish refugee named Sophie who had a concentration camp tattoo on her arm.

"It was like a mandate," he said about the vision of Sophie. "With absolutely no hesitation whatsoever, my adrenalin shot through my body, and I leaped out of bed, performed some desultory ablutions, went right over to the place where I work. I sat down at 8 that morning and wrote steadily for four or five hours the first part of *Sophie's Choice*."

Writing and the creative process were what Styron was there to talk about, and that's the track he stayed right on.

"I've read a lot about the creative process. It's a mysterious phenomenon. I don't know what makes it work or what makes it malfunction, because it seems to malfunction as often as it works. But I submit to you that there is something utterly mysterious about the unconscious. When, after total blanking out a memory, after almost literally forgetting completely this girl whom I'd known for so many years before, she reappeared to me and I still can't explain it." And four-and-a-half years later, *Sophie's Choice* was published, to stay at the top of the best-seller list for forty-seven weeks.

"I am throwing this out as a commentary on the creative process and the mysteriousness of the dynamics and the strange energies which propel us all who want to be writers to write," he said. "And I submit in addition to this that it is this kind of mystery, rather than any hard definition of what writing is, that makes writing such an enormously fascinating and challenging, and in the end, I hope, triumphant human occupation."

During the question and answer period the subject of loneliness of the writer, which had come up several times in Styron's talk, was brought up. "I don't think there is any way out of it. It's a thoroughly masochistic sort of punishment," he said. "It's self-flagellation. I suppose a lot of it is the desire to flog yourself to the point where the words you put down are as close to the truth as can be. Some writers endure the agonies because they are not willing to settle for second best; they want to be the best every word along the way. I think the loneliness comes out of that struggle."

Being so familiar with the agony of loneliness, William Styron had much to say on the subject. "I'm not a competitive writer, like Norman Mailer wanting to win the track race from his contemporaries, or Hemingway. But I am a writer trying to be the best writer it is possible for me to be. And this imposes a large and lonely responsibility. Loneliness goes with the territory, and there's no way out of it."

He laughed. "I have never written a story in my life that I did not think that, toward the end, I would have to add a suicide note. A lot of it is striving for perfection — the desire to flog yourself to the point where you get as close to the truth as you can."

He added: "People, characters for our stories, are all around us, surprising and strange and wonderful. In the early 1950s I was visiting a friend at his house in Malibu. Staying in the beach house next to us was J. Edgar Hoover. We peeked through the fence and there was the head of the FBI painting the toenails of his longtime male friend."

At the end: "I am a great believer in writers' conferences like this and have nothing but scorn for those who sneer at them."

Characters Will Make Your Story

O kay, you've got the paper in the typewriter, or the word proces-
sor turned on, or the pencil sharpened.
What to write about?
Tom Wolfe observes:

> The young person who decides to become a writer because he has
> a subject or an issue in mind, because he has "something to say," is a
> rare bird. Most make that decision because they realize they have a
> certain musical facility with words. Since poetry is the music of lan-
> guage, outstanding young poets are by no means rare. As he grows
> older, however, our young genius keeps running into this damnable
> problem of *material*, of what to write about, since by now he realizes
> that literature's main arena is prose, whether in fiction or the essay.

I assume you have a story either started or in your mind.

What is your subject? It does not have to be a lofty one—it does
not have to be either about war or about peace or nuclear fission or
voyages to the moon. Remember great works of fiction have grown
out of little more than a stolen bicycle, a burnt sled, a phony necklace, a
madeleine cookie, a stone in a snowball, and a discontented housewife
(Zavattini's *Bicycle Thief*, Orson Welles's *Citizen Kane*, De Maupassant's
"The Necklace," Proust's *Remembrance of Things Past*, Robertson Davies's *The Fifth Business*, and Flaubert's *Madame Bovary*).

Virtually any subject is worthy; *The Color Purple*, theoretically a
"little story" about humble people, touched me more than *Gone with
the Wind*'s big canvas about Southern gentry at war.

A writer should be able to ennoble, or at least dignify, almost any
subject. As Flaubert wrote to a friend:

If the book I'm having such difficulty writing turns out well, I'll have established, by the very fact of having written it, these two truths, which to me are axiomatic, namely: first, that poetry is purely subjective, that in literature there are no beautiful subjects, and that therefore Yvetot is as good a one as Constantinople; and that consequently one can write about one thing as well as about any other. *The artist must raise everything to a higher level*: he is like a pump; inside him is a great pipe reaching down into the bowels of things, the deepest layers. He sucks up what was pooled beneath the surface and brings it forth into the sunlight in giant sprays.

But even before subject matter you should be thinking: About *whom* do I wish to write? Who are my characters and what are their problems? Because, as we hear time and time again at our Conference:

Characters make your story!

All right, presumably you have your characters in mind. Do you like them or dislike them? More important — will the reader like them or dislike them? That is important!

"They're okay. They're average. They're like a lot of people I know. Like you or me."

Zzzzzz!

Like a lot of people *you* know! But the reader hasn't met these fictional characters yet. And besides, a lot of people we know, I don't want to know, until I get to *know them*. But in a story, a novel, I want to: Either like. Or dislike.

This is important! Pick up a pencil or a pen and physically, actually, write this down:

Making the reader like or dislike the character is generally half the battle. Sometimes, very rarely, as with Raskolnikov in *Crime and Punishment*, we neither like nor dislike the protagonist but we understand him and are *interested* in his fate.

Clear-cut, black or white, for a short story; gradations, mutations, strata, levels of understanding, for a novel.

All right: Introduce me to these friends of yours; I'm going to be spending x-amount of time with them so I want to know whether I like them or not. If I like them I'd like to see more of them, that is, read more about them. You say your heroine wants to earn enough money to send her daughter to a school for the handicapped because the child is a genius in music. I'd like to see how she accomplishes that difficult task especially since she is in a wheelchair herself. Hey, I like her already!

What a strange phenomenon this business of fiction is! If we see someone with a problem in real life we generally try to avoid them; in fiction, we instantly take them to our hearts and want to know all about them and see them reach their goals, whatever they may be.

So your first chore is to decide who your main character is and then set about to make us like or dislike him or her, or at least to become interested in him or her.

But we should know what he or she looks like physically, his or her age and so forth. *How* to do this is what makes one writer different from another. Ludlum will describe a character in a different way than Saul Bellow, Kay Boyle differently than Danielle Steel. Thomas Hardy takes two pages to describe Eustacia Vye in poetic terms where Dashiell Hammett might do it in two hard-boiled lines. Joseph Moncure March in his narrative poem *The Wild Party* sums up a main character, a showgirl, with these lines:

Her body was marvelous
a miracle had fused it.
The whole world had seen it
And a good part had used it.

Browning characterized the speaker *and* the subject in one line in *My Last Duchess* when he had the arrogant duke dismiss his late young wife with the casual words "She had a heart too soon made glad."

Somerset Maugham said that one shouldn't just list all the physical features of a character, just enough to leave the impression of whether the person was attractive or not. (Yet he seldom followed his own advice.)

Here are three very attractive people described in a straightforward, inventorial style by Hemingway. This is the reader's first look at the three protagonists of the famous short story "The Short Happy Life of Francis Macomber." To hell with lyricism or imagery, Hemingway just tells it as it is:

"You've got your lion," Robert Wilson said to him, "and a damned fine one too."

Mrs. Macomber looked at Wilson quickly. She was an extremely handsome and well-kept woman of the beauty and social position which had, five years before, commanded five thousand dollars as the price of endorsing, with photographs, a beauty product which she had never used. She had been married to Francis Macomber for eleven years.

"He is a good lion, isn't he?" Macomber said. His wife looked at him now. She looked at both these men as though she had never seen them before.

One, Wilson, the white hunter, she knew she had never truly seen before. He was about middle height with sandy hair, a stubby mustache, a very red face and extremely cold blue eyes with faint white wrinkles at the corners that grooved merrily when he smiled. He smiled at her now and she looked away from his face at the way his shoulders sloped in the loose tunic he wore with the four big cartridges held in loops where the left breast pocket should have been, at his big brown hands, his old slacks, his very dirty boots and back to his red face again. She noticed where the baked red of his face stopped in a white line that marked the circle left by his Stetson hat that hung now from one of the pegs of the tent pole.

"Well, here's to the lion," Robert Wilson said. He smiled at her again and, not smiling, she looked curiously at her husband.

Francis Macomber was very tall, very well built if you did not mind that length of bone, dark, his hair cropped like an oarsman, rather thin-lipped, and was considered handsome. He was dressed in the same sort of safari clothes that Wilson wore except that his were new, he was thirty-five years old, kept himself very fit, was good at court games, had a number of big-game fishing records, and had just shown himself, very publicly, to be a coward.

"Here's to the lion," he said. "I can't ever thank you for what you did."

Margaret, his wife, looked away from him and back to Wilson. "Let's not talk about the lion," she said.

Vintage Hemingway!

Quite apart from the physical description, as long as we have this section of a classic story at hand, look at some of the subtle touches:

Why does she look at Wilson *quickly*? Hemingway does not use adverbs in a careless or profligate fashion.

She looked at both these men as though she had never seen them before.

This is a good old device, an excuse to tell the reader what the characters look like. Except that here it is valid because she never *has* looked at them this way before, since she's just seen them in action. (Not at all like the durable, effective, and trite device of the mirror: "Not a bad pair of boobs," she thought, "for an old bag of thirty-one.")

That Hemingway story has this classic provocative beginning:

It was now lunchtime and they were all sitting under the double-green fly of the dining tent pretending that nothing had happened.

In that same story we see how sometimes the unsaid can be power-ful. When Mrs. Macomber shoots her husband, Francis, it might have been tempting to describe what a bullet from a high-powered rifle would do to a human skull. Instead, Hemingway has the guide kneel by the corpse and tell the wife simply: "I wouldn't turn him over."

Now let us look at the way Colleen McCullough describes a charac-ter. This is from her lovely novel *Tim*, which she wrote before her blockbuster *The Thornbirds*. It is the touching tale of a very believable love between a middle-aged Australian woman and a young retarded man of great spiritual and physical beauty. Unlike Hemingway, the author here pulls out all the stops in order to convince us of Tim's handsomeness and, more important—much more important—his ef-fect on the protagonist.

A young man was standing bare-headed in the sun, dispassion-ately watching the desecration of Walton Street; from where she stood some twenty feet away Mary Horton gazed at him, dumb-founded.

Had he lived two and a half thousand years before, Phidias and Praxiteles would have used him as a model for the greatest Apollos of all time; instead of standing with such superb lack of self-consciousness in the backwater of a Sydney street to suffer the oblivion of utter mortality, he would have lived forever in the cool, smoothly satin curves of pale marble, and his stone eyes would have looked indifferently over the awed heads of generations upon generations of men.

But here he stood, amid a slushy concrete mess on Walton Street obviously a member of Harry Markham's building crew, for he wore the builder's uniform of khaki shorts with legs rolled up until the lower curve of the buttocks was just visible, the waist-line of the shorts slipped down until they rode his hips. Aside from the shorts and a pair of thick woollen socks turned down over the tops of heavy, clumping workman's boots, he wore nothing; not shirt or coat or hat.

Momentarily turned side-on to her, he glistened in the sun like living, melted gold, legs so beautifully shaped that she fancied he was a long-distance runner; indeed, that was the cast of his whole physique, long and slender and graceful, the planes of his chest as he swung toward her tapering gradually from wide shoul-ders to exquisitely narrow hips.

And the face—oh, the face! It was flawless. The nose was short and straight, the cheekbones high and pronounced, the mouth tenderly curved. Where his cheek sloped in toward the corner of his mouth on the left side he bore a tiny crease, and that minute furrow saddened him, lent him an air of lost, childlike innocence. His hair, brows, and lashes were the color of ripe wheat, magnificent with the sun pouring down on them, and his wide eyes were as intensely, vividly blue as a cornflower.

When he noticed her watching him he smiled at her happily, and the smile snatched Mary Horton's breath from her body in an uncontrolled gasp. She had never gasped so in all her life; horrified to find herself spellbound by his extraordinary beauty, she made a sudden mad dash for the haven of her car.

By contrast, here is all the description we have to go on for the protagonist in Thomas Harris' *The Silence of the Lambs*, a best-selling thriller of 1988:

Behavioral Science, the FBI section that deals with serial murder, is on the bottom floor of the Academy building at Quantico, half-buried in the earth. Clarice Starling reached it flushed after a fast walk from Hogan's Alley on the firing range. She had grass in her hair and grass stains on her FBI Academy windbreaker from diving to the ground under fire in an arrest problem on the range.

No one was in the outer office, so she fluffed briefly by her reflection in the glass doors. She knew she could look all right without primping. Her hands smelled of gunsmoke, but there was no time to wash—Section Chief Crawford's summons had said *now*.

Pretty skimpy, eh? Yet it's enough for the reader for the time being; we can assume from the clues that Clarice is young, active, and probably pretty. The rest of her, the important part, her character, we get from her subsequent dialogue.

A writer like John Cheever can cram a lot of information in a single sentence, such as this devastating one from the short story "The Worm in the Apple": "She was a pretty woman with that striking pallor you so often find in nymphomaniacs."

Some writers wait until well into the story to describe their protagonist in detail. Some start right off, like this first sentence of Saul Bellow's 1989 novel, *A Theft*:

Clara Velde, to begin with what was conspicuous about her, had short blond hair, fashionably cut, growing upon a head unusually big.

A must is to let the reader know the sex and age of the lead character soon; it is most aggravating to get several pages into the story thinking that Evelyn is a pretty young woman only to discover that he is an aging novelist.

Auden said that no two people ever read the same book. It would be an interesting experiment to take, say, ten people and, after all have read a detailed description of the heroine and hero of a novel, have each make up a portrait with the help of one of those skilled police artists who conjure up criminals' faces from descriptions supplied by their victims. It would be revelatory to find out if the ten portraits came close to resembling each other in the slightest. Then the capper, of course, would be to have the author himself see if any turned out close to the person he had imagined.

Even better than a static description—the character just standing there for his or her portrait, as it were—is to describe him while he is *doing* something, like this description of the protagonist in Peter Matthiessen's wonderful adventure novel *At Play in the Fields of the Lord*:

> Wolfie wore habitually, even at night, a black beret, outsize dark glasses, the green fatigues of one or more foreign armies, and a gold earring in his left ear. He had been talking loudly when he lost his footing in the slime and fell, and because he was drunk he continued talking in mid-air and while still on his hands and knees, as if nothing were amiss. He was still speaking as he rose. He was a broad squat powerful man, with big loose hands and a big shaggy beard, a chest like a nail keg, and small feet, and he was tightly sprung; one had the impression that Wolfie, fitted out with rubber soles, could bound five feet straight up into the air from a standing position.

"One had the impression. . . ."

This is a good device! After listing concrete and specific physical details sum up the person in a metaphorical way, some overall impression. For instance, the following is adequate:

> Homer had a resigned, beaten glaze to his eyes as he trotted down the sidewalk after Brunhilda, his wife of thirty years.

But suppose you made the portrait more emphatic and specific by adding this imagery:

> One had the impression of watching a dog being dragged off to the vet's to be neutered.

Eudora Welty's characters are unforgettable. She came to the Conference three years in a row and delighted everyone with her talent and generosity. Among other things, she answered questions about how she creates a character, whether she draws them directly from life, like her famous jazz piano player in the story "Powerhouse." As she wrote in *One Writer's Beginnings*:

> The characters who go to make up my stories and novels are not portraits. Characters I invent along with the story that carries them. Attached to them are what I've borrowed, perhaps unconsciously, bit by bit, of persons I have seen or noticed or remembered in the flesh — a cast of countenance here, a manner of walking there, that jump to the visualizing mind when a story is underway. (Elizabeth Bowen said, "Physical detail cannot be invented." It can only be chosen.) I don't write by invasion into the life of a real person; my own sense of privacy is too strong for that; and I also know instinctively that living people to whom you are close — those known to you in ways too deep, too overflowing, ever to be plumbed outside love — do not yield to, could never fit into, the demands of a story. On the other hand, what I do make my stories out of is the *whole* fund of my feelings, my responses to the real experiences of my own life, to the relationships that formed and changed it, that I have given most of myself to, and so learned my way toward a dramatic counterpart. Characters take on life sometimes by luck, but I suspect it is when you can write most entirely out of yourself, inside the skin, heart, mind, and soul of a person who is not yourself, that a character becomes in his own right another human being on the page.

Here is a sage piece of advice from E. M. Forster regarding "flat" and "round" characters and how you tell the difference:

> The test of a round character is whether it is capable of surprising in a convincing way. If it never surprises, it is flat.

F. Scott Fitzgerald wrote:

> Begin with an individual, and before you know it you find you have created a type; begin with a type, and you find you have created — nothing.

Novelist John Leggett, a mainstay of our conference, adds to the flat-and-round characters discussion:

A well-known fiction editor for a popular magazine once told me that all the storyteller needs to draw a character is an adjective. *Proud* would do for an example. Then, to tell the story, he lacks only a series of situations, in any one of which the character will behave as pride behaves. The reader gets a sense of satisfaction out of the consistency and recognition, while the storyteller has simplified the task of characterization. What the editor was describing was, of course, a *flat* character, and if he was recommending the adjectival method for a protagonist, he was recommending second-rate fiction.

In fiction of quality, the protagonist is likely to be a *round* character. A round character is fleshed out with a great many different traits and qualities. Though the round character may be the central player, flat characters are sometimes necessary to get the best of stories told.

It is the mark of a classic short story that there be but one major character, so complexity will be properly lavished there. Supporting characters had better be kept simple to prevent their stealing the story's focus.

We readers have a limited capacity for meeting new characters and sorting them out. Nothing is more daunting than confronting, early on in a story, a crowd of strangers without a proper introduction. It is worse if their names are similar. To assimilate a character we need a portrait or a situation which stamps that character in our memory.

Try to avoid creating stock characters: Individualize them! Here's what Leggett says about our old friend — or rather, enemy — the stock character:

The stock character is easy to recognize, familiar to us from a lifetime of mediocre entertainment, yet difficult to avoid in storytelling. When a writer sets out to draw a character, it is second nature to reach up onto the shelf of our fictional experience for them.

What a fusty crowd is up there: the villain, the miser, the poor little rich girl, the country bumpkin, the indifferent clerk, the talkative cab-driver. As soon as we encounter one of their traits, say a downeast Maine twang, we can supply the rest of the formula: the man's economy with words, his diligence in mending his roof, his shrewdness and honesty, his suspicion of strangers.

It is their very predictability that makes these characters stale. We know that real people aren't that way. They are endlessly complex and never wholly predictable. What fascinates us and delights us most in fiction is the portrayal of characters who manage to confound our expectations and yet seem true to life.

An effective and economical way of giving an instant picture of a character is to liken him or her to a famous person, someone whose image everyone is familiar with, be it contemporary, historical, or fictional. The device works but it can be abused. It is one thing to write:

> Dolly swept into the nightclub with all the aura and haughtiness of Marie Antoinette entering Versailles.

But it seems too facile and lazy, somehow, to describe a heroine like this:

> She looked exactly like a young Elizabeth Taylor, with her lavender eyes and black hair and big bust.

It would be more acceptable put into dialogue, if a character were to say the same thing, instead of the author's volunteering it:

> "Hey, know something?" said Burt. "You look like this big movie star what'sherface — kinda lavender eyes like yours — y'know, Taylor, Liz Taylor, that's it, no kiddin', hair, figger, and all."

The conceit seems to be most legitimate and works best when used in a historical sense:

> As he arose indignantly from behind his desk, Mr. Chillingworth needed only a toga and some leaves around his bald head to make him a regal and aggrieved Caesar confronting Brutus.

In like manner, how quickly we can picture in our mind's eye the following character:

> Endicott had a toothy Teddy Roosevelt smile and I expected that at any moment he would shout, "Bully!"

Here is another out of the White House:

> Coming into the elegant living room, I saw my future mother-in-law pouring tea, and with her orange cheeks and bushed out white hair all I could think of was how exactly she looked like the Gilbert

Stuart portrait of George Washington which had hung in my schoolroom.

Joseph Wambaugh uses a presidential figure of speech in his 1987 book *Echoes in the Darkness*:

> Joe Van Nort was more rambling and disjointed than Ronald Reagan without a script.

Look how quickly and graphically Mary Higgins Clark sketches in a minor character in her 1989 best seller *While My Pretty One Sleeps*, with this presidential allusion:

> Peter Kennedy, attorney at law, was frequently asked whether he was related to THE Kennedys. He did in fact bear a strong resemblance to the late President. He was a man in his early fifties with hair more rust than gray, a square strong face and rangy body.

My favorite presidential comparison is humorist James Thurber's remark about his boss at *The New Yorker*, Harold Ross:

> He looked like a dishonest Abe Lincoln.

Try to get *that* image out of your mind!
Or this one:

> Fred looked amazingly like Clark Gable—dimpled white smile, flashing dark eyes, and yes, even the big ears. And he was five feet two inches tall.

Comparing fictional characters to familiar images is an accepted literary device; but be wary of clichés; *she had a smile like the Mona Lisa, she was as inscrutable as the Sphinx, his expression was as stony as the Mt. Rushmore faces* don't do much for the reader. If you wanted to use those figures of speech, you would have to freshen them up a bit, perhaps play around with them thusly:

> Olga's smile would start as a suggestion of one, just a shadow of a smile, like the Mona Lisa's, and then suddenly it would burst out into a great dental grin, like one of Franz Hals' euphoric peasants.

And:

Angus, the most inscrutable Scotsman I ever met, looked like an undriven nail with a perpetually expressionless expression on his cadaverous face that by comparison made the Sphinx look like the Greek mask of comedy.

Similarly:

With very little imagination one could imagine the image of actor Stewart Lonsdale, with his thick eyelids, imperious gaze, and leonine head, being right up there on Mt. Rushmore next to the presidents—except that Stewart's face would be leaning a little to the left so as to upstage Abe Lincoln.

Wambaugh manages to combine modern and ancient, real and fictional, images to create a word picture of a minor character in his true murder book of 1987, *Echoes in the Darkness*:

Many a male customer took a gander at Stephanie Smith when she had her back turned. What they'd see was a voluptuous woman in hot pants and white plastic boots, with dyed hair teased and sprayed to the point of fracture. From behind, Dolly Parton. From the front, a hook-nosed hag from *Macbeth*.

There are many ways to help your reader to see and get to know your main characters so that he will care about what happens to those fictional creatures.

In *The Silence of the Lambs*, mentioned earlier, Thomas Harris doesn't directly characterize Clarice Starling, a fledgling FBI agent; he lets another character do it, which is much more effective than having the author's voice intrude. Harris has the brilliant serial murderer Dr. Lecter (who was also in *Red Dragon*, one of the more sinister and interesting villains in modern literature) size up the young woman from his maximum security cell:

When he spoke again, his tone was soft and pleasant. "You'd like to quantify me, Officer Starling. You're so ambitious, aren't you? Do you know what you look like to me, with your good bag and your cheap shoes? You look like a rube. You're a well-scrubbed, hustling rube with a little taste. Your eyes are like cheap birthstones—all surface shine when you stalk some little answer. And you're bright behind them, aren't you? Desperate not to be like your mother. Good nutrition has given you some length of bone, but you're not more than one generation out of the mines, *Officer*

Starling. Is it the West Virginia Starlings or the Okie Starlings, Officer? It was a toss-up between college and the opportunities in the Women's Army Corps, wasn't it? Let me tell you something specific about yourself, Student Starling. . . .

How much more convincing this method is than if the author himself had ticked off a list of Clarice's characteristics and background information.

Never fail to use your secondary characters wherever possible to characterize your protagonist and to further your plot.

What would playwrights have done over the years without minor characters? The curtain goes up:

BUTLER: "We've best get this parlour spick and span wot wif the young master comin' 'ome from the war!"

MAID: "And 'im bringin' home some French floozie he wants to marry and the missus sayin' over m' dead body and all!"

Homer knew the value of characterizing by minor characters. In *The Iliad* the soldiers are grumbling about the war; they've been in Troy ten long years and they want to go back home to Greece. This is the only war in history where both sides knew exactly what they were fighting for—Helen of Troy—but the soldiers are battle-weary and homesick.Then radiant Helen walks by. Wow! The men stare at her unbelievable beauty, then grab their weapons enthusiastically and charge back into the fight, home and hearth forgotten.

Now we have been made to believe that Helen is indeed the most beautiful creature in the world in a way that all the adjectives in the dictionary could not do.

Which would convince you more of a character's goodness? The following:

Old Andrew Huffington seemed a cold aloof man, but actually he was quite kind and did many nice things for people in the town.

Or do you prefer this?

When Andrew Huffington shuffled out of the barber shop, Max growled, "Old sourpuss!"

"Yeah?" said Bill. "When my wife took sick with cancer last year I got an anonymous check in the mail for five grand for her treatment. Saved her life. Just found out yesterday—my daughter works in the bank—she told me who sent it. Huffington! And I barely know the guy."

Obviously the second is more convincing because no conniving, manipulative writer told you about Huffington; you just happened to overhear it at the barber shop.

If the story is told in the first person by the main character, you can use secondary characters to help reveal the main character's looks and personality, but probably your best ally is the protagonist himself. Huck Finn starts right off telling about himself in a folksy, chatty way:

> You don't know me without you have read a book by the name of *The Adventures of Tom Sawyer*; but that ain't no matter. That book was made by Mr. Mark Twain, and he told the truth, mainly. There was things that he stretched, but mainly he told the truth. That is nothing. I never seen anybody but lied one time or another, without it was Aunt Polly, or the widow or maybe Mary.

Already Twain is starting to characterize Huck, one of the immortal figures of American literature. How different in tone from F. Scott Fitzgerald's opening of *The Great Gatsby*:

> In my younger and more vulnerable years my father gave me some advice that I've been turning over in my head ever since.
> "Whenever you feel like criticizing anyone," he told me, "just remember that all the people in this world haven't had the advantages that you've had."
> He didn't say any more, but we've always been unusually communicative in a reserved way, and I understood that he meant a great deal more than that.

Again, this is vastly different from Holden Caufield's freewheeling first-person spiel at the beginning of Salinger's *Catcher in the Rye* and David Copperfield's earnest but slightly stuffy beginning of his life story, but in all of these examples the character starts to emerge because of *what he says*.

When Edgar Allan Poe's murderer in *The Tell-Tale Heart* tries to tell you in the first paragraph that he may be a little "nervous" but he certainly isn't crazy, you know right away that he's totally deranged.

There is nothing wrong with the author's describing the character, of course. As Steinbeck did when he nailed a sturdy blond prostitute with this felicitous phrase: "She mistrusted language as a means of communication."

But after you the author have *told* the reader about your hero or heroine or villain, you must then have them talk and perform and perhaps think in character to reinforce what you have stated about them. And it is not enough to describe a character once at the beginning of a story or a novel, especially a novel, and expect the reader to retain that image all the way through the piece. If at first a character is described as "grossly fat," for example, you can't just say "Well, that's that, I've described him, I'll get on with the story." You have to remind readers, refresh their mind's eye, as it were, periodically throughout the story. Our porcine character should waddle, lumber, wheeze, heave his bulk out of the chair, or stroke his jowls. (I remember one huge character in an English novel who "immensed his way through the crowd," an expressive new verb.)

The best way of characterizing and describing a character physically is for the writer to show him or her in action, doing something, saying something, interacting with another character, while the author supplies us with the necessary physical statistics. The action can be as commonplace as eating, as Trevanian describes in his novel *The Loo Sanction*:

She ate with healthy appetite, both her portions and his, while he watched her with pleasure. Her face intrigued him. The mouth was too wide. The jawline was too square. The nose undistinguished. The amber hair so fine that it seemed constantly stirred by unfelt breezes. It was a boyish face with the mischievous flexibility of a street gamine. Her most arresting feature was her eyes, bottle green and too large for the face, and thick lashes like sable brushes. Their special quality came from the rapid eddies of expression of which they were capable. Laughter could squeeze them from below; another moment they would flatten to a look of vulnerable surprise; then instantly they were narrow with incredulity; then intense and shining with intelligence; but at rest, they were nothing special. In fact, no single element of her face was remarkable, but the total he found fascinating.

"Do you find me pretty?" she asked, glancing up and finding his eyes on her.

"Not pretty."

Before starting to describe your character physically and to characterize him or her, ask youself: Do I really know him or her? For example, what kind of a car would he drive? The person who drives a beat-up Volkswagen with month-old newspapers in the back is obviously not the same person who drives a convertible Mercedes or a Ford pick-up or a 1930 Rolls.

Here's a good test for you to lay on your character: What kind of a letter would he or she write? You might have her write one, for your own information, even though it doesn't figure in your story.

What a person in your story says and does is what reveals character—just as in real life. Dialogue is your most potent weapon (as we shall see in a future chapter). Look how much Arthur Miller accomplishes in the very beginning of *Death of a Salesman* by a simple exchange of dialogue between Willy and his wife. We know a lot about their lives and their characters immediately.

LINDA, *hearing Willy outside the bedroom, calls with some trepidation:* Willy!

WILLY: It's all right. I came back.

LINDA: Why? What happened? *Slight pause.* Did something happen, Willy?

WILLY: No, nothing happened.

LINDA: You didn't smash the car, did you?

WILLY, *with casual irritation:* I said nothing happened. Didn't you hear me?

LINDA: Don't you feel well?

WILLY: I'm tired to the death. *The flute has faded away. He sits on the bed beside her, a little numb.* I couldn't make it. I just couldn't make it, Linda.

LINDA, *very carefully, delicately:* Where were you all day? You look terrible.

WILLY: I got as far as a little above Yonkers. I stopped for a cup of coffee. Maybe it was the coffee.

LINDA: What?

WILLY, *after a pause:* I suddenly couldn't drive any more. The car kept going off onto the shoulder, y'know?

LINDA, *helpfully:* Oh. Maybe it was the steering again. I don't think Angelo knows the Studebaker.

WILLY: No, it's me, it's me. Suddenly I realize I'm goin' sixty miles an hour and I don't remember the last five minutes. I'm—I can't seem to—keep my mind to it.

LINDA: Maybe it's your glasses. You never went for your new glasses.

WILLY: No, I see everything. I came back ten miles an hour. It took me nearly four hours from Yonkers.

LINDA, *resigned:* Well, you'll just have to take a rest, Willy, you can't continue this way.

WILLY: I just got back from Florida.

LINDA: But you didn't rest your mind. Your mind is over-active, and the mind is what counts, dear.

WILLY: I'll start out in the morning. Maybe I'll feel better in the morning. *She is taking off his shoes.* These goddam arch supports are killing me.

Willy and Linda are not stock characters; they are well-rounded individuals. His feet hurt, even as thee and me. This is so important to remember when you are creating people for your fictional fantasies; at times everyone's feet hurt.

Once you have your characters in mind, you, of course, have to give them names. I often call my fictional characters by the names of the people in real life who inspired them, then at the end of the first draft I go through and change them to made-up names.

Naming the baby, as it were, is important and worth some thought. Different names conjure up different images for different people, but most people would agree that Cecil and Butch are vastly different types. (Wait! Maybe Butch was christened Cecil but got teased out of it when he was a kid!)

Going back to *Death of a Salesman*, can you imagine if Arthur Miller had decided to call the two people Charlene and Maurice instead of Linda and Willy? Or Zazu and Robin? Could they have been the same people and said those same lines?

"Call me Ishmael."

Call me Robert? Ringo? Bruce? They don't quite work.

Babbitt seems so right for that character—is it because it rhymes with rabbit? Can you imagine Adolf Hitler with any other name? Or Roosevelt or Churchill? The name should fit: Robert Jordan is a name fit for a hero, Uriah Heep sounds and is villainous, and Kathy Ernshaw is perfect for Heathcliff. (If the latter had had a first name, what would it have been? Certainly not Harold or Clarence or Irving.) Names go in fashions. Mildred, Mabel, and Maude, so popular in my mother's day, have been supplanted by Lisa, Brooke, and Ashley in my daughter's. A character named Maude or Mabel today would probably be a comic one.

And be careful of comic names. There are actual people out there named Flatula, Aspirina, Rhodadendron, and Ima Hogg, but let's keep them out of all but humorous writing.

We know that there really was an Thomas Crapper who made the first flush toilets and that J. Thomas Looney was the first person to say Shakespeare wrote the plays, but resist the temptation to use such extravagant names in your fiction. The right name is so important: For example, J. Wright Ludington, the Third has more money than Muff Potter, Tiger Rafferty would beat Leslie Brooks Phillips Jr. in a fight, and Bootsie Alexander is a lot more fun at a party than her cousin Mildred Butts. Diana Fluck was Diana Dors' real name, Frances Gumm was Judy Garland's, and Cary Grant was really Archie Leach—what contrary images we get when we compare the alternates. Isn't it lucky that Ernest Miller Hemingway wasn't christened Archibald Gumm Fluck—*A Farewell to Arms* and *Death in the Afternoon* by Archibald Gumm Fluck?!

Some summing up about characterization:

Do not choose a boring character for your protagonist. This piece of advice seems so obvious, yet at the Conference we see many stories at whose center is an uninteresting character. They always fail. The character need not be bizarre, not terribly out of the ordinary—he need not be an astronaut, she need not be running for the Senate—Babbit was a salesman and Emma Bovary was a housewife. But they must be interesting for one reason or another.

Sinclair Lewis once told me: "One day I decided to write a novel about the biggest bore who ever lived, called *The Man Who Knew Coolidge*. I succeeded, and it was the most boring book ever written."

What makes a character boring in a story? Probably pretty much the same things that make a person boring in real life. Among other things, a boring character whines and complains repeatedly about his or her situation and talks too much.

Your main character should never feel sorry for him- or herself. Even if he finds himself in Auschwitz. He should make the best of the situation or, still better, he should *do* something about the problems bestowed on him by the author. He should not be passive; a passive protagonist is boring. He should not let things just happen to him. He should make things happen!

He does not have to be educated, but he should think interesting thoughts. For an example, read Huck Finn's convoluted but well-meaning thoughts on slavery.

The protagonist should not be inept; we don't like to read about people who bumble through life, losers who can't cope. They should be good at *something*. Dustin Hoffman in *Rainman* was autistic and almost helpless, but he was a whiz at calculating. Try to imagine that story if he hadn't had that skill, or some comparable skill.

We do not like to read about wimps and doormats — unless it's a The-Worm-Turns story (like Melanie in *Gone with the Wind* when she helps Scarlett shoot the soldier), in which case we revel in the change. A classic case is James Thurber's "The Catbird Seat" wherein Mr. Martin, the mousy clerk, frames his office tormenter. Another is John Cheever's "The Five-Forty-Eight" where the hapless secretary gets her revenge on her heartless seducer.

We like to read about resourceful characters coping with difficult situations: Crusoe alone on his island, Perry Mason up against it in court, Kunte Kinte against the slavers, Santiago versus the giant marlin, Robin Hood against the sheriff's forces, Scarlett in the midst of the Civil War. The list goes on and on.

Someone once wrote that a foolproof story situation was an ordinary person in an extraordinary surrounding or an extraordinary person in an ordinary surrounding (*Alice in Wonderland* being an example of the former, Sheridan Whiteside in *The Man Who Came to Dinner* an example of the latter.)

Let's take a look at a resourceful and sane character in a very difficult situation — a nuthouse. We know from the moment we meet McMurphy (actually, we hear him before we meet him) that he is a mover and a shaker. We are interested in him and his problem instantly and therefore we want to read more of the story, which is, of course, Ken Kesey's *One Flew Over the Cuckoo's Nest*. Here we see the protagonist as seen through the eyes of the narrator, the half-breed Chief Broom:

> But this morning I have to sit in the chair and only listen to them bring him in. Still, even though I can't see him, I know he's no ordinary Admission. I don't hear him slide scared along the wall, and when they tell him about the shower he don't just submit with a weak little yes, he tells them right back in a loud, brassy voice that he's already plenty damn clean, thank you. . . .
>
> He sounds big. I hear him coming down the hall, and he sounds big in the way he walks, and he sure don't slide; he's got iron on his heels and he rings it on the floor like horseshoes. He shows up in the door and stops and hitches his thumbs in his pockets, boots wide apart, and stands there with the guys looking at him.
>
> "Good *mornin'*, buddies."

And, of course, Kesey has just barely begun to describe and characterize McMurphy. Notice how he plays off the minor characters, which he will do all through the book.

Ken Kesey does a masterful job of *individualizing* the many other characters in his book. At the heart of the story is Authority and Conformity in the guise of McMurphy's nemesis, Big Nurse. (To underline the importance of names, try to imagine her being named Dolly Madison, say, or Binky Schwartz, instead of Nurse Ratched.)

Kesey also accomplishes that difficult task of individualizing and characterizing and even letting the reader know what the first person narrator looks like, the wily Chief Broom, a great character who is faking dumbness to fool the staff of the mental institution. Here is the way he—and, of course, we—see Nurse Ratched:

> By the time the patients get their eyes rubbed to where they can halfway see what the racket's about, all they see is the head nurse, smiling and calm and cold as usual, telling the black boys they'd best not stand in a group gossiping when it *is* Monday morning and there *is* such a lot to get done on the first morning of the week. . . .
>
> ". . . mean old Monday morning, you know, boys . . ."
>
> "Yeah, Miz Ratched . . ."
>
> ". . . and we have quite a number of appointments this morning, so perhaps, if your standing here in a group talking isn't *too urgent* . . ."
>
> "Yeah, Miz Ratched . . ."
>
> She stops and nods at some of the patients come to stand around and stare out of eyes all red and puffy with sleep. She nods once to each. Precise, automatic gesture. Her face is smooth, calculated, and precision-made, like an expensive baby doll, skin like flesh-colored enamel, blend of white and cream and baby-blue eyes, small nose, pink little nostrils—everything working together except the color on her lips and fingernails, and the size of her bosom. A mistake was made somehow in manufacturing, putting those big, womanly breasts on what would of otherwise been a perfect work, and you can see how bitter she is about it.

In short order, Nurse Ratched and McMurphy will clash—one more example of how important it is to *show* your characters in action, to present them up against adversity or other characters the way Kesey has here, the way he lets us hear how they talk as McMurphy and Ratched speak in situation after situation, scene after scene.

If you want to get to know your characters better, ask yourself: *"How would they behave in a quarrel?"*

Do they keep their cool? Explode? Try to kill the other person? Attempt to smooth it over? Lie? Come out with terrible truths? Shrivel?

A good experiment: Try out the quarreling bit on the characters in *your* story. You might even end up incorporating the exercise into your novel or short story.

Ken Kesey's book shows once again the importance of characterization. Also (do we dare say it one more time?), that *characters make your story*.

We'll let Norman Cousins, who made such a valuable talk at our Conference some years back, put it in a more eloquent way:

> Too many current novels put situations ahead of people. It is felt, apparently, that characters exist for the purpose of accommodating a plot, thus minimizing the human potential and demonstrating the limitless possibilities of personal shrinkage. This is not the way to write good novels, much less great ones. There is nothing wrong with the audience; it is not true that people find the real world so dramatic that they can see no excitement in the product of a writer's imagination. *Give readers a book with people they care about and they will queue up to shake the author's hand.* (My italics.)

The noted film director Budd Boetticher, author of *When In Disgrace*, once invited a famous producer to view the first rushes of a new film. In the screening room the lights went down and on the screen one saw a speeding car appear at the top of a steep hill. The automobile careened around one curve after another and finally went screaming off the edge of a cliff to crash and explode on the rocks 100 feet below.

The lights in the room came on, and someone exclaimed: "Isn't that the greatest opening of a film ever?"

The producer puffed on a cigar for a moment and then asked: "Who's in the car?"

Then he added: "If you'd only had the young lieutenant kiss his wife and little daughter goodbye before getting in the car and . . ."

Before we start any plotty stuff with our story, any great dialogue, any spectacular action stuff, or any stuff at all, let's ask ourselves one vital question: *Who's in the car?*

It has never been said better.

We mentioned how well Ken Kesey *individualizes* his characters. This should not be confused with *characterizing*, as I learned from Sinclair Lewis. When I once asked him what the difference was, he summed it up thusly: "Let's say your protagonist is a legless man coming down the street propelling himself along on one of those little platforms with wheels. That is individualizing your character in the extreme — how many stories have legless men as main characters? But you have not characterized him yet—he must do that by his speech and actions. For example, if in passing a blind man, he fumbles into his threadbare shirt, finds a quarter, his last quarter, says 'God bless you,' and gives it to the man, he is characterized as well as individualized. If, instead, he curses the blind man, reaches up and steals his pencils and whacks the Seeing Eye dog on the nose, he is characterized as another type of person."

As a little bonus to this chapter, here is a set of rules for writing a story, any "tale," which Mark Twain wrote for his scathing essay, "Fenimore Cooper's Literary Offenses." Twain showed that Cooper (an enormously popular author in his own day) managed to break every single one of them.

1. A tale shall accomplish something and arrive somewhere.

2. The episodes of a tale shall be necessary parts of the tale, and shall help to develop it.

3. The personages in a tale shall be alive, except in the case of corpses, and that always the reader shall be able to tell the corpses from the others.

4. The personages in a tale, both dead and alive, shall exhibit a sufficient excuse for being there.

5. When the personages of a tale deal in conversation, the talk shall sound like human talk, and be talk such as human beings would be likely to talk in the given circumstances, and have a discoverable meaning, also a discoverable purpose, and a show of relevancy, and remain in the neighborhood of the subject in hand, and be interesting to the reader, and help out the tale, and stop when the people cannot think of anything more to say.

6. When the author describes the character of a personage in his tale, the conduct and conversation of that personage shall justify said description.

7. When a personage talks like an illustrated, gilt-edged, tree-calf, hand-tooled, seven-dollar Friendship's Offering in the beginning of a paragraph, he shall not talk like a Negro minstrel in the end of it.

8. Crass stupidities shall not be played upon the reader by either the author or the people in the tale.

9. The personages of a tale shall confine themselves to possibilities and let miracles alone; or, if they venture a miracle, the author

must so plausibly set it forth as to make it look possible and reasonable.

10. The author shall make the reader feel a deep interest in the personages of his tale and in their fate; and that he shall make the reader love the good people in the tale and hate the bad ones.

11. The characters in a tale should be so clearly defined that the reader can tell beforehand what each will do in a given emergency.

A tale can be interesting, the characters believable — but the reader won't read enough of it to find this out if the language of the story is awkward or unclear. To prevent this, Twain's rules require that the author shall:

12. *Say* what he is proposing to say, not merely come near it.

13. Use the right word, not its second cousin.

14. Eschew surplusage.

15. Not omit necessary details.

16. Avoid slovenliness of form.

17. Use good grammar.

18. Employ a simple, straightforward style.

HERBERT GOLD

The Difference Between a Lie and a Short Story
or
There is a Difference Between the Wolf in the Tall Grass and the Wolf in the Tall Story

Everyone tells stories. But there is a difference between people who tell stories that you want to listen to and ordinary dreams or fantasies. What is the difference?

The first thing is that my dreams or your dreams are boring to other people. The chief cause of divorce is not beating or alcoholism, but telling your dream at breakfast. Fascinating as your dream is to you it is boring to everybody else. Yet we love stories. What is the difference?

The difference is that a dream simply expresses a need, a grief, but it has none of the aspects of communication. What a story does is take a dream and make it significant.

Thelma Sideberg wrote of Kafka that he was half insane; but he kept his sanity by telling his dreams. He brought his dreams back as booty from the night.

A writer uses various techniques which we don't use when we are dreaming or we are having fantasies. A lot of people don't understand the difference between dreaming and storytelling or dreaming and lying.

The essence of a story is that it's a lie that tells the truth. It's not just a lie that is told in order to deceive; it's not an operational lie; it's not a lie in order to make someone let up, or not to nag, or not to punish you in some way.

Thus it is a lie that reveals something about the world.

The story has to be told economically. Every word has to count. In the dream it doesn't work that way, but when you write a story every word has to be precious.

Tom Williams wrote a story about the Korean War, in which he wrote a scene that didn't work. His Master Sergeant was up there looking north from the parapet toward the North Koreans and he described the Master Sergeant as being "mean, nasty, and brutal." And I said, "Tom, that doesn't say anything. That tells me what you think of him, but it doesn't tell me anything about him." We talked about getting something to happen that says what he wanted to say, not *telling* it, but making it happen. And Tom being a gifted writer came back the next week and in place of that sentence ". . . mean, nasty, and brutal sergeant was up there . . . ," he had a little bit of dialogue. And it went something like this: "Hey, Sarge, what ya doing up there?" And the sergeant looked back at him and said, "Oh, eatin' chocolate and killin' people."

It takes no more space than the description of his feeling, but it tells you that he's mean, nasty, and brutal. It tells you that he's overweight. It tells you that he's not from Boston. It gives you a part of the country that he comes from, in general, not this town or this state. It tells you that he has a pack of cigarettes rolled up on his upper arm. It hints that he might have a tattoo. And no dialect, the rhythm of the sentence and what he said, the connection of various greeds—a guy who is always shoveling chocolates in his mouth and likes to kill—it's all in one line. And there are no adjectives describing it. That's what a storyteller who is interested in communication, who gets out of his dream and communicates, does.

Unlike a dream, writing is related to the religious act. Greek tragedy came out of the Greek temples. Writing is not just communication, it is also communion.

When I read a story about a misery, like divorce, that I've been through, I feel a little purged. That is Aristotle's notion. He said tragedy—but he meant good writing, good stories, good novels—purges us of pity and terror.

Making Your Characters Work for You

*H*ere is Shelly Lowenkopf, a distinguished editor, writer, and teacher who for years has run the late night sessions at the Conference, the exciting so-called Pirate Workshops which generally go on till two o'clock in the morning. He has some good advice on how to make your characters work for you:

The characters you create must earn their way at all times or they do not belong in your novel, short story, or any of the dramatic formats. After they have gained admission, characters must be watched closely, even suspiciously, to make sure they don't take their status for granted or try to lead a life of leisure.

Nothing can interfere more with the procession of dramatic events in a story than characters who get along well.

Agreement produces stasis and if nothing happens there is no story. Characters may appear to be in accord provided there is some suspicion that the termites of doubt are chomping away at the foundation: then there is a story.

The entire premise of Neil Simon's *The Sunshine Boys* is based on two old vaudeville comedians, once a successful team, who broke up their act because they could no longer stand one another. They have become fashionable again, providing their families, friends, and associates with motives to reunite them. Another example of this vital point is the acrimony to be found in *King Lear*. Imagine a *King Lear* in which the daughters are good friends, love their father dearly, and want him to leave his money to the poor. Tolstoy addresses another facet of this concept in the ominous first line to *Anna Karenina*: "Happy families are all alike; every unhappy family is unhappy in its own way." A work does not begin until the characters, in attack or defense

of some goal which will be revealed later, are on the verge of foment-
ing some kind of revolution, engaging in a running internecine battle
or, better still, are wresting the lead from the author and telling the
story they want told.

Here are some techniques to help you manage your characters,
to keep them at each others' throats and your readers turning your
pages to see what happens next:

**Keep to an absolute minimum all instances where one character
appears alone.** Single-character situations often lack tension or conflict. They germinate such passive conditions as soliloquies, flashbacks,
speculation, large outpourings of background, and author intrusion,
but they do little to advance the story at hand. Shakespeare, who
well understood that two or more characters are needed to bring
excitement to a scene, kept his soliloquies down within the range of
about thirty seconds and then, to prove that rules are made to be
broken, we cite Jack London's masterpiece "To Build a Fire" which
features only one character (and his dog) in its entirety.

Think in terms of scenes. Even in the compact form of the short
story the basic dramatic unit is the scene, an arbitrary span of time in
which characters explore relevant information. In a locale chosen to
provoke menace, opposition, or irony, the scene becomes the arena
in which characters do things to one another, withhold information
from one another, or in some way attempt to pursue a goal. Sometimes they are successful, often they are thwarted. Ideally, each scene
will suggest the next turn of events. Scenes frequently end with the
fate of a character hanging fire, some vital question or issue posed.
Think of the scene as a vehicle, the elevator which is stalled between
floors, carrying two or more characters who are at odds or who have
opposing visions of what is right.

**Scenes are often exchanges of power between two or more char-
acters.** A character who has something another wants has power and
bargaining position that may produce compliance but may just as well
cause intense resentment. A character who wants something must pay
a price or put up with circumstances that are not normally acceptable
but which must now be endured—until something snaps. Remember
the first line of Poe's "The Cask of Amontillado," which relates to one
kind of power, and note how the protagonist, using another kind of
power, manipulates the vanity of his antagonist to bait a deadly trap.
The exchange of power is at the very heart of dramatic tension; it
applies as much to characters who are close (friends, lovers, and
mates) as it does to antagonists who may be demagogues, ideologues,
and miscreants or merely firm in their opposition to the protagonists.
We tend to make ourselves vulnerable to the former and wary of the

latter. By our understanding and judicious use of this concept, we need never lack effective motivation in our characters.

Front-rank characters — protagonists and antagonists — are more workable and interesting as they become less ordinary and agreeable. Memorable characters have goals, attitudes, and qualities which keep them from conventional responses. They are briny, perfervid, driven beings caught up in some quest or vision. In the world of reality, men and women who are successful in the arts and sciences often reveal on close inspection some qualities of eccentricity; some of our favorite writers, poets, and performers have abrasive personalities and are not noted for the harmony of their personal lives or their ability to be good friends. The focus necessary to excel in any endeavor often comes at the expense of conventionality. When creating characters, proceed accordingly. *Les Miserables* would lose most of its bite if a laid-back Inspector Javert limited his pursuit of Jean Valjean to weekends and holidays; there would be no dramatic thrust if Captain Ahab was less than full-throttle in his seek-and-destroy mission against the white whale; there would be no *Maltese Falcon* if Brigid O'Shaugnessey, Caspar Guttman, and Joel Cairo had stopped short of murder and duplicity in their quest for the fabled black statuette.

When you create your major characters, visualize each one applying for a job he or she wants very much but for which he or she is not all that well qualified. Give yourself over to the project. Some characters will be honest and forthright about their qualifications, but you will quickly learn how far others are willing to go to get what they want. At the same time you will learn another key concept: Most front-rank characters have a hidden agenda, some skeleton in the closet, or some secret goal. This is as true of the pestered, beleaguered characters in the James Thurber stories as it is of the heavily fated individuals in the Faulkner novels.

Front-rank characters should have some defect, some conflicting inner polarity, some real or imagined inadequacy. Without his gigantic nose Cyrano de Bergerac would be just another soldier looking for ways to advance his career, not nearly the romantic presence and idealist he is. As it now stands, he was forced to become a superb swordsman and to develop his skills at poetry and satire. He was also given ample opportunity to note how cruel the Fates can be, enhancing his own humanity and romantic image.

Bernard Malamud's novel, *The Natural*, would have been a more conventional and predictable work instead of the moody, surreal outing it became if the protagonist, Roy Hobbs, were attempting to begin a career in major league baseball at an age when most players are fearful that their best days are behind them. Instead, Hobbs had already begun a successful major league career which was tragically foreshortened by an act of senseless violence. Hobbs' goals and attitudes produce a result that goes well beyond a novel about sports and becomes an highly symbolic minor classic.

Matthew Scudder, the private eye creation of Lawrence Block, had a running battle with alcoholism and was told to quit drinking or die. Even so Scudder continued to deny his condition until he experienced a severe blackout in *Eight Million Ways to Die*, where he finally admits his powerlessness over alcohol. Interestingly enough, this was the most successful of all the titles in the Scudder series. A prolific writer, Block did not produce another Scudder title for some years and even then had to resort to a prequel, a story that jumped back to a time before Scudder admitted and attempted to cope with his defect. When Scudder's problem was removed, so was the tense edge.

Another mystery writer, Dennis Lynds, has produced a successful series of novels in which Dan Fortune, who lost his left arm in early manhood, became a private detective. Although there is violence in many of the Dan Fortune adventures, his physical handicap is not for the sake of melodrama and, indeed, Fortune has become notably more cerebral in recent years.

Mark Antony, the soldier, clashed internally with Antony, the lover, in his dealings with Cleopatra, who was herself not free from the same kind of struggle. Not surprisingly, the duty-bound facets of each created a wrenching conflict.

Howard Roark, the protagonist of Ayn Rand's *The Fountainhead*, had a powerful inner conflict between his desire for personal integrity and the need to prevent his visions as an architect from being diluted.

Moral flaws also help produce dimensional front-rank characters. Consider the varied likes of the devious Randal P. McMurphy, in *One Flew Over the Cuckoo's Nest*, Fagin and Bill Sykes in *Oliver Twist*, the ambitious Macbeth, and that paradigm of opportunism, Becky Sharp, in Thackeray's novel *Vanity Fair*. With the possible exception of Sykes (even his dog didn't like him), all had demonstrable consciences, which produced demonstrable conflicts, and concern for their outcome.

Front-rank characters in a long form work should undergo some kind of change. Short stories, one-act plays, and TV sitcoms are more likely to be incidents or episodes in which there is no time for character development. This does not preclude a realization or attitude that may lead to change. A major character who has not learned from his or her experiences is simply not as interesting or convincing as those who have. Longer works allow and even encourage the process of exploring complexity and suggesting a movement in behavior or attitude. What better way for the author to inject some personal message or conviction. The enormously prolific and successful Frederick Shiller Faust, best known for his writings as Max Brand, had a simple formula for dealing with characters: The good become bad and the bad become good. This kind of character development insures effective storytelling and promotes an outcome that is not readily predictable. And having declared that the protagonist must change, we are reminded once again that there are no fixed rules by the thought that Don Quixote, after his long and adventurous journeys, remains the same at the end of the novel as he was in the beginning.

Give your characters worthy opponents. Storytelling is essentially a clash of wills and attitudes, ending with an accommodation that is often minimal and ironic. Admirable protagonists accomplish little or nothing when they prevail over a shallow antagonist, but even a small (and thus more realistic) victory over a peer is significant and satisfying. Tempting as it is to identify with the protagonist all the way through, the effective writer knows that for at least one draft, it becomes profitable and instructive to side with the antagonist for a better understanding of that character's motives. Arthur Laurents was brilliant with this concept in his novel *Turning Point*, in which two dear friends, an aging prima ballerina at the end of her stage career, and a dancing teacher who gave up a career as a ballerina to marry and have a family, are engaged in combat. The reader is scarcely able to determine who is protagonist and who is antagonist. As a consequence, after considerable conflict, the reader loves both.

Let one or more of your characters tell the story. Point of view is important; it keeps the author from intruding, promotes the delicious result of irony, and more directly involves the reader by an artful mixture of ambiguity and indirection. Two such diverse examples as Ring Lardner's short story "Haircut" and Marguerite Duras' novel *The Lover* show the intimate effects of a first-person narration. The former uses a barber to narrate a series of events to a nameless customer, the latter has an older woman telling a story of her youth as though it were a memoir. Multiple point of view allows characters of different attitudes and agendas to present their version of an event, often with hilarious results. Third person point of view allows the writer to portray an event or series of events as though they were happening right now to a group of characters.

Your writing will take an exponential leap forward if you screen your characters with a cynical eye, work them relentlessly, then sit back and record what they tell you.

EUDORA WELTY

It was a surprise to find out that the small, gracious woman with the soft voice was the giant of American literature, Eudora Welty. Famed mystery writer Ross Macdonald ended his introduction by saying, "It seems a kind of miracle that she came from Jackson, Mississippi, to speak to us here in Santa Barbara."

"I'd like to clear the air about symbols," she said at the very beginning. "The novel exists within the big symbol of fiction, not the other way around." And in elaborating: "One way of looking at Moby Dick is that his task as a symbol was so enormous, he had to be a whale.

"Communication is going on when you can believe the writer. Belief doesn't depend upon plausibility, but it's a quality that makes reliability." And at another point she said, "Style is the product of highly conscious effort that is not self-conscious."

During the question and answer period, one woman asked, "What about being a woman and a writer?" And with a shy little laugh came the reply, "It doesn't bother me a bit. I don't really feel limitations in writing as a woman. I feel I can see the point of view of a man. Once you've leaped into looking at the point of view of another person, I don't think it matters whether it's a man or a woman.

"By nature I think I'm a person who writes about the interior feelings in life. Each writing experience is so different. You go through it as though you've never seen it before.

"I don't write autobiographically, because it doesn't fill the bill for me. I can make up characters who can better dramatize what is needed. All characters in novels only live and breathe within the scope you've given them. That isn't the way we live."

F I V E

Characterization Versus Conflict — Which Is More Important?

*W*hile characterization is very important and is ultimately what makes for great literature, your story will go nowhere without that all-important, *sine qua non*, element: CONFLICT (or adversity or trouble or confrontation or whatever you choose to term it).

Let's prove it, by reducing everything to simplistics:

A man and a woman live in a cottage with their baby and a dog. Do we have a story yet?

No.

Why not?

No conflict.

Okay. They go away for the day and leave the child in the care of the dog, a little nervously because there are wolves around.

Do we have a story yet?

Yes. The beginning of one.

Why?

Because of the threat of harm to the baby. *Conflict!*

Is it a nice baby? Doesn't matter—it's a baby, helpless, and there's the vague threat of wolves.

Is the father nice? Does he read Proust, tie fishing flies and empty the garbage? Doesn't matter—his child is threatened, so we like him. Is the mother a fine woman, does needlepoint, crossword puzzles, and belongs to the PTA? We don't know anything about her and it doesn't matter; we empathize with her because she is a mother and, more important, she is potentially in trouble. Is the dog a nice dog? Sure he is—they trust him to guard the baby, don't they? Have we got a story going now? Yes. We have the elements.

Okay, the husband comes home and is greeted at the door by the dog. With bloody jaws. Beyond him the crib is overturned. In a tragic rage the man takes his axe and kills the dog. Then they discover the dead wolf and the alive and well baby. They are at once glad and sad.

Now, in this story—a very, *very* old folktale—we know nothing about the character of the man and the woman, their looks, their age, nothing. No idea even of what the cottage looks like. Yet still we care, don't we? Why? Because there was foreshadowing of conflict, then conflict, then terrible conflict. Added to that there was the gut-wrenching emotion of *injustice* to the dog.

The feeling of *injustice* is one of the first and most potent emotions we feel in childhood and carry into maturity. First it's: "Mommy punished me unjustly!" Outrage! Then: "Jimmy hit Tommy and he didn't do anything!" Ultimately: "They electrocuted Sacco and Vanzetti and they didn't do it!"

No wonder we react to the unjust death of the dog.

You could also write this from the wolf's point of view; you see, he was a *nice* wolf and just wanted to make friends with the dog. A terrible, terrible injustice was done to that wolf.

But that's another story, as Kipling might have said had he thought of it. Meanwhile, think about this very simple little lesson; did you feel some emotion from that brief story? Pity? Anger?

That is what fiction writing is all about: to arouse emotion in the reader. As Sinclair Lewis told me so long ago:

"People read fiction for emotion, not information."

It is up to you to touch that emotion. *Conflict.* Aim for the heart!

Supposing we were to start a story or a novel in this way:

March is a cold and blustery month.

Have I got your interest? I doubt it. Would you go for this?

March in Paris is cold, especially in the early morning.

Hey! I got a flicker of interest from you. Paris! Not a big flicker, but a flicker. Problem is, I don't get very excited about the idea of Paris early in the morning, do you? On the other hand, not a whole lot has been written about cold Paris mornings; maybe it will be more interesting than I thought. On the other hand, maybe I'll watch TV . . .

Let's try a new tack:

It is cold at 6:40 in the morning of a March day in Paris.

Now I am more interested, aren't you? I mean, not exactly grabbed by the throat, but something apparently happened of interest at a specific time in a specific month in an interesting city and maybe, just maybe, I should read on a bit further.

Supposing we add one sentence:

A man is about to be executed.

I think now we would be hooked. But let's look at the complete opening paragraph of Frederic Forsyth's 1971 runaway best seller, *The Day of the Jackal*, to see how deeply he sank the hook and how adroitly:

> It is cold at 6:40 in the morning of a March day in Paris, and seems even colder when a man is about to be executed by firing squad. At that hour on March 11, 1963, in the main courtyard of the Ford d'Jury a French Air Force colonel stood before a stake driven into the chilly gravel as his hands were bound behind the post, and stared with slowly diminishing disbelief at the squad of soldiers facing him twenty metres away.

We are compelled to read further. Are they really going to shoot him? Who is he? Will someone save him at the last moment? We identify with that very human "slowly diminishing disbelief." Forsyth has aroused our *curiosity* via *conflict!*

James Frey, a Conference workshop leader in 1989, maintains in every class that "The three greatest rules of dramatic writing are . . ." (and then he shouts for emphasis), "*Conflict! Conflict! Conflict!*"

Or, as Peter De Vries maintains: "Every novel should have a beginning, a muddle, and an end."

The "muddle" is the heart of your tale.

Now, an execution, as in *The Day of the Jackal*, is a violent act, a rare phenomenon which most of us know nothing about, and hence we are magnetized by a description of it.

But you do not need an act of violence to attract the reader's attention. Conflict does not, necessarily, mean violence. Look at the wonderfully sly way *Madame Bovary* begins; the novel starts not with the protagonist but with her future husband, Charles. He is a little boy and it is his first day of school and he is the butt of all jokes from the other students and the teacher. This is one of the most universal of experiences—we have all had a "first day" in some surroundings which we perceive as hostile and scary. Our heart goes out to little Charles because he is uncomplaining, because of the odds he is up against, and from thenceforward we like him and will follow him willingly to the ends of the earth. Or at least to the end of the novel. We are just as quickly interested in the outcome of Charles' first day in school, perhaps more, as we are in the fate of the man about to be executed in Forsyth's novel.

This amazing but simple process is known as:

Putting a likeable character in a bad situation.

Character plus conflict equals readability!

And I shall repeat endlessly:

Aim for the heart.

Here's workshop leader Joan Oppenheimer summing up some vital elements for writing almost any type of story:

Always remember the 5 C's: character, conflict, contrast, caring, change.

First, stories need a unique, intriguing *character*—credible, interesting, flesh and blood. Readers want someone they can follow gladly for four hundred pages.

Readers want a character they *care* about. That isn't saying this is a person they care *for*. But they must care what happens to this character, whether he wins or whether he loses. Sometimes, they'll hang around just to see him done in, and may cheer when it happens. Wise writers give readers characters they care about. If you as a reader don't give a damn about the people in a book, you aren't going to waste a lot of time reading it.

Let's have *conflict* for a character (have you perhaps heard that before?); that's what makes us turn the pages. There are hundreds of conflicts possible to choose, physical and mental and emotional, and many ways to deal with them.

A short story usually involves only one or two problems and nothing too serious to handle well in a limited number of pages. A book may contain a variety of problems. In modern fiction, it's wise to begin with immediate conflict, certainly on the first page and in the first paragraph or first line if you can get it in there. Try for at least a hint of conflict to come.

Let's have contrast in a book, beginning with *contrast in settings*. I don't want to spend the whole book in somebody's kitchen, somebody's office, even in somebody's bed. No, you don't have to fly me from New York to London to Paris to Tokyo. You don't have to take me from earth to the moon. I'll willingly spend time in one small town or even in one house, for the most part, if something's going on, if I move from place to place, from room to room, as the action continues.

Let's have *contrast in characters*. I don't want a whole bunch of near-saints or a bunch of unrelievedly evil sinners either. People are a blend of good traits and bad. Mix them up and you get a real person, a human being.

A sympathetic character has unsympathetic traits (even as you and I). When he's cranky, he yells at the people he loves. He procrastinates. He exaggerates. He brags on occasion. He tells the same stories over and over. He's sloppy or a compulsive neatnik.

If you draw your character with other, interesting, admirable traits, the flaws only serve to make him lovable and human. People are rarely predictable, always complicated. *Contrast* makes them more interesting as well as more believable.

Villains not only have nasty habits like stealing and beating up on their kids and killing people, they have good traits, as well. The guy who robs a bank and pauses on the way to his getaway car to put some loot in the blind man's cup or help an old lady across the street—hey, he's interesting.

Is a Mafia hit man credible if he's also a sucker for babies and kittens? Well, he could be if he's drawn with care. It would affirm something almost everyone believes, that there's some good in everybody. Works the other way around, too. There's bad in all of us, too. Some of us are merely better than others at hiding our less attractive traits.

So let's have contrasting qualities in every character. Let's have *contrast, too, between characters.* You don't want everybody in the story to have red hair or the ability to tap dance or a passion for strawberry yogurt. You don't want everybody to have the same kind of personality—outgoing or withdrawn—the same dreams or ambitions, the same problems. Mix up your people. Orchestrate your cast of characters. Two totally opposite people play off each other. The result is two characters who seem much more vivid and real than they would if they were alone on the stage without the illuminating definition of contrast.

You're going to want *contrast* in dialogue, too. Every character speaking in a slightly different way, ideally, as people do. Work on contrast in mood, atmosphere, pace. These variations add texture and richness, refreshing the reader, keeping him turning the pages.

Change. Characters must change by the end of a book. People change and are changed by life, by experience, by each other. You aren't the same person you were yesterday, not even precisely the same as you were this morning or five minutes ago. You are changed physically by functions of the body. You are changed mentally, emotionally, spiritually by thought and through every action you take. You are changed by interaction with others.

In the course of a 200-to-800-page book in which a character is born, lives to a certain age and dies, that character inexorably undergoes a lot of changes. In the course of a book that covers only a year, a few weeks, even a few hours, your character still must have grown and changed by the end of the story, must have learned something, must be different in some way—if only in a small, subtle way. He's changed his mind about something: about another person, about himself or about life in general.

Don't overlook the importance of this last element in the list of five c's. Some books fail on this point alone because the main character is the same at the end of the book as in the first pages. In some books, the characters change too much, straining the credibility factor. Again, as in all five of these elements of fiction, it's a matter of balance.

The heroine may note early on that the brakes in the car are getting soft—or hear that the woods surrounding her isolated cabin are dry as tinder. Readers will know there's trouble ahead.

These are blatant, flag-waving plants, but the reader feels clever when he picks up on them, and surprisingly, it doesn't detract from suspense. It adds to it somehow, the reader reading faster now, knowing there's action ahead, trusting the writer to deliver.

In writing, you often plant ideas in the reader's mind in order to make subsequent incidents believable. Readers will believe almost anything if it's consistent with information they've already received.

K E Y N O T E R

ELMORE LEONARD

A character comes along in my story. I introduce a character—I sort of audition my characters—let's see if they work or not. A character might have a speaking part but no name. Until he talks so well I decide I got to do more than give this guy a name, I gotta make this guy a star, and he becomes the third lead. Another character may be thrown out—not thrown out, demoted, just sort of there. The character serves a purpose, but he's just sort of —there.

My favorite characters are the ones who just bust in, fool me.

I'm very conscious of the point of view. Two people, one of them listening, really listening to the other, the other one just talking. I'll try a scene from the man's point of view, then the woman's, then a third person's—pick the best.

What I started to do about 1953 was get up about five o'clock in the morning and I'd write from five on before I went to work writing Chevrolet ads. I'd do two pages, figured a page an hour. I failed in the beginning. At first it took me about two months to get out of bed. Then when I'd get out of bed I'd pick something up and start reading instead of writing. Then I made a rule I couldn't put the coffee on until I'd started to write, at least a paragraph, to get into it. And that way I'd write two pages a day. And maybe at work I'd write sometimes in my drawer, my hands in my drawer and write on my book. Somebody'd come by, I'd get my hands out of the drawer.

I get a kick out of some my recent reviews: "The aesthetic subtext of Leonard's work is the systematic exposure of artistic pretension." *New York Times*.

So there!

But what I'm most happy about is that I'm being recognized for what I set out to do—to tell stories simply and with economy. I can look back at the first story I ever sold thirty-three years ago and I hear the voice I was trying to develop. I knew what I wanted to do even then, but it took years of studying the craft to not only learn but to get the confidence to stay with my approach to writing.

I'm very conscious of the rhythm, of the flow of the words on the page. I like to see a lot of white space on a page. When the story is really moving there's a lot of white space. I want it to be easy to read. I use "he saids" and "she said" mostly for beats, for pauses, rather than for identification. You sometimes want that little pause in time in between lines of dialogue.

A piece in *Time* magazine said that in my books grammar was irrelevant. Actually, it's not irrelevant—it's expendable. Out it goes if it gets in the way. My stories are told from the point of view of my characters–and most of my characters are ungrammatical. I have a real warm feeling for all my characters, even the bad guys, and when I finish a book I often find myself thinking about them, wondering what they're doing, maybe sitting around like mannequins waiting for me.

My most important piece of advice to all you would-be writers: *when you write, try to leave out all the parts readers skip.*

Dialogue

"And what is the use of a book," thought Alice, "without pictures or conversation?"

*I*n our stories and novels we can do without the pictures but we cannot do without conversation. I can think of only one great story where there is no conversation, either spoken or implied, and that is Jack London's "To Build a Fire," (which breaks several rules.)

Dickens said that every author must be an actor—that is, you have to act out the parts your characters play, put yourself in scene after scene in their place, and make them do and say what they would in such a situation.

You know what has to be said, what the reader will want to know about the character, what details are necessary to advance the plot, and dialogue is one of the best weapons in your arsenal to accomplish this. But you must not reveal that this is being done for the reader's benefit. The effect should be that the characters are talking solely to themselves and the reader has just happened onto the scene and is eavesdropping.

Elizabeth Bowen, the British author of such prestigious novels as *The Death of the Heart,* put enormous importance on dialogue. Here are some notes she made, emphasizing that dialogue must (1) further the plot and (2) express character:

Should not on any account be a vehicle for ideas for their own sake. Ideas only permissible where they provide a key to the character who expresses them.

Dialogue requires more art than does any other constituent of the novel. Art in the *celare artem* sense. Art in the trickery, self-justifying distortion sense. Why? Because dialogue must appear realistic without being so. Actual realism—the lifting, as it were, of passages from a stenographer's take-down of a "real life" conversation—would be disruptive. Of what? Of the illusion of the novel. In "real life" everything is diluted; in the novel everything is condensed.

What are the realistic qualities to be imitated (or faked) in novel dialogue?—Spontaneity. Artless or hit-or-miss arrival at words used. Ambiguity (speaker not sure, himself, what he means). Effect of choking (as in engine): more to be said than can come through. Irrelevance. Allusiveness. Erraticness: unpredictable course. Repercussion.

What must novel dialogue, behind mask of these faked realistic qualities, really be and do? It must be pointed, intentional, relevant. It must crystallize situation. It must express character. It must advance plot. During dialogue, the characters confront one another. The confrontation is in itself an occasion. Each one of these occasions, throughout the novel, is unique. Since the last confrontation, something has changed, advanced. What is being said is the effect of something that has happened; at the same time, what is being said *is in itself something happening*, which will, in turn, leave its effect.

Dialogue is the ideal means of showing what is between the characters. It crystallizes relationships. It *should*, ideally, be so effective as to make analysis or explanation of the relationships between the characters unnecessary. Short of a small range of physical acts—a fight, murder, lovemaking—dialogue is the most vigorous and visible inter-action of which characters in a novel are capable. Speech is what characters *do to each other*.

Here is some great dialogue from the seventh century B.C. that Elizabeth Bowen would approve of:

The Laconians were sparing in speech and emotion. A foreign conqueror sent a message: "If I come to Laconia, not one brick will stand on another." The laconic reply was "If."

Like the Laconians, characters should, on the whole, be under- rather than over-articulate. What they *intend* to say should be more evident, more striking (because of its greater inner importance to the plot) than what they arrive at *saying*.

Those last two sentences of Elizabeth Bowen's are very important; commit them to memory. Here's a blatant example of why:

"Jack, old buddy, if I work my way tonight around the superbly trained squad guarding the vital bridge, I could maybe get to one of the stanchions, plant the dynamite, perhaps six or seven sticks, run a long wire back to the river bank, and then detonate it safely."

Jack poured a drink.

"Bill, I doubt if you can pull this feat off safely, given the superiority of numbers of their soldiers, the terrain, and the other factors. I advise strongly against the attempt. Though I wish you good luck, as an old friend of you and your wife, Mary, I hope you talk yourself out of it."

Prolix, stilted, unnatural and lacking in tension! Obviously introduced to inform the readers of facts they must know if the plot is to advance. Terser, tighter, more realistic sounding would be the following, which makes the reader work a little harder in understanding what exactly is going on and hence involves him more in the story.

He suddenly saw the way it could work. Tonight. "I can do it," Bill said.

"The bridge?" Jack snorted a laugh. But he looked worried. "You're out of your gourd, old buddy."

It can work, Bill thought. Sneak around to the right of the hill! When the garrison's at dinner, plant 'em, get out quick. "Six or seven 72's should do it."

"And a long long wire, eh?!" said Bill. "You're out of your gourd."

"I can do it!"

"You're out of your bloody gourd."

"Bill, I know they got a few guys around it—"

"Few? Would you believe two dozen of the best scum they've got?"

"I can do it." Bill thought of Mary. How would she take it? The news of his death.

Jack stood up, poured himself a drink and with a catch in his voice said: "You dumb sonofabitch. Good luck."

For revealing character, there is no substitute for the voices of the characters themselves.

"Voice makes character," says novelist John Leggett.

And voice makes us like or dislike a character the moment he or she speaks. Witness:

"Good morning, Mr. Murdock!" said the secretary cheerily.

"Find me something good about it," growled the old man, "and I'll get you nominated for the Pulitzer Prize."

As contrasted with:

"Good morning," snarled the secretary.

"Young lady," said the old man with a cheery wink, "every morning that I don't wake up with a lily on my chest is a good morning!"

We've met four entirely different people in these two exchanges. What they say and how they say it will characterize the people in your story or novel; by his or her spoken word shall we know them.

The dialogue need not be witty, though that is sometimes called for.

It need not be profound, though that is nice sometimes as long as it doesn't put us to sleep. If a character is termed profound, we must be given the illusion, at least, that he talks profoundly. (Here's where minor characters can come in handy. For example, the other teachers can exclaim over the profundity and reputation of the new professor; thereafter, anything he says will seem oracular.)

In all cases the dialogue must be enhancing the characters' personalities, setting the scene, foreshadowing, or advancing the story. Witty dialogue alone will not justify an entire novel or story; even a comic master like Peter de Vries, with his wonderfully funny dialogue, subordinates the one-liners to his story and character. Oscar Wilde and Noel Coward and Neil Simon are always thinking plot and character, no matter how flimsy the vehicle; the bon mots, witty sallies, and one-liners are icing on the cake.

Despite the axiom that actions speak louder than words, nothing reveals people so much as their utterances. If you can combine the two — especially if they are contradictory — you'll have instant interest:

"Oh, yes, Mrs. Hampton, your little pet will be just fine," the veterinarian purred into the phone cocked on his shoulder; at the same time he was injecting the lethal needle into the poodle's leg and winking at the horrified nurse.

"But there is nothing wrong with that animal!" cried the nurse.

As we have said earlier, if you can make your reader feel like or dislike for a character, you are most of the way there in your characterization. In just two short lines of dialogue in the above example, you have been made to dislike the vet, like the nurse, and feel sorry for the dog and its owner.

How potent, how economical, and how permanent dialogue can

be! That veterinarian could never do anything in the rest of the story to make up for that scene, to make us like him.

In a similar manner, look at how Joseph Wambaugh in *Echoes in the Darkness* nails the slimy and sinister high school principal, Dr. Jay C. Smith:

> Jay Smith had a full, smooth speaking voice and always enunciated crisply. His most dulcet tone was reserved for attractive women.
>
> "Do you use Warriner's *Grammar?*" he asked the young widow as she squirmed a bit. Many women reported feeling that his eyes were always asking lewd questions.
>
> "Yes, I do," she answered, just as his phone rang.
>
> "One moment, my dear," he said and picked up the telephone.
>
> And the teacher started wishing for silver bullets because he was transformed!
>
> "This is *Colonel* Jay C. Smith," he snarled. "And we *will* bivouac at oh five hundred, do you understand?"
>
> Bang went the telephone and just that fast the wolfman disappeared.
>
> It was a velvet frog who said, "Yes, my dear, it's a *very* good grammar book and I'm delighted to see that you think so."

Would you buy a used car from that man? Would you think him capable of murder? That is what the author wants you to think. Notice, incidentally, the fictional techniques Wambaugh employs throughout that passage as he reconstructs a true crime from available facts, adhering loosely to those facts but taking many liberties.

Good dialogue generally has tension, often stemming from the situation. Here is Robert Ludlum, a master of tension and suspenseful dialogue, in a scene from *The Bourne Conspiracy:*

> "Who *sent* you?" asked the Oriental of mixed blood, as he sat down.
>
> "Move away from the edge. I want to talk very quietly."
>
> "Yes, of course." Jiang Yu inched his way directly opposite Bourne. "I must ask. Who sent you?"
>
> "I must ask," said Jason, "do you like American movies? Especially our Westerns?"
>
> "Of course. American films are beautiful, and I admire the movies of your old West most of all. So poetic in retribution, so righteously violent. Am I saying the correct words?"
>
> "Yes, you are. Because right now you're in one."

"I beg your pardon?"

"I have a very special gun under the table. It's aimed between your legs." Within the space of a second, Jason held back the cloth, pulled up the weapon so the barrel could be seen, and immediately shoved the gun back into place. "It has a silencer that reduces the sound of a forty-five to the pop of a champagne cork, but not the impact. *Liao jie ma?*"

"*Liao jie . . .*" said the Oriental, rigid, breathing deeply in fear.

In this passage there is much more dialogue than exposition. One of the questions most asked at the Conference is: "How much dialogue should there be?"

One could answer glibly "fifty percent," but of course it varies from story to story and scene to scene. The writer simply slides into dialogue when the story calls for it, when it is demanded, when it will enhance what is going on; when two or more characters come in contact it is rare that there would be a situation when they would not speak. Some situations, obviously, call for more dialogue than others; there will be more conversation and less action between guests at a cocktail party than between soldiers on a dangerous patrol in a Vietnam jungle.

No one is better at infusing quiet—and sometimes not-so-quiet— tension in the dialogue around action than Elmore Leonard. Here is the classic opening of his *Freaky Deaky*:

Chris Mankowski's last day on the job, two in the afternoon, two hours to go, he got a call to dispose of a bomb.

What happened, a guy by the name of Booker, a twenty-five-year-old super-dude twice-convicted felon, was in his Jacuzzi when the phone rang. He yelled for his bodyguard Juicy Mouth to take it. "Hey, Juicy?" His bodyguard, his driver and his houseman were around somewhere. "Will somebody get the phone?" The phone kept ringing. The phone must have rung fifteen times before Booker got out of the Jacuzzi, put on his green satin robe that matched the emerald pinned to his left earlobe and picked up the phone. Booker said, "Who's this?" A woman's voice said, "You sitting down?" The phone was on a table next to a green leather wingback chair. Booker loved green. He said, "Baby, is that you?" It sounded like his woman, Moselle. Her voice said, "Are you sitting down? You have to be sitting down for when I tell you something." Booker said, "Baby, you sound different. What's wrong?" He sat down in the green leather chair, frowning, working his butt around to get comfortable. The woman's voice said, "Are you sitting down?" Booker said, "I *am*. I have sat the fuck down. Now you gonna talk to me, what?" Moselle's voice said, "I'm suppose to tell you that when you get up, honey, what's left of your ass is gonna go clear through the ceiling."

Yes, there are several sticks of dynamite under Booker's chair set to go off when he gets up, and, as it turns out, he has to go to the bathroom very badly and wants to get up—has to get up—desperately. What reader could resist going on?

Besides being a model of how to begin that sort of a novel, there are other things to be learned from Leonard's excerpt. The voice, for example, the tone of the writing which is set in the first punchy sentence. And look how much we learn about Booker's life and lifestyle in a minimum of words. How simple, how effective the foreshadowing: "Baby, you sound different."

Here is how that one thought could make all the difference in what otherwise would be mundane conversation:

"Good morning, Betty," said the cheery voice on the phone. "How goes it—off to work?"

"Yes, Dorothy, just leaving," she said. "Another day, another dollar. What's with you?"

This kind of idle dialogue, no matter how familiar and true to life, will deter the reader from having the slightest desire to go on reading. Let's borrow a little of Leonard's technique and rewrite that conversation:

"Morning, Betty." The voice on the phone might have seemed cheery to a stranger. Someone who didn't know Dorothy Slack the way Betty did. "Off to work?"

"Another day, another dollar." Then "Dorothy—" Betty hesitated.

"Yes?"

"You sound different."

"Well, I don't know why," came the quick answer. Too quick. What had happened last night after she'd left the house?

The reader's curiosity is aroused by the contradictions. Something is going on. We want to know more.

Notice the words left out of Leonard's beginning, the way people speak in real life, one of his characters' trademarks. They talk with the *whats* gone ("The hell kind of a name was that?" "You talking about?"), a stylized distillation of normal sloppy speech. One of Leonard's characters says: "Jack, what's money? I got enough to last me the rest of my life if·I die Tuesday." Another recalls the advice of the man who taught him how to rob hotel rooms: "Always look nice and always ride the elevator. You run into somebody on the stairs they gonna remember you 'cause you don't see nobody on the stairs as a rule. But a elevator, man, you so close to people they don't see you."

If I were trying to write a tough-guy or suspense novel of any kind, I would read all of Leonard's books. There is a lot to be learned about dialogue and action from them, just as there is from the earlier novels of James M. Cain: *Double Indemnity, Serenade,* and *The Postman Always Rings Twice.*

Robert B. Parker, in his novels about private detective Spenser, also features wise-guy dialogue around brisk exposition. This is from his 1989 book *Playmates* and is typical:

"God," I said, "you're beautiful when you're decisive" . . . I gave her the complete smile. The one where my eyes crinkle at the corners and two deep dimples appear in my cheeks. Women often tore off their underwear and threw it at me when I gave the complete smile. Ms. Merriman didn't.

Spenser's job is to investigate possible point-shaving crimes by some basketball players, but he doesn't get much help from the team coach, Dixie Dunham. "What the f--- are you doing?" Dunham yells when Spenser shows up at the gym. "What a clever way to ask," Spenser replies.

Parker then inserts his obligatory nose-to-nose standoff: "You're a big strong guy," Spenser tells the coach, "and you're probably in shape. But I've been doing this most of my life and if we have a fight I will put you in the hospital." "How many times your nose been broken?" asks the coach, and the usual bravado begins. Parker always removes verbs when his characters talk tough, as in "How much you weigh now?"

If I wanted to write about young swingers of today and learn how some of them talk and think among themselves, I would read Jay McInerney's 1988 novel *Story of My Life.* The dialogue is distressingly realistic. (For a sample, see the chapter on "Point of View.")

Elmore Leonard told our students at the Conference, "All the information you need can be given in dialogue." Here is proof of that in John Collier's short story "Wet Saturday." It begins with a few expository lines to let us know that Mr. Princey "detested his wife, his daughter, and his hulking son," and that Millicent, his cloddish daughter, has done a "shocking and incredibly stupid thing."

Mr. Princey turned from her in revulsion and spoke to his wife.

"They'd send her to a lunatic asylum," he said. "A criminal-lunatic asylum. We should have to move away. It would be impossible."

His daughter began to shake again. "I'll kill myself," she said.

"Be quiet," said Mr. Princey. "We have very little time. No time for nonsense. I intend to deal with this." He called to his son, who stood looking out of the window. "George, come here. Listen. How far did you get with your medicine before they threw you out as hopeless?"

"You know as well as I do," said George.

"Do you know enough—did they drive enough into your head for you to be able to guess what a competent doctor could tell about such a wound?"

"Well, it's a—it's a knock or blow."

"If a tile fell from the roof? Or a piece of the coping?"

"Well, guv'nor, you see, it's like this—"

"Is it possible?"

"No."

"Why not?"

"Oh, because she hit him several times."

"I can't stand it," said Mrs. Princey.

"You have got to stand it, my dear," said her husband. "And keep that hysterical note out of your voice. It might be overheard. We are talking about the weather. If he fell down the well, George, striking his head several times?"

"I really don't know, guv'nor."

"He'd have had to hit the sides several times in thirty or forty feet, and at the correct angles. No, I'm afraid not. We must go over it all again. Millicent."

"No! No!"

"Millicent, we must go over it all again. Perhaps you have forgotten something. One tiny irrelevant detail may save or ruin us. Particularly you, Millicent. You don't *want* to be put in an asylum, do you? Or be hanged? They might hang you, Millicent. . . ."

There is tension and conflict and information and character delineation and foreshadowing in that dialogue.

How nicely dialogue flows when there is conflict between the speakers! Not long ago I made a note of this conversation I heard when sitting behind two women on a bus in San Francisco:

"No way!" said the young woman.

"We are going to get you the greatest dress at Magnin's, hon,"
said the older woman.
"Not going through with it," the younger woman said through
gritted teeth. "He's so old!"
"Why of course you are!" the older woman said. "You're going
to have a beautiful house and a Mercedes and—"
"Mah-uh-ma! He's old! He's ugly! I don't like him and—"
"You hush!" The mother's voice was steely hard now. "We are
going to get a great dress, the best dress at Magnin's, and you are
going to marry him and that's it and you just shut up and think
good thoughts!"

There were volumes expressed and unexpressed in those brief sentences; I wanted more, and I hated to see the two get off the bus. What a
lesson in writing that was! For example, if they hadn't been in conflict I
wouldn't even have eavesdropped. Think of how commonplace and
boring it would have been had the conversation gone like this:

"Oh boy, Mother, I'm so excited!"
"Yes, darling, and what a dress we're going to get you!"
"I'm so grateful, Mother dear. Sure, he's a little older and not
much to look at, but he's so sweet and generous and I'll make him
a great wife, I'll make that old mansion ring with laughter!"

No conflict, no interest: Zzzzzzz. . . .
Keep notes on good dialogue. I keep index cards in my pocket
and jot down fragments no matter where I come across them. The
other night I heard a tender little line from an old movie, *Easter Pa-
rade*, on television; after listening starry-eyed to Judy Garland singing
a song, Fred Astaire says to her with surprise in his voice and some
reproach:
"Why didn't you tell me I was in love with you?"

Here's how dialogue alone can characterize three people:

"Hey Bill! Want to see something funny—something to liven up
this boring party? I just put four jiggers of rum in Gladys Jones'
Coca-Cola!"
"You didn't! Penny, she's been sober for so long! She's been
out of the sanitarium for five years!"
"I know, isn't it fun? Watch her—she's about to drink it, look!"
"But—if she drinks it—she'll go on a binge! She'll never stop.

And she's worked so damned hard to put her life back together. I'm going over there and stop her!"

"You do, Billy-poo, and I'll tell your wife all about us in Vermont last summer. . ."

What is "summary dialogue"? That is where the author *describes* the dialogue rather than recording it sentence by sentence. Summary dialogue can be very useful at times, especially when the actual dialogue would be tedious to the reader because he already knows the information.

"Tom! Oh, Tom!" She came into his arms sobbing, her clothes torn and singed from the fire. And little by little the story came out in choking words, about how the fire started, how she'd found Jed, the itinerant they'd taken in and been kind to, standing there laughing with the can of gasoline in his hand.

"You poor baby," Tom murmured, holding her close.

Presumably, in this version, the reader has already "seen" the described action and doesn't need to hear it twice in detail. But if this were all new to the reader, as well as to Tom, we would want to hear the actual words for ourselves, like this:

"Darling! Your clothes—what happened?"

"Awful!" she managed to gasp. "Jed—it was Jed—I couldn't believe it—our house, our beloved house. . . Hold me, hold me."

"Jed? What'd that bastard do?"

"After all we've done for him! I found him standing there—just standing there with a can of gasoline—"

"I'll kill him—"

"And Tom, he was laughing! Yes, laughing as our house burned to the ground!"

"You poor baby," he said, holding her close, and already choosing the weapon with which to kill Jed.

Once again, don't have your characters talk in long, perfect, complete, grammatical sentences: "Well, daughter, first we shall go to town, and then, after having dined well at Delmonico's, we shall, if there is time, take in a moving picture show. . . ."

Too stilted! Chop up the sentences! Leave out words! Read the conversations out loud to get a realistic sound.

I once heard a director give this advice to an actor on how to deliver an important line: "First, think! Then do something. Then speak."

This might be good advice for a writer of fiction, especially when it comes to pivotal or very dramatic moments:

> No use putting it off any longer. Jack went over to the younger man.
> "Rob — I'm afraid — well, we've reason to believe that your wife was on that boat, the one that went down."
> *My God! Karen!* Rob went to the table and poured a drink with trembling hands. "You're — you're not sure?"

Be careful about overdoing names when characters who know each other are talking:

> "Gee, Everett, here we are in Venice!" she said.
> "Yes, Molly, we certainly are."
> "I'd never believed it a month ago, Everett, would you? And look — there are Susan and Jim! Hi Susan, hi Jim!"

Don't be worried that the readers won't know who is talking to whom; they will, if you've written the dialogue correctly.

A bugaboo with beginning writers who are just starting their romance with words is dialect and phonetic spelling, especially when dealing with fictional characters of limited education. *Wuz, becoz, lissen, luv, sed,* and *sez* don't sound much different from the words they're derived from and generally belong in comic strips.

A minor character saying things like "oi say, Guvnah," might give one a flavor of old London but would be tiring if the protagonist of an entire story or novel spoke like that. The flavor of an English accent might be suggested in this way a few times and then dropped:

> "I'm bored," Reginald declared; it came out *oim bawd* the way he said it.

Paul Theroux in *My Secret History* has his English girl say:

> "Oh, do leave Andrew alone," Rosamond said. "You're just putting him off."
> I loved the way she chewed the word *orf.*

Or one might use expressions that the English use which we don't:

> "Low ceiling — mind your head."
> "Whilst you were gone, I waited for the lift."
> "I'd best go now."

And so with any language: Capture the essence with a few words or phrases, but don't overdo it.

Last month in Tahiti my pretty waitress kept saying: "Anything is it that you want, Monsieur?"

If I were to put her in a story I would have her say that repeatedly—right up to and including any sex scene—and there would be no need for oo-la-la-ing or oui-oui-ouing to get across to the reader that English was not her first language.

It is fun to write dialect and certainly *y'all, gonna, wanna, agin, y'know, hyar,* and dropping g's and the like are valid to indicate the sound of colloquial or regional speech in moderation.

Without going overboard on the colloquial or spelling variations, see how Steinbeck manages to convey the way George and the retarded Lennie speak in *Of Mice and Men:*

Lennie looked timidly over to him. "George?"

"Yeah, what ya want?"

"Where we goin', George?"

The little man jerked down the brim of his hat and scowled over at Lennie. "So you forgot that awready, did you? I gotta tell you again, do I? Jesus Christ, you're a crazy bastard!"

"I forgot," Lennie said softly. "I tried not to forget. Honest to God I did, George."

"O.K.—O.K. I'll tell ya again. I ain't got nothing to do. Might jus' as well spen' all my time tellin' you things and then you forget 'em, and I tell you again."

"Tried and tried," said Lennie, "but it didn't do no good. I remember about the rabbits, George."

Certainly Alex Haley put some dialect and arcane expressions to effective use in *Roots,* but a whole story or novel with virtually every other word being changed can be tiring. Remember the Uncle Remus stories?

"Aha!" sez Brer Fox, sezee, "you'r dar, is you?" sezee. "Well I'm gwineter smoke you out, ef it takes a month. You'er mine dis time," sezee.

Brer Rabbit ain't saying nothing.

"Ain't you comin' down?" sez Brer Fox, sezee.

Brer Rabbit ain't saying nothing.

Then Brer Fox he went out after some wood, he did, and when he came back he heard Brer Rabbit laughing.

"W'at you laughin' at, Brer Rabbit?" sez Brer Fox, sezee.

"Can't tell you, Brer Fox," sez Brer Rabbit, sezee.

"Bett tell, Brer Rabbit," sez Brer Fox, sezee.

" 'Tain't nuthin' but a box er money somebody done gone an' lef' up here in de chink er de chimbly," sez Brer Rabbit, sezee.

"Don't b'leeve you," sez Brer Fox, sezee.

This may indeed be an accurate approximation of how they sounded in the Old South, but a little of it in print goes a long way. Just as pure hillbilly goes a long way in a short time. In *How to Talk Pure Ozark* by Dale Freeman, he goes into spelling and pronunciation of certain words, ones I hope creep into your manuscripts rarely. In this hardy dialect, *bag* is used as in "He bagged her to marry up with him"; *dork*, what it gets when the sun goes down; *flar*, a rose is about the prettiest flar there is; *hern*, it ain't hern, it's his'n; *oral*, your car needs two quarts of oral; *rah cheer*, he was born rah cheer; *retch*, as in "If I'd knowed it was you I'd have retch out and wove."

Do not be afraid to give your characters speech mannerisms. This helps to individualize them. Captain Queeg in *The Caine Mutiny* substituted *kay* for the word *okay* throughout the story. Scarlett O'Hara said "fiddleedee" regularly. John Mortimer's incorrigible barrister character, Rumpole, calls everyone "Old darling." Barkis in *David Copperfield* is constantly assuring people that "Barkis is willin' "; Dickens is masterful at individualizing by speech peculiarities and mannerisms. Remember Inspector Clouseau and his "deggy" (doggy) and the organ grinder's "mingy" (monkey) and his hotel "rhewm" (room)?

Playing with the spelling of spoken words to individualize the speaker can be rewarding if not overdone. This is from my novel *Matador:*

"Oh, that's a long way off," she said. Only it came out, "Hats a-hong hay aw," because now she was looking into her compact mirror and applying lipstick.

If a speech mannerism or special way of saying a word reveals something about a character to the reader, by all means take advantage of it.

"Organ's nice," she ventured.

I almost asked "which organ" until I realized that she was referring to the western state she came from.

Here's an excellent use of colloquial phrases, plus dialectal spelling to approximate Australian speech of a certain class and region, by Kathy Lette from "Girls' Night Out":

Last Saturdee was Alexis's fourf birfday party. Grub was s'posed to come. But he never fronted. And I rung him at home and his best mate said, "Oh, he's gone to pick up his tuxedo, he gets married today." And like, the woman he married had free children to him that I didn't even know about. . . . So I, um, got drunk and gate-crashed the wedding reception and fronted up to him. Like, I wasn't upset for myself, understand. I couldn't give a stuff. But for Alexis. Like that's a rool horrible fing to get married on her birfday. And the coach was there. Like I'm an Aries and well, this stupid . . . coach, he's new and just doesn't like me. This coach just started draggin' me out of the reception place for no reason. He's a rool idiot and Grub turned round and laughed right at the wrong moment. Like I'm gettin' dragged out of the place and he turns round with a big smile on his face and I just turned round and clocked him. Bloody oath I hit him. Broke his nose. I give him the best hit you've ever seen. Wiv one punch I fractured his nose and split all his mouth open. See, I, like had free bruvvers and they used to bash me.

There's a fine line between catching the accurate sound and rhythm of speech through spelling alterations and idiosyncrasies of idiom, and something that turns out distorted and distracting and farcical:

The first night in the castle the reporter said: "Aw hell, Count Dracula, thassa lotta metaphysical baloney."

The count drew himself up and replied in measured tones: "Metapheezical *purrhops* — bahloney *purrhops* not."

Let us end this chapter with some entertaining and expert dialogue by James Thurber, whose ear for speech never failed him even when his eyesight did. This is about Walter Mitty, a meek little man who spent his days fantasizing in order to blot out his drab existence and his harridan of a spouse. Here, in "The Secret Life of Walter Mitty," he waits in a hotel lobby for his wife who is shopping:

He picked up an old copy of *Liberty* and sank down into the chair. "Can Germany Conquer the World Through the Air?" Walter Mitty looked at the pictures of bombing planes and of ruined streets . . .

"The cannonading has got the wind up in young Raleigh, sir," said the sergeant. Captain Mitty looked up at him through tousled hair. "Get him to bed," he said wearily, "with the others. I'll fly alone." "But you can't, sir," said the sergeant anxiously. "It takes two men to handle that bomber and the Archies are pounding the hell out of the air. Von Richtman's circus is between here and Saulier." "Somebody's got to get that ammunition dump," said Mitty. "I'm going over. Spot of brandy?" He poured a drink for the sergeant and one for himself. War thundered and whined around the dugout and battered at the door. There was a rending of wood and splinters flew through the room. "A bit of a near thing," said Captain Mitty carelessly. "The box barrage is closing in," said the sergeant. "We only live once, Sergeant," said Mitty, with his faint, fleeting smile. "Or do we?" He poured another brandy and tossed it off. "I never see a man could hold his brandy like you, sir," said the sergeant. "Begging your pardon, sir." Captain Mitty stood up and strapped on his huge Webley-Vickers automatic. "It's forty kilometres through hell, sir," said the sergeant. Mitty finished one last brandy. "After all," he said softly, "what isn't?" The pounding of the cannon increased; there was the rat-tat-tatting of machine guns, and from somewhere came the menacing pocketa-pocketa-pocketa of the new flame-throwers. Walter Mitty walked to the door of the dug-out humming "Auprès de Ma Blonde." He turned and waved to the sergeant. "Cheerio!" he said. . . .

Something struck his shoulder. "I've been looking all over this hotel for you," said Mrs. Mitty. "Why do you have to hide in this old chair? How did you expect me to find you?" "Things close in," said Walter Mitty vaguely. "What?" Mrs. Mitty said. "Did you get the what's-its-name? The puppy biscuit? What's in that box?" "Overshoes," said Mitty. "Couldn't you have put them on in the store?" "I was thinking," said Walter Mitty. "Does it ever occur to you that I am sometimes thinking?" She looked at him. "I'm going to take your temperature when I get you home," she said.

Thurber's felicitous onomatopoeia to approximate the noise of the flame throwers, a sound he uses with variations throughout the story to imitate different machines, is inspired—and pure Thurber.

TONY HILLERMAN

Here are two rules of writing that I wish someone had told me when I started thirty or so years ago. One is don't make a career out of writing first chapters as I almost did. The second is that you don't have to be able to outline a plot if you have a reasonably long life expectancy.

When I decided I wanted to write fiction, I had the impression, and I still have it really, that the first paragraph and the first sentence and certainly the first chapter were critically important. I think I must have spent six months writing and rewriting and polishing and repolishing a first chapter. I'll admit it's an extremely good first chapter; I still have it in a filing cabinet at home, along with a good many other first chapters because it took me a long time to learn that by the time I'm well launched in a book, the first chapter I've written to start it really begins to be irrelevant. It tends not to have much to do with the book that I've started by the time I'm in Chapter Five.

A lot of writers, and lots of good writers, outline in great detail. But the system of more or less letting the story grow, seems to me to give you the advantage of letting your characters develop in a way that seems real and natural. You can get very well acquainted with characters. You feel after a time that you really know them.

To give you an example of how it works for me is a book called *Fly on the Wall.* This was the second book I wrote and I still firmly believed that common sense and good practice and decency dictated that you outline a book before you wrote it. Everybody told me this. And so while I was not able to do it, as I wrote it, as I got deeper in the book, I would go back and take what I had written and extract an outline from it. So it seemed at least I was outlining it. I fooled myself a long time this way.

This time the hero, the protagonist, is a political reporter. He's gotten into the state capitol intending to get into the Bureau of Revenue office and extract some information from a tax return, which is of course illegal. He's been tipped off that the information is in this specific file and he's been told that two doors will be left unlocked so he can get it. There are people who want him to have it. He gets into the building, and if you read mysteries you know it's a trap.

The state capitol is one of those labyrinth buildings, five or six stories, and like too many state capitols, it has marble floors. I've made a great thing in establishing mood out of the sound you make in this silent building walking on the marble floors.

The reporter, who is very nervous, has taken off his shoes when he got into the building, in the basement, because he didn't want to make so much noise. He was feeling guilty about what he was doing anyway. He takes them off, leaves them on top of a Game and Fish department display case intending to go back and get them, obviously. In eluding the trap, I have him running down the hallway. I'm thinking, wait a minute, these guys have guns and here it's three o'clock in the morning, what's going to cause my reader to believe they don't simply shoot this bird? We've got to get the lights turned off. So I create a janitor's closet. He ducks into that and sure enough there's a switch box. And he pulls the switch and turns off the power. That's the beauty of writing fiction instead of nonfiction. So now I've got him in this janitor's closet. Light's off. I have him stuck there.

Now I think, it's quiet in this building, totally quiet. Even though he's barefoot, he makes some noise and they know about where he is. So how'm I going to get him out of here? How is he going to get out of this building?

And I couldn't think of a way of getting him out of there. He and I spent, I'd say, five weeks in that janitor's closet.

Finally, I'm having him feel around for something to use as a weapon. So I go to a janitor's closet and look. And you see such things as great sacks of toilet paper and soap and stuff that wouldn't be useful. And finally it occurs to me — what if I convert to liquid soap? Liquid soap and marble floors. So I have him leave the janitor's closet and he runs down this marble hall and this marble stairway with the top off the liquid soap, dribbling liquid soap after him. It almost makes your teeth hurt to think of it, the guy chasing him, hitting this liquid soap on these marble stairs. The sort of thing I could never come up with ever in a million years had I outlined.

I read other mystery writers. I read both for inspiration and . . . right now I'm going back and reading Graham Greene because the kind of book I'm doing needs some of the tricks Graham Greene uses. I shamelessly steal ideas, devices, techniques, methodology, good habits from everybody I can find. I think the best way to teach yourself to write is by reading, and reading not for the meaning but for how-did-the-guy-get-that-effect. And I do that all the time.

Setting

*O*ne of the fine things about writing a story or a novel is that you are your own art director; you can do what you want with that set. An African setting? A few scrubby trees, a Kilimanjaro-type mountain in the background, and some grass huts in the foreground, and voilà, you've got it—we are in Kenya, Zimbabwe, Tanzania, or wherever. Paris? A table at a sidewalk cafe, a kiosk to one side, Notre Dame and its chimes in the background and you are there. (Remember, you are also the sound effects engineer, plus the lighting crew and Best Boy.)

But how do you create the setting and how much setting is needed?

Again, there are no absolutes, no fixed rules; you must find what works for you and your particular story. Obviously if your story is laid in Chiang Mai, Thailand, since we don't know much about that place, we are going to need more physical description than if we are in New York City or a California suburb.

In either case, I would follow one rule: Subordinate the setting, no matter how exotic or attractive, to the characters and plot. Sinclair Lewis's admonition is relevant here: "When I want to learn about the Azores, I'll read the National Geographic, not a novel!"

For atmosphere, one of the best American novels, one that really puts you the reader right there in the midst of the headwaters of the Amazon jungle, is Peter Matthiessen's *At Play in the Fields of the Lord*. But no one would say, "You've got to read this great book about the Amazon—you'll learn all about the Ucayali River and Pucallpa and what the Jivaro Indians eat and the flora and the fauna."

What they say is: "You can't put it down, great characters Wolfie and Moon, wonderful action."

The jungle, while a vital character in the drama, is secondary. It is like *Stones for Ibarra*. If you examine Harriet Doerr's best seller you'll see that you cannot separate setting from characters, and that at the end of the story you know the Mexican village as well as you know the inhabitants.

In days gone by it was frequently the custom to start with a static geographical description:

> The purple hills jutted menacingly behind the little cottage with the blue smoke curling from its chimney and the cow munched its hay contentedly in the corral while the chickens clucked nearby.

Why not take that same boring description and throw some life into it by the simple expedient of having someone, some character, view it? By doing so we will get a *twofer* — that is, a two-for-one. We get the physical description so we know where we are, but we also might learn who our main character is, his or her sex, and that there is some problem about which we will soon be hearing more:

> As Smedrood strode angrily up the steep path into the hills already growing purple in the twilight, the big man stopped and turned around for one last look. Blue smoke was curling from the chimney of the cottage and he could make out Brownie in her corral waiting to be milked. Who would do it now that he had left? Who would feed the chickens he could see clucking about the front yard? He didn't give a damn — he was gone for good, and to hell with Mildred, helpless Mildred, may she rot in hell.

You see how painless the scene-setting is when you weave exactly the same geographic and physical information in with action of a character; readers might skip over the description in the first version in their eagerness to find a character and get on with the beginning of the story, but they can't skip over the second; they want to know what's going on.

Thomas McGuane is not averse to giving us a beautiful description of the setting in his stories, as in this paragraph from his 1989 novel, *Keep the Change*. But observe how quickly the author relates setting to character and the man's character-revealing reaction to the natural beauty:

> The huge cottonwoods along the river had turned purest yellow, and since no wind had come up to disturb the dying leaves, the great trees stood in chandelier brilliance along the water courses that veined the hills. Joe had to stop the truck to try to take in all this light.

Here is how Louis L'Amour, in *Passin' Through*, sets the scene, lets us know in a few lines what state his hero is in, whether it's day or night, his means of travel, that there's wind, that he's in the high country, a bit about his character, a good deal about his immediate past, and an indication of his future—his goal and motivation:

> He topped the high ridge on a wild blue roan with a skull and crossbones brand. He was a drifter, reckless and hard, a man without fear and without a name. The Colorado high country he rode was breathtaking, but all he had on his mind was vengeance. For the night wind stung his neck where the rope burns were still raw. Some good citizens from the last town left him twisting slowly from an unjust noose. They made a big mistake when they didn't finish the job.

I would not like to be in the shoes of those "good citizens in the last town."

Hemingway also was a master of setting a scene with a minimum of words. When you finish *For Whom the Bell Tolls* you feel you have been in Spain in the midst of a terrible war. Similarly, the poetic and subtle opening of *A Farewell to Arms* not only puts you in this place in Italy where the poignant love story will take place, but it creates a mood and a vague foreboding:

> In the late summer of that year we lived in a house in a village that looked across the river and the plain to the mountains. In the bed of the river there were pebbles and boulders, dry and white in the sun, and the water was clear and swiftly moving and blue in the channels. Troops went by the house and down the road and the dust they raised powdered the leaves of the trees. The trunks of the trees too were dusty and the leaves fell early that year and we saw the troops marching along the road and the dust rising and leaves, stirred by the breeze, falling and the soldiers marching and afterward the road bare and white except for the leaves.

Here is the beginning of Ray Bradbury's much-anthologized "The Lake," an early story he considers a landmark in his career. It would be difficult to cram much more setting into a single place, yet Bradbury infuses the description with so much poetry and integrates his characters so well into the surroundings that it is not only painless but a delight. It is the kind of writerly section one reads first for information about the tale and then again for the pleasure of the flow of the words themselves and the imagery. But you will notice when reading any one of Ray Bradbury's hundreds of stories that he may revel in words and phrases, but he never forgets to subordinate the setting or the imagery to the story and the characterization:

> They cut the sky down to my size and threw it over the Michigan lake, put some kids yelling on yellow sand with bouncing balls, a gull or two, a criticizing parent, and me breaking out of a wet wave, finding this world very bleary and moist.
>
> I ran up on the beach.
>
> Mama swabbed me with a furry towel. "Stand there and dry," she said.
>
> I stood there, watching the sun take away the water beads on my arms. I replaced them with goose-pimples.
>
> "My, there's a wind," said Mama. "Put on your sweater."
>
> "Wait'll I watch my goose-bumps," I said.
>
> "Harold," said Mama.
>
> I put the sweater on and watched the waves come up and fall down on the beach. But not clumsily. On purpose, with a green sort of elegance. Even a drunken man could not collapse with such elegance as those waves.
>
> It was September. In the last days when things are getting sad for no reason. The beach was so long and lonely with only about six people on it. The kids quit bouncing the ball because somehow the wind made them sad, too, whistling the way it did, and the kids sat down and felt autumn come along the endless shore.
>
> All of the hot-dog stands were boarded up with strips of golden planking, sealing in all the mustard, onion, meat odors of the long, joyful summer. It was like nailing summer into a series of coffins. One by one the places slammed their covers down, padlocked their doors, and the wind came and touched the sand, blowing away all of the million footprints of July and August. It got so that now, in September, there was nothing but the mark of my rubber tennis shoes and Donald and Delaus Schabold's feet, down by the water curve.
>
> Sand blew up in curtains on the sidewalks, and the merry-go-round was hidden with canvas, all of the horses frozen in mid-air on their brass poles, showing teeth, galloping on. With only the wind for music, slipping through canvas.

Jack London wrote about exotic places, places the average person hadn't been to and probably would never know, so the amount of space he allotted to setting was usually far above the normal. Nevertheless, he never forgot that he was writing about people first and foremost—people in conflict with other people, or people in conflict with nature, or people in conflict with themselves. In what is considered to be one of the most perfect short stories ever written, "To Build a Fire," it is man against Nature, the killer cold of Alaska. Notice how he gets his protagonist mentioned in the first sentence—and a hint of foreboding in the fifth sentence:

> Day had broken cold and grey, exceedingly cold and grey, when the man turned aside from the main Yukon trail and climbed the high earth-bank, where a dim and little-travelled trail led eastward through the fat spruce timberland. It was a steep bank, and he paused for breath at the top, excusing himself by looking at his watch. It was nine o'clock. There was no hint of sun, though there was not a cloud in the sky. It was a clear day, and yet there seemed an intangible pall over the face of things, a subtle gloom that made the day dark, and that was due to the absence of sun. This fact did not worry the man. He was used to the lack of sun. It had been days since he had seen the sun, and he knew that a few more days must pass before that cheerful orb, due south, would just peep above the sky-line and dip immediately from view.

Hemingway liked to say that he learned to write from Flaubert's *Madame Bovary* and Mark Twain's *Huck Finn* but it is hard to believe that he didn't learn a great deal from Jack London's spare, virile prose as well.

A jungle novel usually requires a good deal of "set designing." But V. S. Pritchett in his 1937 novel, *Dead Man Leading*, creates a very real, un-Tarzanlike Brazilian jungle world with a few convincing details, even though he'd never set foot in Brazil:

> Johnson looked blankly and then turned away, saying nothing. He looked over the heads of the people at the settlement. There were big-footed negroes, Indians easily and vacuously laughing, fat men wearing sun-glasses like beetles over the eyes, and pyjama coats. The flies were thick on the refuse scattered over the shore. On the sandy high ground above the flood-level of the water were a few thatched huts and adobe houses. The two men walked across a sunlit stretch. Under the thatch of their open huts, men in pyjamas were asleep in their hammocks, and the women, ragged and scratching themselves, moved to hide in the enclosed compartments. There was just this palm thatch propped up by four poles and the box at one end for the women. In the doorway of one of the adobe houses an Indian lay asleep. Beside him, propped in

the sun, a live boa-constrictor was tied neck and tail to a stick. The only sounds in the settlement were men's shouts—from the drinkers in a furious tavern, and then the slow clapping of wings on a roof, like dusty and ragged rugs being shaken. These were the wings of the vultures.

John Leggett created an entirely different world in his *Who Took the Gold Away*: the complex microcosm that was Yale in 1938. In short order we get to know what the campus, the dorms, and the classrooms looked like, but always through the eyes of the narrator and his best friend—who perhaps isn't his best friend. He sets the tone in the very beginning:

> Considering what Yale was like in 1938, it is remarkable that Pierce Jay and I should have known each other at all.
>
> In that year, when we were both freshmen, Yale was a goldfish bowl in which we fluked about, earnestly unfurling our aspirations. The telling marks on a man were his prep school, his dress, and what he did with his leisure. Grace, detachment, not seeming to care and, above all, being with acceptable companions—these were prized.

In this novel, setting was vital, paramount, an active character in the drama about the dovetailing lives of the two characters. Yet in some stories and novels setting is almost unimportant.

As Leggett, a workshop leader at our Conference since the beginning in 1972, tells his workshops:

> It is surely possible to tell a good story with no scene, no setting at all, no indication of where we are, just as we might expect to enjoy a play presented on a bare stage. If the characters and narrative are strong enough they will hold our interest without any background.
>
> But of course all events occur somewhere, and often the place where they occur has a profound influence over what occurs. The landscape of a story, its atmosphere, its feeling of harshness or mildness, of gloom or cheer, of beauty or ugliness, is likely to affect the characters and the way they lead their lives.
>
> Setting would be critical to a story about a prisoner or to one about castaways adrift in the Pacific Ocean and very likely to one about a high-school graduation in an Appalachian coal town.
>
> A story's setting is what puts us there, gives us readers a sense of being in the situation with the characters. If it is set in Hondu-

ras, we should feel hot, sweaty, and thirsty. We should see the sun
baking the town square and the steam rising from the back of the
little burro tethered at the side of the church. We should smell
the *zozo*, the native delicacy of fish heads and banana skins, as it
sizzles over the charcoal.

A setting, deftly portrayed, not only tells us where we are but
gives the story a sense of truth, the credibility we speak of as verisimilitude. It does wonders for that troublesome disbelief and the
reader's willing suspension thereof.

Deft portrayal of setting is a matter of selectivity, of choosing
only a few details and letting the reader supply the rest. We readers come to a story with plenty of scenic equipment and become
restive if prevented from using it by a storyteller who paints the
whole set for us and lists the furniture and the contents of the
drawers as if we were tenants to be held accountable.

People whose lives are affected by fiction, who live with one
foot in the real and the other in a fictional world, tend to store
up their scenic memory without differentiating between the two.
That, it seems to me, is one of the particular enrichments of reading and writing stories. We don't see the dreary little Southern
community and its poverty-stricken surroundings that appears
before us. Rather, we see Yoknapatawpha County and wonder if
that could be Flem Snopes there on the porch, with his hat down
over his eyes?

But the real purpose of scene is its contribution to the story's
total, emotional effect. If it isn't adding to that, the scene will be a
distraction from, and a detraction to, the story.

An autumnal setting can add a sense of ending and loss to a
story about a doomed love, just as a spring setting can add a sense
of anticipation to a story about adolescence. Setting can be put to
ironic use, too, so that the springtime setting could add poignance
to a story about death.

To some stories the scene hardly matters. They would be essentially the same whether they take place in Chicago or Coon
Rapids. But in a great many of the best stories, scene carries all
the weight of a major character.

That would be true of course of a story where the setting is an
actual antagonist, a tale of the sea or wilderness. It would be
equally true of a setting which is a psychological or social adversary as in a Southern gothic tale in which the customs and memories of a community create the human conflict.

In one of his always lively Conference workshops that I sat in on,

John Leggett quoted a famous contemporary author as declaring in a teaching session:

"*No* weather, please!"

Leggett didn't necessarily agree, but he understood what the writer was getting at; there is a tendency for the beginning writer to go too deeply into the weather as part of the story, the it-was-a-dark-and-stormy-night-syndrome, rather than focusing on the characters' reactions to the weather and nature and the setting in general.

Chekhov is a writer's writer and everyone who aspires to good writing should read him. "The Lady with the Toy Dog" would be a good place to start if you haven't read Chekhov, as it is one of the most believable and touching love stories ever written. It is the story of two people unhappily married to unsuited mates who meet first at the seaside resort of Yalta, and continue to meet there every two or three months. Here, as in all his stories, we have a great sense of place; Chekhov gives us a vivid picture of Yalta, but always in and around his characters' actions and in the most economical and telling fashion.

Here, in a letter to a friend, Chekhov says everything about setting that needs to be said. It is worth memorizing—I don't believe it has ever been expressed better:

> In my opinion a true description of Nature should be very brief and have the character of relevance. Commonplace descriptions such as "the setting sun bathing in the waves of the darkening sea, poured its purple gold, etc."—"the swallows flying over the surface of the water twittered merrily"—such commonplaces one ought to abandon. In descriptions of Nature one ought to seize upon the little particulars, grouping them in such a way that, in reading when you shut your eyes, you get the picture.
>
> For instance, you will get the full effect of a moonlit night if you write that on the milldam, a little glowing star point flashed from the neck of a broken bottle, and the round black shadow of a dog or a wolf emerged and ran, etc. . . .

But having said that, you must remember that all through literature there are many purely descriptive passages, including in Chekhov's writings, that transcend mere setting and backdrop, that are quiet little gems in themselves. I think of paragraphs from Flaubert, Twain, W.H. Hudson, Tom Wolfe, Hemingway, Paul Theroux, and small paragraphs like this one from Forster's *Passage to India* describing a first look into the Marabar Caves:

> There is little to see, and no eye to see it, until the visitor arrives

for his five minutes, and strikes a match. Immediately another flame rises in the depths of the rock and moves toward the surface like an imprisoned spirit: the walls of the circular chamber have been most marvellously polished. The two flames approach and strive to unite, but cannot, because one of them breathes air, the other stone.

PAUL ERDMAN

The author of *The Crash of '79* and six other runaway best sellers has spoken at the Conference twice. The erstwhile banker told us how after a "commodity trading irregularity" in Switzerland he was put into jail.

Many writers, Cervantes, O. Henry, Koestler, et alios, have turned to writing in jail.

"The jail they put me in was a medieval monastery. The graffiti on the walls was in Latin. I could order meals from any restaurant in town, with wine, for which of course I paid. There was TV and radio. It was very charming, but after a few weeks it got boring. So I decided to write. Since a Swiss jail has no research facilities, a novel seemed to be the answer. I've always read novels. I still read seven or eight every week. I came to the conclusion that the U.S. dollar would be massively devalued and the price of gold would skyrocket, and so I decided to write a novel about that. It was enormously successful. Now, I don't mean to urge you to go to jail in order to become a successful novelist. On the other hand . . ."

Style and Language

'He's supposed to have a particularly high-class style: "Feather-footed through the splashy fen passes the questing vole" . . . would that be it?'
'Yes,' said that Managing Editor. 'That must be a good style. At least it doesn't sound like anything else to me.'
          — Evelyn Waugh, *Scoop,* 1938

*I*t has been said of Somerset Maugham that he had so little style that that, of itself, was a style. What is meant is simply: no frills. Just the facts, ma'am. Just the noun and the verb please, with as few modifiers, adjectives, adverbs, similes, metaphors, et cetera, as possible to convey the meaning.

When Elmore Leonard spoke at the Conference in 1985, he urged us to be very sparing with our fancy similes and metaphors. "I myself almost never use them. They tend to call attention to the fact, one I always try to hide, that there is a writer, a guy behind all this, who is making it all up with words, a puppeteer. I want it to all sound real, as though it were truly happening right now."

But then look at Raymond Chandler, Truman Capote and Ross Macdonald who used the most elaborate and clever imagery, and that was *their* style.

Tom Wolfe said recently:

In college, at Washington and Lee, I decided I would write crystalline prose. That was the word: *crystalline.* It would be a prose as ageless, timeless, exquisite, soaring, and transparently dazzling as Scarlatti at his most sublime. It would speak to the twenty-fifth century as lucidly as to my own. (I was, naturally, interested to hear, years later, that Iris Murdoch had dreamed of the same quality and chosen the same word, *crystalline,* at a similar point in her life.) In graduate school at Yale, I came upon the Elizabethan books of rhetoric, which isolated, by my count, 444 figures of speech, covering every conceivable form of wordplay. By analyzing the prose of writers I admired — De Quincey, I remember, was one of them — I tried to come up with the perfect sequences of figures and make notations for them, like musical notes. I would flesh out this perfect skeleton with some material when the time came.

Such experiments don't last very long, of course. The damnable beast, material, keeps getting bigger and more obnoxious.

If you try for style *per se*, it most probably will come out sounding phoney, whereas if you write what is truly meant and truly felt, lo and behold, you will read back over the piece and discover there is a unique style, unique because you are not exactly like anyone else.

The style is the man or woman, the style is the writer, the style is the words you choose, the style is *you*.

James Hilton, author of the beloved *Goodbye, Mr. Chips*, has written about style:

So far as "style" goes, I am a functionalist; if a sentence represents exactly the idea I wish to convey, I am satisfied with it. I dislike "style" that has a look or sound of having been stuck on afterwards, or "style" that employs unusual words with no intention but to startle the reader, send him to a dictionary, or give the snobbish feeling that because he cannot understand what he is reading he is therefore improving his mind enormously.

Apropos of that, I remember with shame that when I was writing the last part of my novel *Matador*, I learned the word "brobdingnagian" and used it instead of "gigantic" or "huge" for no other reason than to show off; I am sure the sentence and the action came to a halt at that point and the reader was reminded that there was a writer at work on his sensibilities and hence some of the effect would be lost. Style has never depended on big words; one has never had to reach for a dictionary when reading Hemingway or Fitzgerald.

Faulkner, a great stylist himself, said that a writer who has a lot to say hasn't time to worry about style. Evelyn Waugh, always an inimitable stylist, wrote: "Properly understood, style is not a seductive decoration added to a functional structure; it is of the essence of the work of art. The necessary elements of style are lucidity, elegance, and individuality. . . ."

When pinned down and asked how he managed to achieve that graceful, seemingly effortless style, Waugh merely shrugged and answered: "Oh, I just put down the words and push them around a bit."

The late Argentine writer Jorge Luis Borges has amplified those thoughts as follows:

At the beginning of their careers many writers have a need to overwrite. They choose carefully turned-out phrases; they want to impress their readers with their large vocabularies. By the excesses of their language, these young men and women try to hide their sense of inexperience. With maturity the writer becomes more secure in his ideas. He finds his real tone and develops a simple and effective style.

Joyce Carol Oates thinks that style comes second to story:

> I think that's one of the problems with the really elegant writers; you stop reading and start admiring the words. So you lose the narrative flow. I don't want that to happen.

Style, like literature, is an academic word; it comes after the act. I do not believe that great writers set out to write "literature." Stendhal, when he wanted to limber himself up for his day's work and put his clear-eyed, quick-marching prose in good order, did not read "literature." He gave himself a dose of the *Code Napoléon*. He liked its no-nonsense clarity.

Hemingway said, "Prose is architecture, not interior decoration."

And Thomas Hardy maintained that "the whole secret of living style, and the difference between it and dead style, lies in not having too much style."

W.H. Hudson was the most seductive of non-stylists: "How does he get his effects?" muttered Joseph Conrad, "He writes as the grass grows."

In other words, when you sit down to write, do not consciously try to be stylish, to be fancy, to be erudite, to write "literature." The English essayist C.H. Sisson warns: *"The avoidance of 'literature' is indispensable for the man who wants to tell the truth."*

For Flaubert, style was the observing of specific detail and drawing for the reader a picture in words of *that* object or *that* person. The great short story writer de Maupassant received a famous piece of advice from his master, Flaubert, which has influenced many writers, including London, Hemingway, and Fitzgerald. It is worth reading and rereading:

> . . . we have fallen into the habit of remembering, whenever we use our eyes, what people before us have thought of the thing we are looking at. Even the slightest thing contains a little that is unknown. We must find it. To describe a blazing fire or a tree in a plain, we must remain before that fire or tree until they no longer resemble for us any other tree or any other fire.

"That is the way to become original."

After repeating over and over again this truth, that there are not in the entire world two grains of sand, two hands or noses that are absolutely the same, Flaubert made me describe in a few sentences, a being or an object in such a way as to particularize it clearly, to distinguish it from all the other beings or all the other objects of the same race or kind.

"When you pass a grocer sitting in his doorway," he used to say to me, "or a concierge smoking his pipe, or a cab-stand, *show* me that grocer and that concierge, the way they are sitting or standing, their entire physical appearance, making it by the skillfulness of your portrayal embody all their moral nature as well, so that I cannot confuse them with any other grocer or any other concierge. And make me see, by means of a single word, wherein one cab-horse does *not* resemble the fifty others ahead of it or behind it.

Particularize is the key word in Flaubert's advice. *Individualize* with specific detail. The specific detail that you select as significant to your story will culminate in your true style.

Truth and sincerity is what style is all about. Think of *The Color Purple*. One would hardly call the letters that the ignorant protagonist wrote to her absent sister "stylish," yet they had style because of the power of longing and love and truth that was inherent in each, as well as the personality and dialect of the girl. The old-time journalist Adela Rogers St. Johns would never be termed a literary stylist, yet for decades she was a best-selling writer. She came to our Conference in 1976 and urged the students to keep it simple:

I have always believed that what you say is more important than how you say it. Certainly it is better to write well than to write badly, but too often I find people worrying desperately about how to say something that isn't worth saying anyhow. I have wished more time was spent on thinking, feeling, knowing people, and less on the thought of style and construction, which has to be second at least.

No amount of technique can repair an engine that isn't under the hood, and no glory of style, knack with words, or fancy writing can conceal the horrid barrenness and vacuum where sincerity, passion, and a great need and desire to tell a story that will make people laugh or cry or fight ought to be.

The one thing we hear said over and over by speakers at the Conference is: Learn from other writers' styles, but don't set out to copy any one of them. I suppose Hemingway's is the style most aped because, with its seeming simplicity, it is the easiest to copy—badly. Here is Steinbeck on this subject and how ruinous it can be for a beginning writer:

> In my time, Ernest Hemingway wrote a certain kind of story better and more effectively than it had ever been done before. He was properly accepted and acclaimed. He was imitated almost slavishly by every young writer, including me, not only in America but in the world. He wrote a special kind of story out of a special kind of mind and about special moods and situations. When his method was accepted, no other method was admired. The method or style not only conditioned the stories but the thinking of his generation. Superb as his method is, there are many things which cannot be said using it. The result of his acceptance was that the writers did not write about those things which could not be said in the Hemingway manner, and gradually they did not think them either.

Paul Horgan warns writing students:

> The young writer is often more effective with style than with substance. The older, experienced writer commands substance—and mourns the time when style was all.

And here is an editorial from Isaac Asimov's *Science Fiction* magazine which says it all:

> Many beginners are obsessed with STYLE; they want to know if their style is "good," or "right," or even if there is "enough of it."
> Style is that use of language that creates a vivid, full-color image, with sound and smell and other sensory effects, in the reader's mind; *and that is all*. It is *not* there for its own sake, nor to tell the reader how smart the author is. Remember: what lasts in the reader's mind is not the phrase but the effect the phrase created: laughter, tears, pain, joy. If the phrase is not affecting the reader, what is it *doing* there? Make it do its job or cut it without mercy or remorse.

One of the most popular workshop leaders in fiction at our Conference is novelist Anita Clay Kornfeld. She urges her students to find their own style by using "picture-making words that strut and shriek and march right across the pages!"

The *right* word, as Mark Twain said, is the author's eternal quest; he also said the right word was as different from the almost right word as lightning from the lightning bug. Flaubert was merciless and tireless in his striving for the right word:

> Whatever one wishes to say, there is one noun only by which to express it, one verb only to give it life, one adjective only which will describe it. One must search until one has discovered them, this noun, this verb, this adjective, and never rest content with approximations, never resort to trickery, however happy, or to vulgarisms, in order to dodge the difficulty.

Norman Cousins spoke to us at the Conference about his love affair with words over a lifetime as an editor and a writer:

> It is not true that one picture is worth a thousand words. It takes only a few words—if they are the right words—to ignite the imagination and produce pictures in the mind far more focused and far more colorful than anything within the range of electronic communications.

At the Conference we try to get the writers to focus on the verb and cut down on adverbs and adjectives. In 1880 Mark Twain wrote to a schoolboy essayist:

> I notice that you use plain, simple language, short words and brief sentences. This is the way to write English—it is the modern way, and the best way. Stick to it; don't let fluff and flowers and verbosity creep in. When you catch adjectives, kill most of them—then the rest will be valuable. They weaken when they are close together; they give strength when they are wide apart. An adjective habit, or a wordy, diffuse or flowery habit, once fastened upon a person, is as hard to get rid of as any other vice.

Of course, do not cut out *all* adjectives but use them judiciously:

Tom patted the big, fat curly friendly brown dog.

Ask yourself which of those adjectives, if any, are essential to your scene. Some must be eliminated, because they are overloading the noun, canceling themselves out, numbing the reader. Perhaps verbs could take the place of some of the adjectives:

A brown shape appeared and the dog wagged its tail as Tom ran his fingers through its curly fur.

On about the third rewrite, maybe you as the writer would ask yourself: Is it important that I know that the fur is curly or that the dog is brown? Maybe the only important thing is that we know the dog is *friendly*, and we achieve that by the wagging tail.

Some adjectives may be essential to the thrust of your sentence or paragraph. Less likely to be essential are your adverbs. The beginning writer tends to modify every verb with an adverb. If the verb is exactly right and the dialogue is exactly right and we know the characters, one usually does not need an adverb:

"I'll kill you," he snarled viciously.

We don't really need the adverb, do we?

"Oh sure, and I'm Greta Garbo!" she said facetiously.

We don't need the adverb there, or here:

"Who cooked up this mess—Julia Child?" he asked sarcastically.

Sometimes adverbs *are* needed, but if the character is well-drawn and the dialogue is right we need never use a word like *sarcastically*.

An adverb is sometimes vital, especially when it is needed to contradict the way the reader would expect a character to speak or behave.

If a young man said to his bride "I love you," an adverb like *tenderly* might not be needed. But if a big bellowing stevedore were to say those words to his kitten, the adverb would be essential. If the same Neanderthal said "I love you" to his new girlfriend, the reader might want very much to know whether he said it:

savagely, gently, questioningly, timidly, chokingly, flatly, warily, or *sensuously.*

The novelist Oakley Hall, in his book *The Art and Craft of Novel Writing*, discusses a passage from D.H. Lawrence's *The Horse-dealer's Daughter*:

Lawrence makes effective use of the adverbs *floutingly* and *sumptuously*. The passage would lose much if they were deleted:

The great draught horses swung past. They were tied head to tail, four of them, and they heaved along to where a lane branched off from the main road, planting their great hoofs floutingly in the fine black mud, swinging their great rounded haunches sumptuously, and trotting a few sudden steps as they were led into the lane, round the corner.

Lawrence uses fine adverbs and many adjectives, but each of them tells us something, intensifying the picture rather than blurring it; defining, and qualifying.

Often, however, modifiers preceding a noun will weaken it rather than make it more specific, and writers do well to remember Voltaire's admonition: "The adjective is the enemy of the noun."

We should all tape that last sentence to our desks.

In all writing, the use of adjectives and adverbs depends upon the situation and a writer's instincts, and there are no hard and fast rules.

But on one point all writers agree: Strive mightily to find the right verb.

The man went down the road.

We get no picture of the action at all, do we? *Went* is a nothing verb. Suppose he *hurried* down the road? Better. At least we see *some* action in our mind's eye. How about *ambled, strode, trotted, tiptoed, lurched, staggered, slunk, limped, shuffled, fled, minced, flounced,* or *sped* down the road? Each of these verbs creates a strong and different mental picture obtainable with no other word combinations. The all-important verb!

P.G. Wodehouse, who created the immortal Jeeves tales, knew the power of the verb and made good use of it; Jeeves, the canny and resourceful butler, always appears surprisingly and unannounced in front of his employer, Bertie Wooster:

Jeeves flowed in with the tray, like some silent stream meandering over its mossy bed.

He trickled into my room.

He had shimmered in.

He floated noiselessly through the doorway like a healing zephyr. . . . This fellow didn't seem to have any feet at all. He just streamed in. . . . Then he seemed to flicker, and wasn't there any longer.

In "The Artistic Career of Corky," Bertie provides his most penetrating analysis of this effect:

> "Sir?" said Jeeves, kind of manifesting himself. One of the rummy things about Jeeves is that, unless you watch like a hawk, you very seldom see him come into a room. He's like one of those weird birds in India who dissolve themselves into thin air and nip through space in a sort of disembodied way and assemble the parts again just where they want them.

You can see how much more effective Wodehouse's verbs are than bland ones like *went* or *entered* or *came*.

Even the simplest of action can spring alive with a good verb. In Elmore Leonard's 1989 *Killshot*, he tells the reader that the outboard motor "grumbled in the water." That is using the language imaginatively and, of course, he does that throughout his book.

In the area of language improvement, one of the prime concerns of the workshop leaders at the Conference is to nudge students out of the habit of clichés. As one of the teachers advises his students with only a trace of a smile:

> "Avoid clichés like the plague!"

Every Conference sees its share of: *drunk as a lord, thin as a rail, brown as a nut, his heart beat a tattoo in his chest, he felt as low as a snake's belly, his blood boiled, his blood ran cold, light as a feather, cold as a fish, stiff as a board*, and so forth.

Clichés are all right, of course, in dialogue since most of us talk in clichés much of the time:

> "Hey, Tom, long time, no see!" he said. "Keepin' your nose to the old grindstone? All work and no play, you know—we're not getting any younger, time sure flies, doesn't it, but you look fit as a fiddle . . ."

But clichés in the author's words should be avoided like—well, er, like the plague. *Eyes like limpid pools, beestung lips, bedroom eyes, eyes at half mast, an hourglass figure, an aquiline nose, sinister eyes, a heart as big as all outdoors, was all heart, his word as good as his bond, a toothbrush mustache, hands like hams, a burly cop, strong as an ox, weak as a kitten, eyes that crinkled when she smiled, a chill ran down his spine, a smile that lit up the whole room*, et cetera, et cetera.

A cliché is a tired expression that is still around because it was pretty good when new. While Shakespeare seems to use a lot of clichés, they weren't clichés then because he either invented them or was the first to put them in print:

> vanished into thin air, something rotten in Denmark, in a pickle, refuse to budge an inch, too much of a good thing, without rhyme or reason, play fast and loose, hoodwinked, a fool's paradise, lie low, tongue-tied, at one fell swoop, an eyesore, the long and short of it, etc. etc.

The time to catch the clichés is in the rewrite. Sometimes you don't have to totally discard the cliché but can reshape it. For example, the last one in the above group could be changed from "a smile that lit up the whole room" to:

> When she smiled it was as though the switch to a whole row of kleig lights in the room had been thrown.

That would not be great, but it would say what you wanted to say and still dodge the cliché. How to express the thought "chill down the spine" without resorting to the cliché? Play around with the same basic idea only with different words, as Joseph Wambaugh does here in *Echoes in the Darkness*:

> So the casket got hooked to chains and raised up by the backhoe. It had been a long day in that graveyard by the time they got the casket out of the grave and swinging around in the crisp spring air. Then the chain slipped and the coffin shifted, and it was like someone dropped ice cubes down their backs that slipped right into their underwear. It was the *sound* of the resident of that coffin when he did a 360-degree roll.

Brown as a nut is so familiar that *as a nut* makes the compared object no browner than just saying "brown" by itself. One might, however, take the cliché, expand it a bit, and be specific:

> The old woman's skin was the color of a walnut shell and just as wrinkled.

Here's how Joseph Wambaugh, a speaker at our 1989 Conference, adroitly handled that ancient cliché *cold fish eyes* in his true crime book of 1987, *Echoes in the Darkness*:

It took a full week for the new principal to walk into her office and introduce himself.

"You've never seen such a pair of eyes in all your life," she said often. "There was no *feeling* in them. You might think you've known a few people with cold fish eyes, but not like his."

They were *not* fish eyes. They were eyes that newspaper editors in later years loved to isolate for effect. They were referred to as "reptilian," but that was not correct either.

Jay Smith was tall, middle-aged, with receding dark hair, a weak knobby chin, and a rubbery sensual mouth. He was *not* an attractive man. Some thought that Jay Smith looked like an obscene phone call.

Strange, even though the author tells us that they weren't fish eyes or reptilian eyes, that is the impression we come away with.

Wambaugh, incidentally, is a master of the *In Cold Blood* technique, the novelizing of true criminal cases. Anyone interested in that genre should read his *Onion Field* and *The Blooding*, and of course, the prototype, Truman Capote's *In Cold Blood*.

A student in my class last year wrote this tired line: *I'd rather dance than eat.*

We kicked it around and she renovated it to: *I'd rather rhumba than eat a rum baba any old day.*

I myself would have preferred a simple sentence like: *I like to dance a lot.*

You may point out the fact that many best-selling novels today are cliché ridden. How do they get away with it? The answer is that they probably have such well-defined characters, stock or otherwise, in such interesting predicaments, with such human conflicts, that the reader becomes engrossed in the outcome and overlooks the lazy writing. And that is what it is, lazy writing, for it is easier to toss off "hair the color of wheat" than to look for some better, less hackneyed, comparison; it is always easier to make a familiar generality than to look for a telling specific.

Judith Krantz has a style of her own, and whether you write lush sentences like hers, convoluted sentences like Faulkner, terribly long-then-short sentences like E. L. Doctorow, terse ones like Hemingway, ones with punch like Elmore Leonard, or flamboyant ones like both Tom Wolfes, your own individual style will creep through and establish itself if, and this is a big if, you are expressing exactly what you mean to convey in clear language.

One more admonition—be stingy with your exclamation marks. As F. Scott Fitzgerald says: "An exclamation mark is like laughing at your own joke."

Ted Berkman teaches biography and autobiography at the Conference, but he has written a great deal of fiction (the best seller and film *Cast a Giant Shadow, To Seize the Passing Dream*, etc.). He loves words and shares his affection with his crowded workshops. I once heard him say fervently, "Words are as beautiful as wild horses, and sometimes as difficult to corral." Here he is to wind up this chapter on style:

Professor William Strunk Jr.'s admonitions on style have for half a century guided countless authors of fiction and nonfiction through the labyrinths of composition. I had the good fortune to be a student of Willie Strunk's course, "The Elements of Style" at Cornell in the faraway days when Big Red football titans dominated the Ivy League.

Strunk's "little book," first privately printed in 1919, published more widely in 1935, and expanded in the '50s and '70s by *The New Yorker*'s E.B.White, has become a miniature bible for professional writers. In the semantically slovenly age of television, its strictures on grammar, organization, and usage are more relevant than ever.

Willie himself projected an aura endearingly Victorian. His pumpkin-round head and steel-rimmed glasses, the thin, meticulously plastered gray hair neatly split down the middle, and his cranky, half-croaked pronouncements linger in memory like the smile of the vanished Cheshire cat. In his trim country-squire tweeds he was a literary artifact of the nineteenth century: Humpty Dumpty, or one of the solemn eccentrics peopling Alice's tea-table in Wonderland. The Mad Hatter, perhaps.

On a more immediate level, he was the classic absent-minded professor. I still chuckle recalling the morning he popped onto his podium in peg trousers, natty brown jacket and pink shirt—but minus his trademark bow tie. Shirt buttoned tightly at the neck, he lectured for an hour, oblivious to the oversight and to the delighted smiles it evoked.

Never was Willie forgetful, however, of his maxims on language. Delivered with biting precision between pursed lips, these issued in a steady stream: "Be clear. Be concise. Be forceful. Know where you're going. Avoid windy locutions, repetitive mannerisms. Save your most important point for last."

Nor was the professor shy about handing down extracurricular opinions. His small moustache bristled as he complained about George Gershwin being allowed to share the Pulitzer Prize for *Of Thee I Sing*. "An ordinary songsmith," he hissed. "My son tosses off better tunes every evening." Happily, Willie's reputation does not rest on his musical expertise. Rereading the "little book" today, I am astonished at how many of Strunk's literary precepts I have tried to follow, and how many still echo in my teaching.

Inevitably every Strunk disciple, set loose on the hard path of personal experience, develops corollaries to the master's doctrine. E.B. White, in his added chapter to *The Elements of Style*, discourses engagingly on the subtleties of rhythm, cadence, and cultivating a sensitive ear. At the risk of treading in the footsteps of a giant, I would add a few notes of my own culled from long labors in the verbal vineyard as reporter, broadcaster, lyricist, screenwriter, biographer, and occasional fictioneer.

Flexing its muscles at the top of my approved list is the verb, preferably short and Anglo-Saxon. The verb in itself has style. Verbs drive a narrative forward, pump blood through its veins, gather around them the necessary nouns, adjectives and adverbs. They define action and underline emotion, thereby promoting my number two concern: pictures.

The writer, especially in fiction, is painting with words, stringing together visual images as fresh and arresting as he or she can make them. Almost as much as the screenplay scenarist, the novelist is aiming ultimately at the gut, although some cerebral detours my be necessary in order to get there. In the perennial search for vividness and color, a writer's best tools are concrete, specific details that speak to the senses: "The cold, wet nose prying under my palm," as the poet Ralph W. Seager put it, "not a dictionary of dogs . . . the snowflake, not the glacier." That's where style comes from.

Are you trying to convey a character? Don't settle for a police-poster chart of height, weight, and hair color; pick a handful of highlights and compress the whole person into them. Saul Bellow can suggest a complete personality in the twist of a lip, the heavy pink flesh of a thigh; his fierce, narrow-beamed authorial gaze has been likened to a "spiritual X-ray." *That* is style.

And don't get hung up on the niceties of a first draft. Give yourself free rein, letting your initial vision run untrammeled, without censorship from the judgmental left brain.

But once you've got the draft down, be prepared to take it apart. Ruthlessly and repeatedly. "Tediousness," observed Samuel Johnson, "is the most fatal of all faults." Two pages—the right two pages—can tell more than four hundred bad ones. As my late colleague Ed Murrow, certainly a stylist of note, liked to say, "Keep it crisp." If readers want stupefaction, they can get tranquilizers. At today's prices, it's cheaper than a novel.

So have the blue pencil and scissors and Scotch tape ready, and wield them without mercy. You're not a pro until you can "kill your darlings," edit out your most treasured inspirations if they violate your larger purpose.

And keep writing, playing with words—in letters, notebook impressions, profiles, vignettes, reflections on relationships, looking for your own style. This is the writer's equivalent of the pianist's five-finger exercises, or the painter's endless pencil sketches outside the Café de la Paix. Behind every sharply etched character in a novel lies a multitude of earlier experimental portraits on which the author honed his or her skills; behind every published page of fine prose there are probably three hundred pages of unpublished preliminaries.

Nothing you write is wasted. Minimally, you will be acquiring a facility that will pay off in years to come. The ghosts of literary immortals will be beckoning you onward.

And the ghost of Willie Strunk will be grinning over your shoulder, watching your style assert itself.

A last thought on style, from Julian Barnes' delightful *Flaubert's Parrot*, in which he paraphrases Flaubert's ideas:

> Do you still think the novel divides, like Gaul, into three parts—the Idea, the Form, and the Style? If so, you are taking your own first tremulous steps into fiction. You want some maxims for writing? Very well. Form isn't an overcoat flung over the flesh of thought . . . it's the flesh of thought itself. You can no more imagine an Idea without a Form than a Form without an Idea. Everything in art depends on execution: the story of a louse can be as beautiful as the story of Alexander. You must write according to your feelings, be sure those feelings are true, and let everything else go hang. When a line is good, it ceases to belong to any school. A line of prose must be as immutable as a line of poetry.

K E Y N O T E R

WILLIAM F. BUCKLEY JR.

He has come twice to the Conference. At the first in 1977 he had only recently come to the writing of fiction after a lifetime of nonfiction. He confessed to being dismayed to look out in the audience and see Eudora Welty, Ross Macdonald, William Styron, and other literary luminaries.

"It would be tedious to elaborate upon my own disqualifications to address this group, so I'll simply plunge ahead and tell you everything I know about fiction writing. Rest assured it won't take long."

In discussing reviews of his first novel *Saving the Queen*, he said that his favorite came from the *Kansas City Star*. "On one point at least we can console ourselves," the reviewer said, "inasmuch as the hero of Mr. Buckley's novel is handsome, witty, and rightminded, it is obviously not autobiographical."

One strict rule he set for himself was to work on the novel for two and a half hours a day. The book was written in Switzerland with mornings dedicated to journalistic tasks, afternoons to skiing, and work on the novel in the late afternoon until seven o'clock. "If you feel as I do that writing is a terrible pain, there is absolutely no point at all in protracting the pain. Under these circumstances I write faster. If you are impatient, you tend to insist on movement. I think it is extremely important for a beginner's writing *to move*. It's one thing to read a languid novel if it's written by a master. The only thing I did permit myself to luxuriate over was my own impatience — and since my own impatience is highly cultivated, my book, my trivial novel, moved."

He added at one point: "In terms of technical difficulties, I kept forgetting the names of my characters. I also have a terrible fear of description. I'm not good at it, color of eyes, hair, width of the mouth, and so forth, so I decided since I don't have it — I'll just leave it out."

And: "Nabokov, my neighbor, a writer I revere, told me I must have some O.S.S — some obligatory sex scenes — so I threw in a couple."

When asked "What kind of mental gears did you have to shift from years in nonfiction to fiction?," he answered:

"It made me a lot lazier. At one point I reminded myself of Mozart, who was so physically lazy when he composed in bed that if a bit of air carried off a sheet of manuscript, rather than picking it up, he'd recompose the page."

As for his great output: "At a purely mechanical level, impatience says I'm going to write 1,000 words a day, instead of saying I'm going to write as many perfect crystalized words as possible. I know authors who stop writing their own books to write books about the difficulty of writing books."

Theme, Thesis, Moral, or Premise

Don't start with a thesis. Start with people. You can't ever make a good play out of an idea. For young playwrights, it's important that they start with the psychological urgency and make the assumption that, if there are symbols, they'll turn up.

*T*his is Edward Albee, one of our great playwrights (*Who's Afraid of Virginia Woolf*, etc.), speaking. Many writing teachers talk about how you have to have a theme before you even start your story, but I don't buy that. I agree with Albee — start with people confronted with problems and by the time you are done with your story/novel/ play your theme will manifest itself.

I find it hard to believe that Tolstoy sat down in front of a blank piece of paper and said:

"I'm going to write a novel called *War and Peace* — or should I call it *The War and The Peace?* — whose theme will be . . ."

I think the themes, rightly or wrongly, were supplied subsequently by hundreds of literature professors the world over.

I recently had a letter from Elmore Leonard after I sent him a review of his latest novel:

"I love the *Chronicle Review*'s saying *Killshot* is 'an indictment of civilization and its by-products.' It's almost as good as the one that said the subtext of my work 'is the systematic exposure of artistic pretention'!"

I was pleased and bewildered not long ago to see an old story of mine in a college literature textbook, but I was infinitely more bewildered than pleased since in the introduction, an erudite one, they ascribed all sorts of things to the simple tale — things I hadn't remotely thought of before, during or after I wrote it. Maybe all those things *were* in my subconscious mind before I wrote and I just didn't verbalize it to myself. My feeling is that once the story is written, like murder, theme will out.

And, apropos the outage of murder:

In *Payment Deferred*, C.S. Forester's first big success, the protagonist, a mousy bank teller, poisons a man for his money and buries him in the backyard. Subsequently he makes a lot of money, but he can't move from his dingy house for fear that new tenants or owners will discover the body. Ultimately his unstable wife commits suicide by drinking poison. Police find the poison the husband used to kill the man with, plus other clues which ironically point to the husband, and he is convicted of her murder and hanged.

Obviously the theme is: Murder will out, or, you can't get away with evil in this world. But in his autobiography, *Long Before Forty*, the author tells of how he constructed the story bit by bit, starting with the idea of the effect of a murdered body lying so close to the murderer year after year. The idea of the wife's suicide and the murderer's ultimate comeuppance occurred to him very late in the planning stage. In other words, he did not start with or look for any theme; the theme emerged as he plotted the story, and it is we the readers who ascribe a moral to it. Without being verbalized, the theme or moral is innate in the author; i.e., he wants murderers to ultimately be punished. (Apparently most people do, as witnessed by the fact that the book became a best seller, a successful play and a movie starring Charles Laughton.)

Tell the story excitingly, choose your characters carefully, and the message, whatever it is, will come through.

It would seem that every writer has his or her own idea of theme (or premise or moral or whatever we choose to call the overall conclusion to be derived from a novel or short story).

James Frey, a workshop leader at the 1989 Conference, emphasizes theme in his classes and, in his book *How to Write a Damn Good Novel*, he writes:

The premise of a story is simply *a statement of what happens to the characters as a result of the core conflict in the story.* Consider these examples:

In *The Godfather*, Puzo shows us a reluctant son becoming a Mafia don because he loves and respects the family. The premise: "family loyalty leads to a life of crime." Puzo proved it well.

In *The Old Man and the Sea*, Hemingway sets out to prove the premise that "courage leads to redemption." In the case of the old man it does.

Dickens, in *A Christmas Carol*, shows us a miserly old man who is confronted with his misdeeds by the spirits of Christmas, and who is transformed into a kind of Santa Claus. The premise: "forced self-examination leads to generosity."

Le Carré, in *The Spy Who Came in from the Cold*, shows us that even the greatest of spies can be demoralized by the duplicity of his own government. The premise: "realization leads to suicide."

Kesey's *One Flew Over the Cuckoo's Nest* proves the premise that "even the most determined and ruthless psychiatric establishment cannot crush the human spirit."

Nabokov's *Lolita* proves that "great love leads to death." It does in Humbert Humbert's case.

Flaubert knew premise well. *Madame Bovary* proves that "illicit love leads to death."

Does every dramatic story have a premise? Yes. One and only one premise? Yes. You can't ride two bicycles at the same time and you can't prove two premises at the same time. What if Dickens in *A Christmas Carol* were also trying to prove that "crime doesn't pay" along with his premise that "forced self-examination leads to generosity"? He'd have Scrooge exposed as a crook and punished. Wouldn't work, would it? What if Kesey wished to prove that "love conquers all," in addition to his premise "even the most determined and ruthless psychiatric establishment cannot crush the human spirit"? He'd really have a cuckoo's nest. How could he make his statement about the uncrushable nature of human spirit at the same time? He clearly couldn't.

Why a story can have only one premise is self-evident once you understand the nature of premise. In fiction, the premise is the conclusion of a fictive argument. You cannot prove two different premises in a nonfiction argument; the same is true for a fictive argument. Say the character ends up dead. How did it happen? He ended up dead because he tried to rob the bank. He tried to rob the bank because he needed money. He needed money because he wanted to elope. He wanted to elope because he was madly in love. Therefore, his being madly in love is what got him killed; "great love leads to death" is the premise.

Novelist Thomas Turner states boldly:

Characters come before theme.

He adds:

The theme is a generalization derived from the action of the novel. The writer is making a statement about life. He is trying to make sense out of darkness and chaos.

Since the word "theme" has become so closely associated with the word "moral" and "message" perhaps instead of saying that a book has a theme we should be saying *issue* defined as a matter to be *disputed and decided*. Disputed with whom? By the writer himself. He is resolving a conflict between his own nature and the nature of the world as he knows it. A writer is like a court, deciding an issue by examining the evidence.

Here is the dean of our workshop leaders, John Leggett, an old hand at theme in his half-dozen novels:

"To produce a mighty book," said Herman Melville, who certainly knew about such things, "you must choose a mighty theme."

I remember reading a student's story that was full of incident—mountain climbers about to plunge into a ravine, a skier schussing into peril and a killer waiting in the valley below. In spite of all this action the story was not just boring, but infuriating, because it was impossible to tell what the author meant by it. It turned out he didn't know either. He had no notion of theme.

A story's characters and events take on meaning only when we grasp the author's intent, or at least that the author has one.

All the story's elements—its principal characters, its narrative, its voice, its scene—must fashion and illuminate its theme, which is to say they must provide some insight about human life and human nature.

Shopwornness, the cliché condition, applies not just to characters, but of course to language, to expressions and metaphors, and to ideas and themes. Themes often spread through the storytelling population like an epidemic, very likely germinated by some development in the common culture.

In a recent writing class it seemed that all the young women were writing about adult heroines who had suffered a "battered childhood." As if struck from a mold, each story had a father bent on daughter-molesting and a mother addicted to drink and inattentiveness.

I could not help but think they had sprung from the popularity of family-therapy confessionals. It was even more depressing to realize that this theme taps into the deceptively alluring stream of self-pity. What a mistake it is to imagine that self-pity, such a lovely wallow for the originator, is appealing to anyone else. For a character, or a narrative voice, an air of self-pity has all the appeal of warts.

It is often said that an author should be able to state the theme of a story in a single sentence. The practice is in disrepute because to do so is likely to reduce the most subtle and complex of themes to banality or bumper-sticker absurdity. Nevertheless, the author must know what he means by the story.

In fact, what a serious author means by a story reveals almost everything about that author, what that author thinks is important in life, what he or she believes about how the world works—or fails to work.

Suppose for example that a writer has a heroine work diligently at her job in the fish cannery and be rewarded by a two-dollar an hour raise and a trip to Vancouver. We recognize this author's world as a relatively benign place, where human beings have some control over their destiny.

But suppose another writer takes this same industrious heroine and has her fired for her pains. As she leaves for home, she even finds that her bicycle has been stolen. We recognize that this writer's world is a far different one, a barren place where human strife is met with cold and indifferent winds.

In any case, theme is not subject matter, not a moral, not a prescription for conduct, not a sermon, nor a course of instruction. It is a revelation of some kind, a discovery the author wants to share with us, and it is most likely to be lured out where we can see it in such change as has taken place in the protagonist's perception of self or the surrounding world.

I recall another student story in which a girl finds her car broken into and her stereo stolen. The girl is crazy with rage, and all she can think to do is call up an ex-boyfriend because he'll know what to do. He does. He calms her, gets the car fixed and talks her out of her anger.

As we read, we realize the girl is still in love with her ex-boyfriend, though he no longer is with her, and the story is about *that* misfortune. In the end, the girl accepts both facts and we realize, with all the force of sudden revelation, that the heroine has been undergoing a major growing-up experience. Now *that's* theme. Telling that by means of a story is about sixty times more compelling and memorable than saying, "One of the lessons we must learn in growing up is how to deal with the loss of love."

My own feeling is that the beginning writer should concentrate on character and conflict and let the themes emerge as they may—and they will, consciously or unconsciously.

Sid Stebel, author of several fine novels including the highly acclaimed 1989 novel *Spring Thaw*, has been with the Conference since its inception in 1972. Here he talks about theme and clarity, or lack of it, in the modern novel, elements he emphasizes in his workshops at the Conference:

How to recognize a story's theme when we read one? Slices of life may demonstrate a writer's skill in focusing on the minutiae of contemporary existence, and sometimes it is true that memorable characters or emotions of powerful intensity have been created. But if, as is too often the case, we're left with a vague feeling of disquiet, as if we've gotten a peeping-Tom's slavering glimpse of strangers' intimacies, without history and without future (*i.e.*, a lack of beginnings and endings), we have a right to wonder what those writers' purposes were in so briefly opening a blind.

I am not so old-fashioned as to suggest that stories need to be told linearly, or that beginnings, middles, and ends can't be juggled in a variety of ways, or even implied, as long as the reader's imagination is steered by the author to certain desired conclusions.

One way of discovering whether a story has been told is if a character has changed. Have the events which a protagonist has endured transformed or enlightened the main character? If not, then it seems to me a given that the author's point, deliberate or not, has been precisely that no matter how much or what traumas have been undergone, the character remains hidebound, armored as an armadillo. Nothing has, or could have, changed this character.

A perfectly valid theme, that. But we need to discover whether that was indeed the author's intent, or whether the author has simply, through laziness or inattention, failed to produce the final catharsis (for the character, if not for the reader), thus producing the resolving chord of the authorial symphony (or concerto, or rondeley, depending upon the scale of the performance).

Theme. Meaning. The hidden agenda. A statement of the underlying issue. Subtext. The author's intent, conscious or otherwise.

It seems to me obvious, or ought to be, that it's the writer's job, not the reader's, to make sense of the fictional world created. The reader will willingly do his part if—it's a big if—the writer has at least removed all inconsistencies from the material. In order to do that, of course, the writer must understand what the material that's been spewed up out of the subconscious is trying to say. I do not mean that the writer has to state the theme explicitly in the written text. But I can virtually guarantee that if the writer sees the theme clearly before the final rewrite, so then too will the reader.

I'm not saying the writer has to dispense with complexity. But complicating the theme, ringing changes on it, does not, repeat not, mean contradicting it or going far afield to give us themes that have no connection with one another. We want our stories woven out of the same cloth, not patched together out of the remnants of the writer's floundering. Even the poorest patchwork quilt ought to have a certain unity in its overall design, not least in the quality of its stitching.

It simply won't do for a writer to cling to ambiguity, counting on us to resolve the story. If the writer knows not only which door the tiger crouches behind, but understands the protagonist so deeply that he can guess which door the protagonist will finally open, then so too will we. What the author knows in his or her bones makes a reader's own bones ache with sympathy.

K E Y N O T E R

ALICE ADAMS

This esteemed novelist and short story writer preferred an interview rather than making a formal talk:

QUESTION: During this week, Ray Bradbury has said that writing is fun, Alex Haley said it is hard but rewarding, and Elmore Leonard said it wasn't fun at first, but it is now that he's successful. Where do you fit in that spectrum?
ANSWER: I think it's more fun than anything. I'd be an idiot if at my age I kept on writing obsessively if I didn't enjoy it. What I don't like are the things connected with it. I don't like the business that surrounds it.

Every now and then a story goes very badly. Or almost always a story does not end up being as marvelous as my initial conception of it. But the actual writing, of course, I love. There's been a lot—too much—said about the agonies of creation. Anyone who feels that way shouldn't write.
QUESTION: What was the theme of *Superior Women*?
ANSWER: I'd be the last person to know what the theme is. Maybe some critic will know. All that interested me was their history. These people are roughly my age. They were in college precisely when I was, and I was interested in what happened to them. My characters are mixtures of me and my friends.
QUESTION: Do you outline your work?
ANSWER: Yes, I do. I outline short stories much more carefully than I do novels. Possibly I should change that in both cases. I don't know. One of the reasons I write novels as opposed to stories, one of the things that continuously interests me about the process of writing novels, is the fact that my original notions change. For

instance in *Superior Women* I develop such an affection for Peg, whom I had really started out being kind of snotty toward.

Stories don't change as much in the process. Maybe they'd be better if they did, I don't know.

Once I was writing a novel about a very handsome man whom I had intended to end up happily at the end as a sort of hero but at some point — I got a very clear message that it was necessary for this man to commit suicide, which he did obligingly.

A short story is comprehensible. I can think about what it's going to be like. I can see the end, unlike a novel.

One problem I find with writing novels is that you almost necessarily rather tire of it. You get a sort of deafness so you can't even tell the good parts any more.

QUESTION: Do you work with an editor?

ANSWER: I sure do. She's a brilliant young woman. I get brilliant input, I would say.

QUESTION: At what moment in the writing do the characters take on their own personality, do they dictate that they should commit suicide?

ANSWER: It can't define that. It could come at anytime. But that's the exciting moment. In a wonderful interview in *The Paris Review* William Faulkner said one of the joys of writing was when a character would suddenly stand up and cast a shadow. But I think the moment when a character will cast a shadow or commit suicide or become more likeable is quite unpredictable or entirely variable.

QUESTION: How long did it take to write *Superior Women*?

ANSWER: That again I should know but I don't quite. It was interrupted. I have a very short attention span. I usually do several things at once, which is to say I'm working on a novel, but I usually have short stories going at the same time. I would say three or four years anyway.

QUESTION: Who is your favorite author?

ANSWER: God, I have so many. Among contemporary authors, Diane Johnson, Cynthia Ozick, Joyce Carol Oates, Alice Walker — it seems to be a group of women. But tomorrow I might give you a different list.

I guess I am rather prolific now. I wasn't prolific when I was younger. In a sense I feel I am making up for lost time. I should have been working harder when I was younger.

Optimally I work in the morning and in the afternoon, and I don't go out to lunch. I find that's a terrible distraction — although I love to. And then I swim and do other things. I can have a lousy morning and a good afternoon or a bad day or a good day; I can't predict an awful day. One depressing fact that I seem to find is that a marvelously productive day of writing is fairly predictably followed by a not-so-great one. I don't work at night usually.

QUESTION: Did you always know you were going to be a successful writer?

ANSWER: Certainly not, and I still don't think of myself as one. I was struck by what Harriet Doerr said this afternoon about being two people: that person is the writer and doing okay, but then one is still one's own terrified person.

QUESTION: Can you describe how your short stories evolve from conception to completion?

ANSWER: They all evolve quite differently. The genesis of each story is quite different. The simplest story that I've written — some of you may have read it — is called "Barcelona." That was a fairly simple recounting of an actual event. I was in Barcelona and someone did run by and snatch my bag. And the man I was with did run after him and he dropped the bag and we got it back. I've never done that before.

Stories can evolve from almost anything. Once we were in a hotel in northern California called Little River Inn. There were nice waitresses, and I began thinking about them and wondering about their lives. So I wrote a story about a waitress at such a place, imagining her life from really wholecloth. That was one of the most entirely made up stories I have written.

I feel strongly that it's a mistake often to read stories or show stories around. It's a mistake that I used to make when I was starting out. This sounds quite paranoid but I found that people would often take the stories as an occasion for the exhibition of some long-standing grudge: "Your story is rotten and anyway I've never liked you." I think extreme caution should be observed in choosing audiences for your stories. You have to be quite certain of the sympathies of the persons to whom you're going to talk because, let's face it, this is a crucially intimate part of oneself.

I used to think outlining my stories in detail was so virtuous. I used to make speeches to the effect that everyone should do that. I even had an outline that I used to give out and that people would copy. But lately I've been trying to get away from that and make my stories a little more fluid. And occasionally they've ended in ways that were a little surprising and quite gratifying to me.

I think generally when you haven't written a great many stories, it's probably better to know how they will end before you start. My first attempt when I was really young and starting to write stories, I used to have a very strong emotion, usually about a very sensitive girl, of course. I would get halfway through and not have the least idea of how it would end, and that made me enormously unhappy. Starting to outline was a great improvement for me.

I do outline my novels, but they get away from me. And it's hard to outline a five-pound novel.

QUESTION: At this point in your career are you ever faced with a rejection slip?

ANSWER: Are you kidding? All the time.

QUESTION: Do you find the market shrinking?

ANSWER: Yes, I do. I have this exceptionally fortunate relationship with *The New Yorker*, but if they don't take it—and a lot of mine they don't—then I'm really up a tree.

QUESTION: Where would they go as secondary outlets?

ANSWER: Well, it depends on the story. Some of them should go to the so-called women's magazines. But then there's a larger group for whom there is really no home. And those are the ones that don't get published or they might end up in some little magazine. There's a magazine called *Shenandoah* that I like a lot and that's been hospitable to me. But it's tough.

Show, Don't Tell

*T*his chapter, along with the all-important one about conflict, might be the most vital to your writing. So many aspiring writers start *telling* rather than *showing* when they set out to create a story. It is the commonest cause of failure, along with lack of conflict.

What does that admonition, *show, don't tell*, actually mean?

As a simplistic example, most jokes that we hear are part tell but mostly show. Take this rather basic one:

> A man was making love to a woman one afternoon. "What's that?" he exclaimed suddenly when they heard the front door bang open. "My god," the woman gasped, sitting up in bed. "My husband!" Quaking, the man heard the heavy footsteps clumping up the steps. "Where's your back door?" the man whispered, jumping up. "We don't have one!" she answered. "Where would you *like* one?" cried the desperate man.

Apart from the debatable humor of the joke, it is a good example of show and tell. Only the first sentence is pure *tell*; the rest of the anecdote is *show*, that is, every effort is made to make you feel that you, the reader, are part of the scene, that you are in that adulterous situation, that you are hearing the door, the footsteps, the desperate conversation. That is *showing*.

Let us *tell* the same story with no showing:

> A man was making love to a woman one afternoon. Without any warning, the woman's husband returned home and came up the stairs. Alarmed, the man inquired as to the rear egress from the building and, upon learning that none existed, he requested that

the woman make a hasty decision as to which part of the structure she envisioned his creating one.

Well, you get the point. Obviously dialogue is a large part of showing. We want to hear what characters say to each other, especially in the dramatic and important parts of a story. If we were writing this scene as part of a story or a novel, instead of a quick joke, we might heighten the effect of the reader's *being there* by showing what the room looked like, what her perfume smelled like, how the fear-sweat glistened on his neck when he heard the husband's footsteps, and so forth. Remember always that vivid, graphic, specific detail is the lifeblood of all your fictional scenes.

Think of *showing* in terms of motion pictures: In a western when the bad guy comes on the screen, a narrator's voice doesn't boom out over the image, "Luke was a mean guy and everyone in town was afraid of him."

What happens is that Luke strides out of the saloon, kicks the dog sleeping on the porch, pushes the town cripple out of the way, and walks down the street as people cringe, sidestep him, and watch him fearfully. Now we have been *shown* that he is not a swell fellow, and our hero better watch out.

In the film *Letter to Three Wives*, when protagonist Paul Douglas gets kissed in the car by Linda Darnell, a subtitle doesn't come on saying: "Wow, he has fallen for her like a ton of bricks!"

The screenwriter had to show that cupid had struck the big lug in a big way. How to do it? The job was done in a simple, lovely way: After she gets out of the car, he sits there dazedly for a long time. Then mechanically he takes out a cigarette, lights it with the car's cigarette lighter, shakes the lighter twice, tosses it out the window, and drives off.

This was far more effective than if he had said "I love her" ten times over. The writer *showed* us!

Apropos romance, it is always an interesting situation when two characters in your story are *shown* to be in love and don't know it. The reader knows that they are truly meant for each other, but they themselves haven't a clue. It is always eminently satisfying when, after some climactic scene, they wake up and realize what we've known all along (because we've been shown), that they adore each other and should live together happily ever after.

Many unimportant parts of a story may be *told* rather than shown in a story, but the reader will feel cheated if not "present" at the important ones, such as the one where the protagonists realize they love each other. We want to be *shown* how it happened: how the air smelled, how her hair smelled, how the gardenia smelled, how the garlic from the stove smelled, and how the crackling eggs frying in the olive oil smelled. Never forget what an important sense smell is in evoking the atmosphere of a scene. (I remember one student's writing Hemingwayesquely: "I saw her standing well and true at the bar and she was gorgeous, smelling of jalapeños and WD-40." Which just might be considered overdoing it.)

If it's a love scene, we want to be *shown*, not told, how that first touch felt—and in a sensual, graphic way. Not like this:

> He reached his hand out, touched her breast and was thrilled to the core.

This description doesn't do a thing for the reader. Why? Because it is telling rather than showing. Let's try showing:

> He reached out his hand tentatively. Her glance made him draw it back. He was trembling. Her perfume was gardenia-scented and it made him bolder. He put out his hand more decisively, this time on her white bare shoulder. She gave a shudder, but didn't move. Do I dare? he thought even as his hand moved down. Her dress was strapless. His little finger slid under the top of her velvet gown. He pushed it down slightly. Still, she didn't pull away. He slid three fingers under the dress and pushed it down more. Now he could see the beginning of the pinkness around her nipple and he found that he was breathing very hard.

Better? Certainly better than "thrilled to the core."

An outline of an action—"and then he went there and got mad and afterwards he took a knife, went back to the house and brooded for several days until he finally . . ."—is not the way to write a story.

A story proceeds by narration of dramatized, closely examined *scenes* with atmosphere and settings and probably dialogue, and appeal to the readers' senses to coax and invite them into the story, to *be* someone in the story, to live the events of the story and thus virtually to enjoy the privilege of living another life or lives with all the attendant problems and joys.

Of course, some *telling* is not only permissible but in many cases desirable and necessary to enhance the *showing*, especially when done as well and vividly as T. Coraghessan Boyle does in the passage from a short story called "Greasy Lake":

> Digby wore a gold star in his right ear and allowed his father to pay his tuition at Cornell; Jeff was thinking of quitting school to

become a painter/musician/head-shop proprietor. They were both expert in the social graces, quick with a sneer, able to manage a Ford with lousy shocks over a rutted and gutted blacktop road at eighty-five while rolling a joint as compact as a Tootsie Roll Pop stick. They could lounge against a bank of booming speakers and trade "man's" with the best of them or roll out across the dance floor as if their joints worked on bearings. They were slick and quick and they wore their mirror shades at breakfast and dinner, in the shower, in closet and caves. In short, they were bad.

That is pure *telling*.

What percentage of your novel or story will be *show* and which will be *tell*? It will vary. The first three paragraphs of my novel *Matador* were pure *tell*—the author speaking—then we slid into *show* and never looked back at *tell*. In O. Henry's famous short story "The Gift of the Magi," he is in and out of *show* and *tell* constantly; the *telling*, the author's intrusion to inform us what is going on, seems unnecessary and dates the lovely little tale. Here's the first page:

> One dollar and eighty-seven cents. That was all. And sixty cents of it was in pennies. Pennies saved one and two at a time by bull-dozing the grocer and the vegetable man and the butcher until one's cheeks burned with the silent imputation of parsimony that such close dealing implied. Three times Della counted it. One dollar and eighty-seven cents. And the next day would be Christmas.
>
> There was clearly nothing to do but flop down on the shabby little couch and howl. So Della did it. Which instigates the moral reflection that life is made up of sobs, sniffles, and smiles, with sniffles predominating.
>
> While the mistress of the home is gradually subsiding from the first stage to the second, take a look at the home. A furnished flat at $8 per week. It did not exactly beggar description, but it certainly had that word on the lookout for the mendicancy squad.

While it is not unknown in fiction for the author himself to step in and *tell* (viz.: Jane Eyre's "Reader, I married him"), it should be an option weighed heavily against the loss of the reader's "willing suspension of disbelief," a diminution of credibility, and a reminder that there is a writer behind all this who is out to manipulate the reader's emotions. The day of the author's addressing the reader directly is over, at least in the modern commercial novel. *The Way We Live Now*, Anthony Trollope's 1875 masterpiece, begins in a way which was fine then but which seems dated now:

Let the reader be introduced to Lady Carbury, upon whose character and doings much will depend of whatever interest these
pages may have, as she sits at her writing-table in her own room
in her own house in Welbeck Street. Lady Carbury spent many
hours at her desk, and wrote many letters ...

Is the difference between *show* and *tell* still not clear? Let's try this:

Jess, dressed like a cowboy, went into the barn and began to milk
the cow, the first time he'd ever stooped to doing it.

That is obviously *tell*. Now let's make it *show*:

Jess strode off with the bucket toward the barn in that peculiar
rolling gait that was just short of a limp, his spurs ching-chinging,
his bat-wing chaps flapping against his bowed legs, and his black
hat with the rattle-snake band tilted back on his thatched head.
The red door squealed in protest when he swung it open, and the
ammoniated stench of the wet hay stung his nostrils. He found
the cow in the darkness, her muley horns lit by a Rembrandt
shaft of light and, patting her bony rump gingerly, he grunted:
"Amelia, this here might be the beginning of a beautiful relationship." She answered with a wary and unconvinced *moo*.

A Dennis-the-Menace cartoon a few years back had Dennis explaining to a friend as they studied his father reading: "A book is like
TV, only you have to think up the picture in your head."
Sage words! Just make sure you give your reader enough visual
clues to help him form a vivid image.
Sometimes *show* appears to be *tell* when it really isn't. The opening
of Elmore Leonard's 1989 bestseller *Killshot* looks like *tell* for a moment. Then you realize that he is *showing* what's in the Blackbird's
head. And in very short order the author is in complete *show*: We are
in that hotel room, we are listening to a conversation, eavesdropping,
and something somehow ominous is afoot. Somebody wants Blackbird to kill someone. One guy wants something, the other guy doesn't.
Conflict, hence—interest!

In the moment the voice on the phone said "Detroi-it" the Blackbird thought of his grandmother, who lived near there, and began
to see himself and his brothers with her when they were young
boys and thought, This could be a sign. The voice on the phone
said, "What do you say, Chief?"

"How much?"

"Out of town, I'll go fifteen."

The Blackbird lay in his bed staring at the ceiling, at the cracks making highways and rivers. The stains were lakes, big ones.

"I can't hear you, Chief."

"I'm thinking you're low."

"All right, gimme a number."

"I like twenty thousand."

"You're drunk. I'll call you back."

"I'm thinking this guy staying at a hotel, he's from here, no?"

"What difference is it where he's from?"

"You mean what difference is it to *me*. I think it's somebody you don't want to look in the face."

The voice on the phone said, "Hey, Chief? Fuck you. I'll get somebody else."

This guy was a punk, he had to talk like that. It was okay. The Blackbird knew what this guy and his people thought of him. Half-breed tough guy one time from Montreal, maybe a little crazy, they gave the dirty jobs to. If you took the jobs, you took the way they spoke to you. You spoke back if you could get away with it, if they needed you. It wasn't social, it was business.

He said, "You don't have no somebody else. You call me when your people won't do it. I'm thinking that tells me the guy in the hotel—I wonder if it's the old guy you line up to kiss his hand. Guy past his time, he don't like how you do things."

There was a silence on the line before the voice said, "Forget it. We never had this conversation."

"This guy was a punk."

That is not Elmore Leonard the author himself *telling* us that this guy was a punk; it is the author *showing* what is flashing through the character's mind.

Tolstoy maintained that in his most successful stories the reader never knew whose side the author was on. This is also true of most of Elmore Leonard's twenty-eight books. He merely sets down the action and the dialogue and lets you make up your mind who you think is a good guy or a bad guy, which action is just or unjust.

Of course, Elmore Leonard knows what he is doing every moment and whom he wants you to like and whom you should pull for. But the slanting is almost imperceptible.

I have been using the terms *show* and *tell*. You could also call it *scenes versus exposition*. The nomenclature doesn't matter; it's the concept you must implant and reaffirm solidly into your brain and into every fiber of your being when you sit down to write. Say to yourself: I am going to conceive of my story or novel in dramatic scenes (*showing*) connected by whatever hard and essential facts must be absorbed by the reader (*telling*).

The funny thing is that you will find that if the scenes (*showing*) are done well enough, you will need less and less exposition (*telling*). And, when you come to rewrite, you will sometimes find that the hard information that you thought vitally needed to be brought out by itself can be subtly inserted into some character's (major or minor) dialogue.

Something, for example, like this:

> She looked around the cocktail party and dimly heard the Silly Girl saying something about "sure, Hamilton was cute, but wasn't it a shame he was double gaited and totally silver-corded and that he would be cut out of the will in nine months unless he got married and had an heir, I mean, really and truly."

As I said, the labels for achieving this goal may be different, but we are all talking about the same thing. James Frey, a Conference staff member in 1989, talks about what he calls *modes*, but we're emphasizing exactly the same thing:

> In my book *How to Write a Damned Good Novel*, I wrote about what I call the three "modes" of dramatic fiction: scene, half-scene, and dramatic narrative. In a scene, the author shows the reader what is happening in real time. The scene plays in the reader's imagination pretty much as it would play in real life. Here's an example of a scene from *Madame Bovary*:

> At dinner that night her husband found that she was looking well, but when he asked about her ride she did not seem to hear him; she sat leaning her elbow on the table beside her plate, between two lighted candles.
>
> "Emma!" he said.
>
> "What?"
>
> "Well, I went to see Monsieur Alexandre this afternoon; he has a mare several years old, but still in fine shape, except that she's a little kneesprung. I'm sure he'd sell her for three hundred francs or so . . . I thought you'd like to have her so I reserved her . . . I bought her . . . did I do right? Tell me."
>
> She nodded. Then, a quarter of an hour later, she asked, "Are you going out tonight?"

"Yes. Why?"

"Oh, nothing . . . nothing, dear."

As soon as she was rid of Charles she went upstairs and shut herself in her room.

At first she felt dazed; she saw the trees, the paths, the ditches and Rudolphe; and again she felt his arms tighten around her while the leaves quivered and the reeds rustled.

But when she saw herself in the mirror she was amazed by the way her face looked. Never before had her eyes been so big, so dark, so deep. She was transfigured by something subtle spread over her whole body.

She repeated to herself, "I have a lover! I have a lover!" and the thought of it gave her a delicious thrill . . .

This scene, like all good dramatic scenes, exploits the conflict (he wants her to respond to him, she refuses); shows emotional growth in the characters (he grows more and more befuddled, she moves from unresponsive to giddy); and comes to some sort of climax and resolution (Emma's repeating "I have a lover" resolves the scene). A scene follows the same sort of development as a story follows: opposition of wills leads to conflict which rises to a climax and resolution.

In the above scene Emma is first lost in thought, ignoring Charles, then she gets rid of him, and finally goes to her room and sees herself flush in the mirror and is thrilled by her sense of being alive and in love.

The conflict in a scene need not be the same conflict as the core conflict of the novel. The core conflict of a novel may be, say, survival at sea in a storm, but some of the scenes might show the conflict between lovers, which impacts the survival story in some way but does not contribute directly to it at the moment.

In the dramatic narrative mode, the author summarizes the action without showing us a scene. Here's an example from *Madame Bovary*:

Charles did not know what to answer; he respected his mother and idolized his wife; he considered his mother's judgment infallible, and yet everything about Emma was irreproachable to him. After the elder Madame Bovary had gone, he would timidly try to repeat, using her own words, one or two of the mildest criticisms he had heard her express; Emma would quickly prove to him that he was wrong and send him back to his patients.

Meanwhile, following theories in which she believed, she made determined efforts to experience love. In the garden, by moonlight, she would recite to him all the passionate verses she knew by heart and sing him mournful adagios accompanied by sighs; but afterward she found herself as calm as before, and Charles did not seem to be any more amorous or stirred up.

Unable to produce the slightest spark of love in her heart by such means, and as incapable of understanding what she did not feel as she was of believing in anything that did not manifest itself in conventional forms, she easily convinced herself that there was no longer anything extraordinary about Charles's love for her. His raptures had settled into a regular schedule; he embraced her only at certain hours. It was one habit among many, like a dessert known in advance, after a monotonous dinner.

Flaubert is relating through dramatic narrative the same values he could have shown in a scene. Charles wants to set his wife straight in view of his mother's criticism, but Emma does not want to be straightened. This is conflict. The climax comes when she "sends him back to his patients." There's emotional growth in Charles. He gets up his courage to criticize Emma and gets quickly put in his place.

Next, Flaubert summarizes Charles and Emma's love life. Emma recites love poems hoping to excite Charles, but he is unresponsive. This is conflict; a conflict which resolves in Emma's giving up.

The third narrative mode is the half-scene, which is a combination of dramatic narrative and scene. The author summarizes the action, moves into a scene at key moments, then returns to dramatic narrative.

Here again, the example I used in *How to Write a Damn Good Novel* is from *Madame Bovary*:

Toward the end of September, Charles spent three days at Les Bertaux. The last day went past like the others, with the big moment being put off from one to the next. [Dramatic narrative to this point; now scene begins.] Monsieur Rouault was accompanying him a short distance before seeing him off; they were walking along a sunken road; they were about to part. The time had come. Charles told himself he must make his declaration before they came to the corner of the hedge; finally, when they had passed it, he murmered, "Monsieur Rouault, there's something I'd like to say to you."

"Go on, tell me what's on your mind—as if I didn't know already!" said Monsieur Rouault, laughing gently.

"Monsieur Rouault—Monsieur Rouault—" stammered Charles.

"As far as I'm concerned, I'd like nothing better," continued the farmer. "I'm sure my daughter agrees with me, but I'll have to ask her just the same. I'll leave you here and go back to the house. Listen to me now: if she says yes, you'd better not come in, because of all the people around; and besides, it would upset her too much. But I don't want to keep you in suspense, so I'll open one of the shutters all the way against the wall; you'll be able to see it if you look back over the hedge."

And he walked away.

Charles tied his horse to a tree, ran back to the path and waited. Half an hour went by, the he counted nineteen minutes by his watch. Suddenly he heard a sound from the house: the shutter had slammed against the wall; the catch was still quivering. [End of scene; return to dramatic narrative.]

He returned to the farm at nine the next morning. Emma blushed when he came in, but she forced herself to laugh a little in order not to seem flustered. Monsieur Rouault embraced his future son-in-law. They postponed all discussion of financial arrangements: there was still plenty of time, since the wedding could not decently take place until the end of Charles's mourning, the spring of the following year.

The winter was spent in waiting . . .

Again, there's conflict. Charles wants to marry. There's a rising conflict as he stammers out his proposal, which is *shown in the scene* rather than being summarized in narrative, followed by a return to dramatic narrative. This is the half-scene technique.

As James Frey points out, half-scenes allow the author to narrate quickly what may happen over a long period of time—in effect, compressing time—and then focus in on the moments of most intense conflict.

Here are some final examples to ram home the show and tell concept. Instead of telling our readers:

Jim was a bastard, lying and cheating on his nice wife, Lydia.

See how much more visual and effective to let readers see for themselves:

"I love you, my darling," said Jim embracing his wife.

"Forever?" Lydia asked wistfully.

"Forever," he whispered fervently, looking past her cheek at his watch; only twenty minutes until he'd be in Marilyn's arms. "Yes, darling, forever."

The reader enjoys observing and discovering things for himself or herself. "Hey, this guy's a louse! I want to read on and see him get his comeuppance!"

George Meredith had no need to tell the reader that his protagonist was narcissistic in his novel *The Egoist*; all he had to do was show Sir Willoughby looking deeply into a lady's eyes and "find reflected there the only person he had ever truly loved."

Sometimes a writer, for emphasis, will *show* and then *tell* or vice versa to underline the point:

> "To pee or not to pee," slurred Ellsworth Whitney, raising his glass of straight Stolie to the others at the bar. "Tha's no longer the question."
>
> As he lurched off toward the men's room, Mary Lou watched him go with loving, troubled eyes. She gave a nervous little laugh.
>
> "Ellie's been working so hard lately," she said unhappily, twisting the little paper napkin into a knot. "Since the accident. Just so tired, that's all. He needs—he just needs a little vacation, that's all he needs." She stood up abruptly. "That damned accident!"
>
> Ellsworth's daily intake had indeed stepped up since the accident, there was no doubt about it, and Mary Lou who truly loved him was worried sick and felt helpless.

The last sentence *does* reinforce the preceding scene but—big question—is it necessary? Isn't it all *shown* in the scene itself? If reinforcement of the idea is needed, you might do better to recruit one of the minor characters at the bar and do some more *showing*, such as adding this:

> Sandra put her hand on Mary Lou's and patted it.
>
> "Honey, why don't you just dump that guy? He's sloshed all the time these days, and using that accident for an excuse. Sure it was awful, but he's dragging you down with him, that's the terrible thing. We all love you and hate to see you go through this."

Or the bartender could wrap it up with:

> "Y'know, I love 'em both but he's been, y'know, different since the—well, since the unpleasantness, y'know, and it's killin' her, it truly is."

Sometimes the difference between *show* and *tell* is so subtle that you almost don't know the disparity. Which is *show* and which is *tell* here?

He rode down to the town, to the Silver Dollar, bent on killing Tom Killion, thinking about the best way to do it though his father had warned against using a gun.

Or here with a larger dose of *show*:

The horse rocked easily under him as it made its way on the moonlit path through the fragrant sage that scraped against his chaps. *He's there, he's gotta be there.* The .45 on a frontier frame was heavy on his thigh but pop's words echoed in his brains: *Use the gun and you're dead!* Pop was right—it was the bowie in his boot sheath that would do it. Just walk up to the bastard at the bar and say, casually: "Hi, Tom Killion—how've you been?" and slide the blade in under his ribs, just above that big belt buckle. Then, in front of him, he saw the lights of the Silver Dollar flicker on the horizon.

The moral of all this is: *Show* whenever possible but don't be afraid to *tell* when it is called for. I have not seen a manuscript yet that erred on the side of *showing* too much!

And always remember Terence's admonition, written around 150 B.C.:

No tale is so good, my Antipho, but can be spoilt in the *telling*. (My italics!)

HARLAN ELLISON

What else is writing but showing off. Writing is the most incredible act of ego anyone can perform. You show me a writer who is humble, I'll show you a hypocrite. The minute you sit down and write something for publication, what you are saying by the act itself is, "What I have to say is important enough for you to read. What I have written is important enough for you to know." That's pure ego. I don't care what a Casper Milquetoast you are in real life, you are saying, "I'm top of the world, Ma."

I'm a writer, folks. That's what I do for a living, for Christ's sake. Day in and day out for thirty years professionally and about fifteen years before that as an amateur, since I was about ten years old. I write.

I'm a professional liar, folks. I don't know any great secrets of the universe, any more than you do. If when I write a story, I'm able to capture one small thing about the human condition and lay it on you in a way to make you say, "Wow, I never noticed that before." For instance, did you ever notice the toilet roll in the bathroom? Women hang it so the tongue hangs down the back; men hang it so it hangs over the front. No one notices that. That's the eye of the writer. That's what I talk about when I come to talk.

The trick is not becoming a writer, folks, the trick is staying a writer. It is the hardest possible life. I do not say this from the lofty glass pinnacle of never having worked at other jobs. I have worked on road gangs, I still have my brick layers' ticket, I have driven truck cross-country. I know whereof I speak. Writing is tough work. As Perlman said, "The muse is a tough buck." Staying a writer for thirty years is probably the greatest achievement of my entire career. Hanging in there, day after day after day, and doing it. And I must tell you that I don't fancy writers' conferences very much because there is a sadness in a great many people who come to them, a longing, an unnatural hunger for something they should not want if they know what's good for them.

Wanting to be a writer is antisurvival if you have any sense at all. If you've got the brains of a yam, folks, the best advice I can ever give you—and I give it to kids in workshops—"Forget this crap. Go learn plumbing. Plumbers are noble people. They do an important service for humanity, which you know if you've ever had your toilet stopped up. Plumbers are honest people; they do an honest day's labor (as long as they're not drunk). And they make a hell of a lot more money than writers."

Columbia University put up the money for a Writers' Guild Survey, indicating of the 35,000 people who call themselves writers, 2,000 made a living from it, if they were lucky. Two thousand made a living writing full time. Of that 2,000, less than a hundred made more than $5,000 a year from it. At the top are writers who make a lot of money. I make a real good living; I'm lucky—I do real well.

Poverty does nothing but make you hungry and desperate. Don't let them cheat you, folks. Never write on spec. Never write for nothing. Engrave it on your eyelids.

Writers are writers. They are not romance writers or mystery writers or science fiction writers or any of the other handy bullshit labels that *People Magazine* needs to stick in front of the word *writer*.

Category writing, if you can avoid it, avoid it, because once you're in it, you're stuck. Once in a while an Elmore Leonard breaks out, once in a while an Ian Fleming breaks out, once in a while a Ross Macdonald breaks out, once in a while a Doris Lessing breaks out.

Don't let them tag you. Let's say for the sake of argument that your mother gets a job part time working for Movable Feast. And she's going through this neighborhood and these stores selling sandwiches. One of these joints is a whorehouse. Your mother in all innocence goes in, and sells some sandwiches. The joint gets busted, while your mother is inside. Your mother is not a whore.

I once made a pit stop in the whorehouse of science fiction. I am not a science-fiction writer. Occasionally I will write a story in which there is some appurtenance or gadget or thing, which may be called a fantasy device or a science-fiction device. This does not make me a science-fiction writer any more than Agatha Christie was a railroad writer just because she wrote *Murder on the Orient Express*.

Categorization is death.

Plotting

The 1989 recipient of the Nobel prize for literature, Spain's Camilo José Cela, likes to tell this story:

"A young man once said to Flaubert, 'Give me a plot, and I'll write a novel,' and Flaubert said: 'Write this down—a man and a woman fall in love. That's the story. Now you have to provide the talent.' What Flaubert was saying, of course, was that you have to tell me who the man is, who the woman is, and why we should care whether they fall in love or not."

The mother of an art student enrolling in one of my portrait classes advised me: "Homer can't draw so good but he sure can shade!" I refrained from telling her that drawing *is* generally shading and shading *is* generally drawing.

In like manner, plot *is* generally character, and character *is* generally plot. The tendency for the beginner is to think up a plot and then tailor a character to fit it. In some professional stories this may be the case, especially in "gimmicky" plots. In a wonderful old story by Marc Connelly, *Coroner's Inquest*, about circus midgets, this was surely the case. Apparently, what show-business midgets fear the most is a second growth that can come in adulthood without warning; this adds just enough inches to keep them from qualifying for show business and not enough to be considered normal. You can see that the author came across this fact so he invented a love affair between two midgets in the circus and a jealous third midget who causes his rival to have a nervous breakdown and subsequently kill himself. The villain accomplishes this, it comes out in the coroner's inquest, by periodically whittling off bits of the other man's cane so that he thinks he is getting the dreaded second growth.

There are many books and stories whose *idea* comes before the *characters*. Take these questions, for example. "Suppose someone were to try to shoot De Gaulle. Who would it be?" or "Suppose someone saw that those airfields in England supposedly getting ready for a Pas de Calais landing were really covered with plywood airplanes and tanks and that the real invasion was to be at Normandy in two days? What kind of character would it be who would want to get the news to Hitler and help win the war for Germany?" (*Day of the Jackal* and *Eye of the Needle*)

But most great stories and books stem from character, no matter how convoluted the plot may become. "What would happen if this old fisherman named Santiago was out in that little boat and he tied on to a huge marlin?" or "What would happen to the spoiled, bored wife of a small-town doctor in France if she took the dashing neighbor as her lover?" (*The Old Man and the Sea* and *Madame Bovary*)

Oscar Wilde said: "It is personalities not principles that move the age."

He might have added, "And it is personalities, not so much contrived twists, that move a plot."

Once you get a character with a problem, a serious problem, "plotting" is just a fancy name for how he or she tries to get out of the predicament. Plot is the solution to the problem. If the character succeeds it's a happy-ending story, if not it's a tragedy. Pretty simplistic, I'll admit. Let's hear what the author of the classic *Laughing Boy*, Oliver LaFarge, has said about plotting:

> Because critics and advisors are accustomed to speak separately of plot and characterization in analyzing fiction, beginners are likely to lose sight of the inseparable nature of the two. Either can arise from the other, but on the whole I believe it is safe to say that plot must fit character, and usually develops from the seedling combination of a character in a situation.
>
> To the reader enjoying the finished story, the plot must appear to be the inevitable product of the characters reacting upon the environment—the situations and circumstances—which the author has devised. The author presents a coward with danger; the coward can't meet it but runs away instead, from which in turn develop further complications leading to the eventual end. The author had foreordained this end, but it appears to arise from the nature of the character, and as a matter of fact, in most construction, has actually done so.
>
> Alternatively, a common theme is the apparent coward who, pushed to a certain point, finds courage, with deep effects upon himself, the attitude of others towards him, and the following events. I say "apparent coward": if the author has made the man hopeless, the reader will reject the sudden regeneration, as he will

if the special conditions that produce a favorable reaction are not convincing in the light of the reader's opinion of that particular character. So, again, plot and situation must arise from the demands of sound characterization. If it does not, it will appear that the coward, or whatever he may be, is merely a puppet jerked arbitrarily in different directions by the writer to suit the needs of a story arbitrarily laid down, and immediately reader and storyteller part company.

I like to think of the plot as *the spine* of your story. In *The Odyssey* the spine is Ulysses' struggle to get back to his home after the ten-year Trojan war; all along the way are separate stories but, like ribs, they are connected to the spine. In *Gone With the Wind* the spine is Scarlett's love for Tara; in *Rainman* it is the Tom Cruise character's craving for the money; in *Romeo and Juliet* it is the feud between the families; in *Hamlet* it is the protagonist's need to kill his uncle; in *Moby Dick* it is the quest for the white whale, etc. Ask yourself, what is the spine of my story? Is it Mary's abiding love for her family, John's driving ambition in business, Penelope's search for a father she lost in childhood?

The protagonist's dilemma is that he or she is up against one or maybe all, of these three basic conflicts that beset human beings:

1. Protagonist against another person or society.

2. Protagonist against Nature; you may substitute God, flood, the supernatural, or anything beyond human control.

3. Protagonist against him- or herself.

The germ of a story can be anything you feel strongly about, which causes a surge of emotion when you think of it; how to convey that emotion to the reader is where your plotting comes in. *Story* is playing the melody of a song on the piano with one finger; *plot* is the orchestral arrangement of it. And different arrangers will have totally different arrangements of the same song, some simple, some complicated, some classical, some jazzy.

"Passions spin the plot," they say. How to start the tapestry on the loom? Should you map it all out, chapter by chapter? Some writers do. Should you know the ending before you start? Some writers do. Should you make a graph so that you know where your climax, denouement, and so forth come? Some writers do.

And a lot of writers *don't.*

Some just put a sheet of white paper in the machine and start. A writer friend of mine says: "Hell, if I knew what was coming next I'd be bored to death."

Elmore Leonard claims that the characters of one novel kidnapped him from his home in Michigan and took him to Florida. "The book was supposed to be about Wayne Colson," says Leonard, "but Colson's wife took it away from him." He adds:

> What happens to me and my plots is that I feel my way along. I have an idea what the next scene is about. I shift points of view. I see the story develop through different eyes. Once I realized what I had here was really a husband-and-wife situation, I had to be carried by Carmen. She was more substantial.

Joan Didion told the Conference that she saw a woman in an airport in Mexico and wrote a whole novel around what she imagined her story might be. Her husband, novelist John Gregory Dunne, came to one of his novels by glibly telling a reporter that he was "writing a novel called *The Red, White and Blue*."

> All I know about *The Red, White and Blue* is that Scott Fitzgerald considered a similar title for *The Great Gatsby*. What will it be about? About 600 pages, I hope.
>
> The result of this fabrication was that my publisher invited me to lunch at The Four Seasons to discuss the work in progress, and the progress I was making on it. The night before the lunch, I sat down at my typewriter in a suite at the Carlyle Hotel that a movie company was picking up the tab for in the misplaced hope that I was paying more attention to the screenplay I was allegedly writing than I was to the novel the producers did not know I allegedly had in progress. In a spasm of fear, I wrote the following sentence: "When the trial began, we left the country." An hour or so later I had reached the point where I could note in my diary the next day, "Lunch w/JE [my publisher]—showed her 1st 3-4 pp RWB." And thus began four years at the factory.
>
> What civilians do not understand—and to a writer anyone not a writer is a civilian—is that writing is manual labor of the mind: a job, like laying pipe. Although I had not written a word, I had in fact thought a great deal about the novel over the course of the preceding year. I knew what the first sentence was going to be, and I also knew the last—it is a peculiarity of mine that I always know the last sentence of a book before I begin. That last sentence I intended to be a line of dialogue, either "No" or "Yes," with the penultimate line its reverse, either Yes or No, not in dialogue. It

was the six or seven hundred pages between "When the trial began, we left the country" and "No" (or "Yes") that seemed a desert I could not irrigate.

Here is John Leggett on the subject of plot:

Stories need a structure or framework to give them shape and hold them together, much as a house or a body does. That framework is the *plot*, and it is made up of four major parts, which can be thought of as the story's bare bones:

The Doormat: The first of these is the basic situation, which I like to call *the doormat* since it is the entryway to the story, grounding us in it and introducing its characters.

On the doormat of the Cinderella story, for example, we find the comely, virtuous heroine unjustly assigned to K.P. by her evil stepmother and two poisonous stepsisters.

Complication: The second bare bone of plot is *complication*, that part of the story in which the main character takes some action to resolve the conflict and instead heightens it, increasing emotions of danger, hostility, indecision, or fear.

Cinderella yearns to attend the ball along with her beastly stepsisters but is thwarted by her stepmother. However, a Fairy Godmother appears with a deal. If Cinderella will agree to be home by midnight, she can make the scene in style. And off she goes, enormously impressing the Prince, who does not know what to make of her hasty, midnight departure nor the glass slipper he finds in her wake.

Climax: The third bare bone of the plot is the *climax*, the peak and turning point of the action, that moment when one force of the conflict prevails over, or gives in to, the other. The Prince, glass slipper in hand, sets off on a house-to-house search for the foot that fits.

Denouement: The fourth and final bare bone of the plot is the resolution, more often known as the *denouement*, the unraveling. It occurs at the story's end, disposing of the characters and settling the issues which, earlier, had seemed so perplexing and charged with emotion.

And Leggett, like all the teachers of fiction at the Conference, knows that:

Conflict makes it go! On the most primitive level it is plot itself, the curiosity about what happens next, that is the source of a storyteller's magic. We are reminded of hairy, antediluvian warriors gathered around the tribal historian, their feeble attention spans firmly held by his grunts, or of Scheherezade saving her pretty neck with a new story for each of one-thousand-and-one Arabian nights.

But plot will not work any magic unless it is energized. The energy is a human emotion. If emotion sleeps, so does the listener. What stirs the emotions is conflict.

Conflict is created when a character struggles. It is most likely to emerge when a main character's desire is thwarted in some way. A main character who wants something badly and is capable of struggling to get it is the sort of person a storyteller will want to cast as a protagonist.

In *The Odyssey*, the major conflict springs from Ulysses' desire to get home. That understandable desire is blocked by the anger of Poseidon, who brings his battery of storms, whirlpools, cannibals, and sirens on line for what is surely the classic set of plot complications and a generous supply of story energy.

Conflict brings change and the outcome of the story or novel will normally result in a change in the protagonist's character.

And Leggett goes on to say:

> Don Juan will think twice before he tries to seduce another woman marine. The undertaker will be more skeptical of the coroner's judgement. The sweepstakes winner will check with the Internal Revenue Service before buying the yacht.
>
> We like, and like to identify with, a character that changes and grows in the course of the story, one who gains some understanding. But we know that in life most of us don't learn a great deal from experience and go right on repeating the same patterns and mistakes, particularly after we are grown.
>
> So, when we portray character change in a story (he learns not to be so arrogant, she learns not to be ashamed of her father) the change must be believable. It must answer to our experience and expectations and not simply the needs of a plot.
>
> When the change is believable, it not only brings the reader an understanding of the character, but it explains what the story is about. How the protagonist changes, or what the protagonist learns, is what the story means.
>
> In classic story structure it is the climax which brings about the change. Most likely it is in the main character's world or perception of it. If it is a grand enough change it produces a catharsis shared by hero and reader alike. Oedipus fulfills the terrible prophecy, kills his father, beds his mother, and is blinded for his pains.
>
> If some fundamental change has not taken place, a story has not been told.

TOM McGUANE

Famous for his short stories and novels (*To Skin a Cat, 94 in the Shade*, etc.) he has also written screenplays (*Rancho Deluxe, Missouri Breaks*, etc.). After his talk to the Conference in 1987 he answered questions.

QUESTION: How did you get started?
ANSWER: I wanted to be a writer very early on. I think one of the reasons is my father was a failed writer. Strangely enough he didn't encourage me; in fact he discouraged me from writing. But I started writing when I was twelve or thirteen years old. It never really came to anything. In fact it went on and on. I wrote *Trial in Terror* for about twelve years straight. I didn't publish it until I was in my late twenties. I reached the point of complete discouragement. I remember having a genuine psychotic anxiety attack when I got a book back from a publisher that had been under consideration for eight or nine months. They were really close to taking it and then they abruptly decided at the last minute not to take it. I was twenty-eight and I had a wife and a child. I remember thinking this is just about as much of this as I can stand. I had no backup plans. I really hadn't learned to do anything else.
QUESTION: What is the difference between journalism and fiction?
ANSWER: I think there is almost no difference. And there is certainly no important difference. Journalism used to be the redheaded stepchild of literature. You could wipe out by writer by saying, "He was journalistic. He wrote newspaperese." Frank O'Connor, writing about the writers he admired, said that in all good writers there was an element of journalism, but that in Chekhov that element was 95 percent. It was the highest praise he could think of. I think that in exceedingly good fiction there is a kind of factuality, a kind of literalness, that requires because of its arrangement so slight an adjustment to transcend itself that if held askew, it looks like journalism.

Literature is seldom about what its subject would seem to indicate. And the difference between those two things is something that is not always clear to the author. And this goes back to what is right at hand because you may be able to write about something that is above your reach by examining those things.

If for example I went back home and wrote about the life of the ranch — I really took a strict view of what went on in the ranch — it would not be possible for me to write about that in a way that was not about death.

I don't know how that would happen but the way that the death of the key man would be refracted through the activities of the things you would see, which would express death much more clearly, more closely to you all, than any sort of mellifluous oratory I could say on his behalf.

Your theme is inherent in what you say; so you don't have to worry about whether what you have to say is important; concern yourself with what you know about.

You can't worry about style. You have some style. But you can't do anything about it. Baseball players can't think about style and step up to the plate. They have to think about the ball. Writers have to do the same thing.

Writers have to arm themselves with anything that will protect them from the blank page. Other people call the blank page paper. Civilians know it as paper. But in their narcissistic and paranoid way, writers want you to know that mere paper is a wall, a terrible wall, and it scares them. So they resort to their education, and their theory, and their habits, their self-discipline. They either climb over it, or go through it.

QUESTION: Do you aspire to work again in Hollywood?

ANSWER: Basically, aspiring to work in movies is aspiring to be a copilot. I can't make an honest deal with myself when I look at the blank page if I can't control the page. I can't make every effort to get at the truth of my life and my experience if I'm going to argue with three other people six months from now about whether it really happened. Someone once said that film will be as important as literature when the materials they use are as inexpensive as pencils and paper. I think that's true. I think it'll be as important as literature when they have the guts to turn it over to individuals. I don't think there is a chance of committee art reaching the level of individual art.

QUESTION: Are there themes or subjects that you're afraid to write about?

ANSWER: I'm sure they're down there. You know that you steal of the life around you as you write, you know that if you steal from certain places that the sources are going to be identified, and you wonder how accountable you want to be for that.

Part of the exploration is to get closer and closer to the danger zones and to try to rise above the fear. Although I think it's important to know that that's not really what writing is for. Writing is not for people to unburden themselves necessarily. That's only good when it's good for the writing. I don't think a confessional approach is necessary. Obviously in literature we have people who can just blurt, endlessly, tell the most awful truths about themselves, and it doesn't bother them. But it also utterly lacks any kind of dramatic tension. It used to wear me out about Henry Miller after the first thrill. Then you read Henry Miller and think, "All right he did that and that and that, and he's clearly not ashamed of it," but the tension is gone.

Action and Narrative

*N*arrative is another way of saying what the actors in our stories *do*—a continuing account of their actions. Generally, by action we've come to mean physical doings in a tense situation, not the goings on in a Noel Coward drawing room farce where most of the action is contained and explained by dialogue alone. Jack London, Hemingway, Ludlum, L'Amour, Sheldon, deal mainly in physical action; Henry James, Maugham, Welty, Joyce Carol Oates, Saul Bellow are more interested in interaction between the characters cerebrally and in relationships. Sometimes you find equal interest, such as in stories by Mary Higgins Clark who combines tense action with exploration of character in her thrillers.

In his autobiography, *A Sort of Life,* Graham Greene talks about how to convey "physical excitement" or action:

> Excitement is simple: excitement is a situation, a single event. It mustn't be wrapped up in thoughts, similes, metaphors. A simile is a form of reflection, but excitement is of the moment when there is no time to reflect. Action can only be expressed by a subject, a verb, and an object, perhaps a rhythm—little else. Even an adjective slows the pace or tranquilizes the nerve. I should have turned to Stevenson to learn my lesson: "It came all of a sudden when it did, with a rush of feet and a roar, and then a shout from Alan, and the sound of blows and someone crying as if hurt. I looked back over my shoulder and saw Mr. Shuan in the doorway crossing blades with Alan." No similes or metaphors there, not even an adjective. But I was too concerned with "the point of view" to be aware of simpler problems, to know that the sort of novel I was trying to write, unlike a poem, was not made with words but with movement, action, character. Discrimination in one's word is cer-

tainly required, but not love of one's words . . .

I seem to remember Hemingway's saying that you should do all your describing of a bar or of a room or a place outdoors *before* the action starts, because once it starts you don't want even the smallest distraction to impede what's going on and what's going to happen next. He followed his own advice in "The Short Happy Life of Francis Macomber" in that everything the reader needs to know about guns and lion hunting and wounded animals and what the terrain was like is spelled out *before* the final dramatic action begins.

Graham Greene would subscribe to Hemingway's advice, because once action starts in a Graham Greene story it is a model of stripped tension and economy of words. In his masterpiece of a long short story, "The Basement Room" (made into an excellent film with Ralph Richardson called *The Fallen Idol*), he has only one short scene of violence. The story is seen through the eyes of Philip, a young aristocratic boy (except for a few daring flash-forward, omniscient observations regarding the effect of the episode on the boy's life — an amazing *tour de force*). His idol, Baines the butler, is having an affair with a young woman when suddenly his vicious wife returns home in the middle of the night to trap them. Philip doesn't quite understand everything except that he loves Baines and hates Mrs. Baines:

> He got out of bed. Carefully from habit he put on his bedroom slippers and tiptoed to the door: it wasn't quite dark on the landing below because the curtains had been taken down for the cleaners and the light from the street washed in through the tall windows. Mrs. Baines had her hand on the glass door-knob; she was very carefully turning it; he screamed: "Baines, Baines."
>
> Mrs. Baines turned and saw him cowering in his pyjamas by the banisters; he was helpless, more helpless even than Baines, and cruelty grew at the sight of him and drove her up the stairs. The nightmare was on him again and he couldn't move; he hadn't any more courage left, he couldn't even scream.
>
> But the first cry brought Baines out of the best spare bedroom and he moved quicker than Mrs. Baines. She hadn't reached the top of the stairs before he'd caught her round the waist. She drove her black cotton gloves at his face and he bit her hand. He hadn't time to think, he fought her like a stranger, but she fought back with knowledgeable hate. She was going to teach them all and it didn't really matter whom she began with; they had all deceived her; but the old image in the glass was by her side, telling her she must be dignified, she wasn't young enough to yield her dignity;

she could beat his face, but she mustn't bite; she could push, but she mustn't kick.

Age and dust and nothing to hope for were her handicaps. She went over the banisters in a flurry of black clothes and fell into the hall; she lay before the front door like a sack of coals which should have gone down the area into the basement.

As an aside, I was fortunate to have dinner with the eminent author in 1960. I was living in Tahiti, he was passing through, someone brought him to my house, and we stayed up most of the night talking. He was fascinating on the subject of writing, but to my discredit I made no notes on the occasion the next day and hence haven't a single idea of what was said. Moral: Keep notes! Keep a notebook! Jot down ideas, characters, names, phrases, etcetera! Start today.

Sinclair Lewis once let me browse through his voluminous notebook which he affectionately called Ebenezer. In its orderly pages were categories such as: German-American names, French-American names, story ideas, random dialogue, characters, and so forth. He had several pages under "titles." Reading them, I felt a thrill to see such classics as *Arrowsmith, Babbit, Main Street, It Can't Happen Here,* and *Dodsworth,* all with a line drawn through them and the word "used" next to it.

If Sinclair Lewis and F. Scott Fitzgerald and just about every other author keeps a running notebook, why shouldn't we? Writers' notebooks are usually interesting to read, especially Arnold Bennett's. For example, he was a loving son but on the way to his mother's funeral, after a light rain, he made a note of an interesting observation: "Some bricks dry quicker than others," and later, through his tears, he added:

Orange light through blinds in front of room. Coffin in centre on 2 chairs. Covered with flowers. Bad reading, and stumbling of parson. Clichés and halting prayer. Small thin book out of which parson read. In dim light, cheap new carving on oak of coffin seemed like fine oak carving. Sham brass handles on coffin. Horrible lettering . . .

But getting back to the writing of action, no one has written better action stories than Jack London. One of the greatest of his tales is the classic "To Build a Fire"; I read it first when I was fourteen and it made a big impression upon me. It tells the simple story of a man and his dog caught in the killer cold of the Yukon. He must build a fire or freeze to death. The lean language and the short sentences detailing the man's every move make us feel that we too are with him in the terrible situation:

> The sight of the dog put a wild idea into his head. He remembered the tale of the man, caught in a blizzard, who killed a steer and crawled inside the carcass, and so was saved. He would kill the dog and bury his hands in the warm body until the numbness went out of them. Then he could build another fire. He spoke to the dog, calling it to him; but in his voice was a strange note of fear that frightened the animal, who had never known the man to speak in such way before. Something was the matter, and its suspicious nature sensed danger—it knew not what danger, but somewhere, somehow, in its brain arose an apprehension of the man. It flattened its ears down at the sound of the man's voice, and its restless, hunching movements and the lifting and shiftings of its forefeet became more pronounced; but it would not come to the man. He got on his hands and knees and crawled toward the dog. This unusual posture again excited suspicion, and the animal sidled mincingly away.

Elmore Leonard owes a lot to Jack London and Hemingway for his hard-hitting, spare, narrative prose. In this excerpt from his best-selling novel *Stick,* notice how Leonard realistically leaves words out of the tough guy's dialogue. In this scene, Cecil, the fired chauffeur, has come drunkenly to make trouble for Barry, the employer, who is having a garden party. Stick, the low-keyed protagonist, has been hired to replace Cecil as chauffeur and gofer; he appears on the scene carrying a can of gasoline:

> Stick walked over to the buffet table. He placed a glass on the edge, unscrewed the cap on the gooseneck spout of the gasoline can and raised it carefully to pour.
> Cecil said, "The fuck you drinking?"
> Stick placed the can on the ground. He picked up the glass, filled to the brim, turned carefully and came over to Cecil with it. Cecil stared at him, weaving a little, pressing back against the cart as Stick raised the glass.
> "You doing? I don't drink gasoline, for Christ sake. Is it reg'ler or ethyl?"
> Stick paused, almost smiled. Then emptied the glass with an up-and-down toss of his hand, wetting down the front of Cecil's shirt and the fly of his trousers.
> There was a sound from the guests, an intake of breath, but

no one moved. They stared in silence. They watched Cecil push against the bar, his elbow sweeping off bottles, watched him raise the fifth of Jack Daniel's over his head, the sour mash flooding down his arm, over the front of his shirt already soaked. He seemed about to club down with the bottle . . .

Stick raised his left hand, flicked on a lighter and held it inches from Cecil's chest.

"Your bag's packed," Stick said, looking at him over the flame. "You want to leave or you want to argue?"

This is the perfect action scene because it not only is entertaining to "watch," but it establishes our character once and for all; we see him being gutsy, laconic, and resourceful. There simply is no substitute for action to characterize.

Leonard could have used a dozen adjectives, similes, and metaphors to describe Stick for us and not have made the points he does in this brief scene.

The cliché "actions speak louder than words" has become a cliché because it is true: Stick speaks only twelve words during the whole episode.

K E Y N O T E R

SIDNEY SHELDON

Few writers have the track record that this best-selling author has in both the TV and novel field. He has come to the Conference twice, always with sound advice:

I decided I had to get an idea, and the way I did it was to sit in a chair in my apartment and not get up until I had an idea. I wouldn't get up for a cigarette, I wouldn't go to the bathroom, I wouldn't do anything. I forced myself to sit in that chair and get an idea, a premise for a movie. And after about two hours I had a premise. And I also had to go to the bathroom badly.

I was writing and producing *I Dream of Jeannie* and at the same time writing all the Patty Duke scripts. I used to write a [TV] script a day. On Saturday I would have my secretary come to the house and I would dictate a complete script. Sunday she'd come back and I'd do another script. And during the week while I was producing and doing other things, I would write a third script.

The facility I take no credit for because I think any talent is a gift, and we ought to be grateful for that gift. And we have to work at that gift. In between hours I did eight Broadway shows. And when we worked on Broadway, I loved it. When I did television, I loved it. When I did movies, I loved it.

And I got into writing novels by sheer accident. One day I got an idea that was so introspective you had to really know what the character was thinking. And I didn't know how to do that in a dramatic form. I decided that the only way to do that was to write it as a novel where you could tell the reader what the character was thinking.

I almost abandoned the idea simply because I was terrified of trying the novel. But I liked it enough so I said I would give it a shot, and I called in one of my secretaries and began. I dictated from nine to twelve every day. Then I put on my producer's hat and did other things. Finally the novel was finished. William Morrow published *The Naked Face*; it sold 17,000 copies.

They seemed to be pleased with that. But I had a show that was being watched by twenty million people a week, and I wasn't thrilled by the figure of 17,000.

Still, I sat down to write another novel. And I had no expectation that it would be more successful than *Naked Face* financially.

The reason that I did that is this: There is a freedom in writing novels that is ecstatic. When you do a movie you have a hundred collaborators. You have stars saying, "I can't read those lines," a director saying, "We're going to play it in the mountains instead of the beach," a producer saying, "We're going to cut the budget—we can't play that scene," musicians creating moods with their music.

But when you write a novel, it's yours. In a sense you're God because you create the characters. You decide whether they live or die, whether they have cancer or are happily married. You can do anything you like. You have no limitations. And that is the only reason I sat down to write my second book.

I work in a way that I don't really recommend for anyone who's not very experienced. When I begin a novel, I have absolutely no plot in mind. I have a character.

I dictate my first drafts. I dictate to a secretary. And as I talk the novel starts to come to life. I really feel that my books are being given to me. I wouldn't know how to sit down and create an idea. None of us know where ideas come from. Yet they come. And it flows. And when it starts to roll, the characters take over and that is a thrilling experience. They tell the story for you, and they go in their own directions.

At the end of the day I would look at the typed page and there would be situations in those pages that I didn't know existed in my head in the morning, new character, dialogue. When I dictate a book, I dictate it completely, dialogue, description, everything.

It takes several months for me to finish that first draft. And when I've finished it, it's all typed up. My secretary gives me the pages. And I go to page one, and I start rewriting.

The first draft can be anywhere from a thousand to twelve hundred pages. I will throw away a hundred, two hundred pages at a time, and rip all the scenes apart, tighten and get rid of characters. Create new characters. And a few months later that draft is finished and retyped. And I go to page one, and I start all over again.

And I do that for a year to a year and a half. I will do up to a dozen complete rewrites. Now I'm sure if I just gave that first draft a little polish the books would be best sellers because of my name, but I feel that would be cheating my readers. I feel obligated to make those books as good as I know how.

My publisher doesn't see a word till I have done my last draft and don't know what to do to make it any better. And then I turn it over to them.

If I write about a place, any place, I have been there. If I write a meal in a restaurant, I've had that meal in that restaurant, or I won't write about it. When I decided that one of my protagonists was going to be an ambassador to Rumania, I flew to Rumania and I met with the ambassador there. Now I learned things while I was there that I never could have learned if I had just read about Rumania. You have to do research.

Not everyone here can afford to go to Rumania, but there is another way to do it. You can talk to people. You want to know about Rumania, find a Rumanian society. Find out who some of the people are and talk to them. Do research. I think it's very important. The reader knows when there's something authentic. You can't fake it.

People have said to me, "I would love to write, but I have five kids and I have no time." But she'll have time to go out to lunch with the ladies or to play golf on Sundays. You do what you want to do. You have priorities in life. And if you really want to write, you'll carve out time whether it's early in the morning, late at night, Sundays, whatever. It could be an hour a week, ten hours a week. If you do a page a day, that's seven pages a week. Finally the novel will be written. But it takes that determination.

And it's worth it because creativity is the most exciting thing in the world. Once we were all a piece of the stars. We were created from that. And there's nothing that will bring us as close to touching the stars as actually creating something. Someone said that a blank piece of paper is God's way of telling us how hard it is to be God. And isn't it wonderful that all of us have the chance to try it?

Basically I consider myself a storyteller. I won't let anything get in the way of the story.

I try to write all my books so that when the reader gets to the end of the chapter, he or she must turn one more page and begin a new chapter. It's a cliff-hanger technique that I love doing because I love to read that kind of book so I like to write that kind of book.

What I do is to put my characters into situations that are so precarious there is no way to get out. And then I figure how to get them out.

What all of us must do is get an idea that excites *us* and then write the hell out of it. Write it as well as you know how. And if you hit a nerve, and it's true, then you have a chance.

Motivation: What Does He Want, What Does She Want?

"First, find out what your hero wants," Ray Bradbury boomed from the podium, one arm lifted like Moses delivering the Commandments, "then just follow him!"

He gave us that dictum the first night of our very first Conference in 1972. It's hard to think of a single better piece of advice for a writer. Recently I was having trouble with a novel I'm writing. It wasn't going any place, despite attractive characters and an exotic setting. I suddenly remembered Ray's admonition and discovered: *I didn't know what my hero wanted! I didn't know what motivated him!*

There was no gasoline in the engine.

Novelist John Gardner says: "In nearly all good fiction, the basic — all but inescapable — plot form is this: A central character wants something, goes after it despite opposition (perhaps including his own doubts), and so arrives at a win, lose, or draw."

If you're having trouble with a story or novel, ask yourself: What does my hero or heroine *want*? As a matter of fact, what do *all* my characters want?

And this is extremely important: Whatever it is that they want, they should want it *very much*. Not just a wimpy, vague "gee, wouldn't it be nice to have a lot of money, or live in Hawaii, or marry Marilyn, or maybe kill my brother."

Make a list right now of the principal characters in your story or novel; after each name write what they want. "To be happy" is not enough of an answer; we all want to be happy; Hitler wanted to be happy; he just had a funny way of going about it. No, be specific — as specific as possible.

MAJOR CHARACTERS	WANTS:
Richard, 46 *Investment Banker*	A divorce so that he can marry Charlene, his young secretary. (He really wants to recover his lost youth in a last desperate fling. He's in "the age of repair.")
Esther, 42 *Housewife*	Loves Richard truly and wants to keep the marriage and home together at any cost.
Charlene, 22 *Secretary*	She loves Richard almost as much as she does three other guys in the office—she wants money and position fast.
Woodward, 46 *Lawyer*	Pretends he wants the best for his two good friends, but what he really wants is for the divorce to happen because he loves Esther.

MINOR CHARACTERS	WANTS
Jimmy and Judy, *11 and 14*	Daddy to shape up, stop making Mommy cry, and get their lives back to normal. Jimmy also wants to make the baseball team and Judy wants to be a doctor.
Esther's Mother, 76	Wants Esther to come to her senses, dump that bum she's never liked, and embrace her new church, Our Lady of the Unusual.

Think of your own story or novel that you're working on. Do you know what your protagonist wants, his or her goal? Is it clear to the reader what that is? Is it a goal that the reader will want the protagonist to achieve? Does a great deal of opposition to attaining that goal stand in the way? Is it something very important to the protagonist? This is vital! Make that list!

What is wanted does not have to appear life-threatening or world-shaking to us the reader; it could be no more than a little girl wanting a graduation dress and not having the money for it, but you must show that it is of supreme importance to *her*.

Ask yourself once again: Does what my hero or heroine want have major importance in his or her life, career, love life, marriage, or relationship to his or her family? If it does not, your story is probably in trouble, and that will probably be the reason for its ultimate cool reception and rejection.

Many editors use the term "too slight" in their rejection letters, which generally means not that the problem is too small and unimportant a subject to humanity, but rather that the writer has not convinced the reader, has not *shown* the reader, that this problem — whatever it might be — is a vitally important one to the protagonist.

Many, if not most, of the unsuccessful manuscripts we see at the Conference fail because the main character doesn't want anything, or at least not badly enough to warrant the word — *motivation*!

The character without motivation, without any pressing goal, the character who lets things happen to him rather than making things happen, is not an interesting character. Get rid of him, or have him change and acquire some motivation out of some dramatic turn in the narrative. According to the old book *The Robin Hood of El Dorado*, Joaquin Murrieta, the California bandit, was a mild-mannered farmer until five miners raped his wife. He then turned wild, tracked down each of those men and killed them. The story started the moment he had motivation — the primitive one of revenge. As Ray Bradbury has urged, the author knew what his protagonist wanted: Joaquin wanted to find and kill those men, and the author and the readers just followed him. The reader should be in sympathy with the hero's or heroine's goal, whatever it is, and hope fervently that he achieves it, overcoming seemingly impossible obstacles. In this case, as in most stories of justified revenge, we are with the bandit-hero and want to see the villains punished.

In *The Count of Monte Cristo*, Edmond Dantes is railroaded into prison on the terrible island the Chateau D'If, and we can hardly wait till he finally escapes and gets his revenge on the four bad guys. Sometimes in a revenge story, the hero will decide that physical revenge is un-Christian and spare the person or persons who wronged him. This was the case in the true story of *Eleni*, the saga of a Greek man who spent most of his life tracking down the sadistic killer of his mother, only to decide not to bother to kill the pathetic old man he finally finds, not to descend to his level. This is called a Purpose Abandoned story. We see it superbly done in John Cheever's story "The Five-Forty-Eight" in which an unstable and vulnerable secretary, seduced and then summarily fired by her sadistic boss the next day, seeks revenge. The reader understands and completely accepts her motivation when she decides to board his commuter train and kill him. She (and the reader) wants him to be humiliated and punished the way she was. At the end of the story she abandons her purpose, decides not to shoot him, and feels vindicated by simply seeing him grovelling and afraid.

Can you think of heroes and heroines who in the same way wanted something very much, who were extremely motivated? Let's put it another way. Can you think of any who *weren't*? I doubt it.

What, for example, did Scarlett most want? (Rhett is the wrong answer; he was secondary. Tara is the motivation throughout.)

What did Ashley, Melanie, and even Belle Watling want?

Think about your favorite books. Don't the heroes and heroines all want something badly? A Danielle Steel heroine desperately wants to marry someone, a Robert Ludlum character desperately wants to find the microfilm, a Jack London character desperately wants to get through the snowstorm to the warm cabin, a Dominick Dunne character desperately wants to be invited to the elite party, a Judith Krantz character desperately wants stardom, a Leon Uris character desperately wants a state of Israel, a Hemingway character desperately wants to blow up the bridge.

Does your main character want something desperately? Or even a whole lot? And is the reader in sympathy with this goal? In my novel *Matador*, one would think that the motivation of my over-the-hill bullfighter, Pacote, would be simple survival, to get through this last fight alive in any possible fashion. But in his character was this need to be great, to be The Number One, which stemmed from his early life of poverty and seeing his sister go into prostitution. This motivation was greater than his sense of self-preservation and leads unswervingly to the book's conclusion. It is not really a tragedy because he achieved his goal—proving that he was the world's greatest—even at the cost of his life.

That brings up the fact that there can be several motivations, especially in a novel, at different times of the protagonist's saga. We could call those mini-motivations, subservient to the Master Motivation. Pacote wanted to live, certainly, but that was a mini-motivation (as was his love for the cheap actress) compared to his desire to be considered great. Sammy Glick, in *What Makes Sammy Run*, has several objectives and distractions, but all are secondary to his manic drive for fame and power. Charles Kane's motivation is a quest for power, but the motivation behind the motivation is his lost boyhood symbolized by a sled called Rosebud.

John Leggett, a workshop leader since the Conference began in 1972, has been an editor for top publishing houses as well as a best-selling novelist and the head of the prestigious Iowa Writer's Workshop, so he knows to emphasize *motivation* in his classes. His book *Ross and Tom* is a study of Ross Lockridge and Tom Heggen, two highly successful writers of the 50s who were highly and similarly motivated: They both wanted to be rich and successful writers, mainly to prove something to their mothers and siblings and the world. They knew what they *wanted* — or thought they did — and both succeeded big; Ross with *Raintree County* and Tom with *Mister Roberts*. But, as F. Scott Fitzgerald said about the American writer, nothing fails like success, and as Truman Capote warned, be careful what you pray for — you may get it. Both writers committed suicide at a young age.

John Leggett always looks first for character motivation in the manuscripts turned into him at the Conference. He simplifies it thus:

> When we talk about character in a story, we invariably talk about that character's *motivation*. Unless we understand why an otherwise docile girl suddenly lashes out at her mother, her behavior strikes us as inconsistent and unbelievable.
>
> But once we understand that Frederica is punishing someone — anyone she can get her hands on actually — for the way her boyfriend has neglected her, Frederica begins to make sense to us. More than that, she is no longer that flat, that stock, that boring character, the dutiful daughter, but a real girl with some spunk and unpredictability. She is considerate most days, but you never can be sure of Frederica.
>
> If you hang out with fiction long enough you begin to see its advantages over real life. One of these is understanding human motivation. In both fiction and life one spends an enormous amount of time trying to puzzle out why people do what they do. In life you can never be sure whether you've got it right and sometimes you can't figure it out at all. In good fiction though, you always discover the reasons people do what they do.

Now, just for fun, serious fun, think of some books and stories or even films you've either read recently or have admired over the years. What was the main character's immediate goal? To get the job? To get the girl in bed? To have a baby? To save a buddy still a prisoner in Vietnam? To be elected? To get into nursing school? To hide from the Nazis in the farmhouse? To get the part in the play?

Then see if you can pinpoint the underlying main motivation. To prove something to her mean mother? To make a rich and successful marriage to spite her peers? To become a great doctor and help humankind? To become an actor so as to have many facades to hide behind? To save her crumbling marriage because she truly loved him?

When examining a character for motivation, play psychiatrist and dig deep. Don't make easy, superficial conclusions, especially in a novel. Be suspicious; question everything, every motive. But remember, in a short story you don't have room enough for much more than one motivation per character, one basic propellent.

And that's what motivation is, *fuel*, the essential energy that makes your story start and go and keep going!

Never cease to examine what the origin of the fuel is; be both cynical and compassionate. Ask what the obvious motive is, then question it. Someone gives millions to charity; is he just a swell guy or is he atoning for turning in his best friend to the Nazis at Belsen? Then, take it a step forward in understanding; suppose we learn that he, our prisoner, did it — ratted — because he felt he had to survive in order to take care of his crippled son back in Warsaw?

Now where are we?

I'll tell you where we are: *involved*! Emotionally involved. Right where the reader should be.

A brilliant *tour de force* is Thomas Harris' suspense novel of a few years back, *Red Dragon* (which has nothing to do with either China or Communism). In this gripping novel he managed by some sort of alchemy to understand, empathize, and even sympathize with the motivation of a brutal serial murderer by exploring how the man's mind got to be so twisted and evil.

That is the kind of godlike, omniscient power that we writers can wield when we do our job right. Heady stuff, addictive stuff. Maybe it's why we keep writing.

K E Y N O T E R

JUDITH KRANTZ

"Never get hung up on openings," Judith Krantz advised the large audience attending her lecture for the ninth annual Santa Barbara Writers' Conference. "I wrote the first paragraph of *Scruples* just before I sent it off to my agent. By the end you know so much more about your characters."

She then went on to explain that she writes every day of the week. "If I don't do that, Monday is such a bad day. Every Monday is like starting a new book. I'm like the Tin Woodman from *Wizard of Oz*. I get rusty over the weekend.

"Good erotic sex scenes are the greatest challenge. They have to be in the context of the book and have to be within the character of the people involved. No sex scenes can be written in cold blood." She said she hadn't realized how erotic the sex scenes were in *Scruples* until she started meeting the American public on her book tours. "There are no new words," she said. "And when you write sex scenes, you can't get too intellectual or you lose the sexuality. I love thinking up new situations and ways to describe the same old acts."

She said that when she wrote *Princess Daisy*, she decided she had shocked more people than she had planned to shock, so there were to be no four letter words in the sex scenes. "And I think those scenes were better than *Scruples*," she said. "Writers have to feel comfortable with the words, just as readers do.

"I had fun writing *Scruples*. I had such fun giving my heroine two hundred and fifty million dollars. I went around smiling for days.

"I'm now having much more trouble writing. I'm challenging myself. But basically I like the act of sitting in front of a typewriter and writing. I get days of absolute exhilaration. It's rather like childbirth. You forget the agonies of writing and only remember the good."

"What comes first, the story or the character?" one woman asked.

"It begins with me asking myself questions. What if I owned the biggest boutique on Rodeo Drive? What would I be like?" Then she said that she had "wanted an umbrella, something all the characters could huddle under. The boutique was that umbrella." The idea led to the outline, which led her into the book. "I don't like to start a book until I know how it ends," she said. "The middle can remain hazy. *Princess Daisy* started as a character. Here it was a person; in the first book it was a store.

"For me, motivation is extremely important," Judith Krantz told her audience. "I have to know what is in the characters' backgrounds, what makes them what they are."

Selective Detail

*V*S. Pritchett, one of this century's great short story writers, states: "Short stories can be rather stark and bare unless you put in the right details. Details make stories human, and the more human a story can be, the better."

Think back on stories or novels you have loved, and recall the attention that the authors paid to details; as you read those books you *knew* the contents of Tom Sawyer's pockets, the subtle differences between Louisa May Alcott's little women, the food that the clan of the Cave Bear ate, the way that Gatsby dressed, the make of gun James Bond carried, the lurch of the Joads' jalopy, the songs they sang at a Corleone wedding, and nearly every significant detail about Emma Bovary's everyday life and loves, for no one extolled the use of selective detail more, or demonstrated it better, than Flaubert.

Here is Joan Oppenheimer on that important facet of descriptive writing:

Beginning writers often toss in a variety of facts when they're writing true experiences, or fiction based on true experiences, just because that's the way it really happened. That's not a good enough reason. Every fact, every incident should mean something, not only by itself, but in the context of the rest of the story. A writer should not record everything that took place. For one thing, much of life is trivial, meaningless. The danger in constructing a story of meaningless trivia is that, if a story is the sum of its parts, the end result won't be worth reading. The wise writer chooses incidents which move the story and the characters along, details which evoke vivid images and elicit emotional reaction from the reader.

Selecting the most vivid, colorful, evocative details can mean more intriguing characters, more visual settings, and far more interesting narrative.

Suppose you begin a scene with the character getting up and eating an enormous breakfast, which you describe in detail. Then your story continues with the character hurling himself/herself into significant action. What's wrong with that? Well, what does the breakfast have to do with the character or the story?

It could mean something, and it might definitely add to the story, if this particular character is the kind who wouldn't budge from the doorstep of hell until he'd had a good solid breakfast, and it's important for the reader to know that. Details about the breakfast provide a clue about a character trait that will have a bearing on the story to unfold. If it doesn't work as a plant, conveying a meaningful facet of the character, such a lengthy description would merely slow the action. Worse, it would interfere with extraneous details about nourishing vittles adding up to nothing more than an inappropriate "aside."

The key word here is inappropriate. Occasionally, even in mystery fiction, the author stops to describe a little sidetrip, one that may be humorous, possibly philosophical, maybe a that's-the-way-life-is incident, always one that will add to the characterization of the main character. The professional writer learns from experience when such incidents add to a scene, a chapter, and carefully selects the best details, keeping the section brief.

Good fiction includes specific detail, the better to enhance a scene, make settings more visual, add dimension to characters. "A lovely place, a beautiful house, a pretty sunset" — they are phrases which convey to the reader nothing but the author's judgments. If the writer has to add how and why the place is lovely, the house is beautiful, etc., it would be far better to explain how and why with the first view of the setting, using colorful, interesting details.

There is a hilarious scene in Salinger's *Franny and Zooey* in which Mrs. Glass insists on talking to her son who is taking a bath. Reluctantly, he lets her come in after he's modestly pulled the shower curtain. In the ensuing action, after she's chatted a bit, she opens the medicine cabinet and makes a silent inventory of the contents of each shelf, a mindboggling assortment, everything from laxatives to acne cream. After the reader's first startled awareness of what she's doing, the recital becomes a wonderful example of lunatic humor. Reread it and observe a master at work, because every item in that lengthy list was almost certainly selected for maximum impact.

It's possible to show a great deal about a character by describing his or her home or office, possibly the desk within that office. There may be an incredible array of papers, folders, clippings, depending on the character's profession and also the reader's conception of that profession. Newspaper, magazine, and book editors are notorious for having overloaded desks. Editors are not generally pictured as tidy people. On the other hand, top decorators or bank officials or advertising executives may have desks totally bare and waxed to a sheen. You'll find the clutter on their secretaries' desks.

But that's the broad picture. Give your reader some specific, revealing detail about this character's desk. You can get a lot of mileage out of family pictures, but how about the picture that's face down on the desk? Or a small gold-framed picture with a single rose in a vase beside it?

In the kind of contradictory detail that may sharpen the reader's knowledge of a character, the office Romeo may have a whole gallery of family pictures on his desk. What kind of message does that send? *Honey, I love to play games, but don't expect me to get serious.* Another type of Don Juan may have the pictures stashed in a top desk drawer, and they come out only when his wife visits the office.

The character who is prim and proper and squeaky clean may have an office which is equally antiseptic and sterile, nothing out of place, no dust, the air smelling of pine or lemon. A glass and plastic or chrome office, everything cold and slick and impersonal, modern and efficient, in muted colors.

But maybe the character has repressed another side of himself, and the writer wants to show that to the reader. He may do that by giving him an office which is cheerful with bright colors and furniture chosen for comfort. Perhaps, within an office which is otherwise modern and elegant, there is one glaring flaw: the ancient oak desk which once belonged to the character's grandfather.

If the writer mentions a bottle in a bottom drawer of someone's desk, he may be hinting that Marian or Marvin has a drinking problem. This is an example of something which is not a casual detail. Be sure it means something in the story, or it might appear as the worst kind of red herring.

The home or apartment of a certain kind of character will echo the details of the office, either warm or cold, according to the image the writer seeks to portray. Are there blazing colors in the pictures on the walls? Framed stitchery? Delicate watercolors? Perhaps there's an apple core in an ashtray. Fresh flowers, or an arrangement of silk roses. Peppermints or licorice in a dish. The smell of lemon or floral air freshener — or fresh-brewed coffee and something spicy cooking on the stove or baking in the oven.

One, two, or three details of setting may go a long way toward building a character. This person is seen far more clearly against the backdrop which he or she has chosen.

Picture yourself in the corridor of an office building. You open a door and a woman looks up at you from the receptionist's desk. She's wearing a red dress. What shade of red? A soft rose, or a bold scarlet or crimson? Is it a tight red dress, low cut? Or is this dress merely a cheerful accent in an otherwise colorless waiting room? A phrase like "a cheap shiny rayon" conveys one picture, while "a lustrous silk" depicts a very different dress—and a very different woman.

When it comes to selecting details to describe your protagonist, think carefully before you give him/her a scar. It's a temptation, because a scar is a detail that's distinctive and most visual. A writer can do a lot with a scar. Yet, to be as effective as possible, that scar must be important to the character as well as the reader.

Possibly, your man is a former football hero. Or maybe he once totaled a car and emerged unhurt except for one tiny cut on his chin. (Does he lead a charmed life, and is this one example?) It may be a scar that interrupts the line of one eyebrow, so that others are constantly aware of it. Maybe he is comfortable with his charming, distinctive scar.

Scars may be ugly, disfiguring, sinister. It might be confusing to the reader, however, if the writer bestows a sinister scar on a character who leads a blameless life. Unless it's meant as a humorous switch, the wimp who looks like Al Capone.

Maybe it's a woman who has a scar. Perhaps a teenager, keenly aware of the X-shaped scar high on one cheek, memento of an accident in childhood. She's self-conscious about it, hating it when little kids ask about it—and they always do—until the day when a very small boy calls her "the girl with a star on her face." It will never again bother her as much.

Scars may be useful for conveying a lot of information about a character, his background, etc. Be sure they're important, that they mean something. They aren't to be thrown in merely to add a little extra color. In the long run, it won't add much if you have to explain that John got the scar on his temple falling out of a tree when he was six, or Jane got the scar on her chin after a dive from her highchair. Few scars are that glamorous or significant—unless the writer makes them so.

Words may balloon instantly into images or concepts in the reader's mind in a combination of reader's conception—and the details furnished by the writer. A grossly fat man may be a gourmet or merely greedy. Is he Nero Wolfe or Santa Claus—jolly, irascible, or

evil? Give readers the details they need to form their own picture—
and opinion.

Bring a kid with bad skin into your story, and the reader often
assumes he's sullen, or shy; perhaps because that's often the case in
real life. (But it isn't always the case.) A tall man with impressive shoulders must be, to many readers, aggressive and confident.

This kind of mind-set can be annoying if it works against what
you intend. The only way to get around this is to tell readers firmly
and immediately (better still, *show* them) that your character may look
a lot like John Wayne, but he's afraid of the dark, or that while this
college freshman is still majoring in zits, he is rarely seen without an
astonishingly pretty girl in tow.

Would you believe a hero (of any age) whose eyes are too close
together? Would you go along with a hero or heroine in a serious
romantic context if he or she had Bugs Bunny teeth, or acutely bowed
legs, or knock knees? Sure, we all have flaws, some of them major,
and that doesn't mean we don't have colorful love lives. But that's
reality. In a serious love story, demeaning details may be an impossible hurdle to pass—unless you have the genius to give the world another Cyrano. In a humorous story, specific and ludicrous details
might work if handled gracefully—and for a good enough reason.

It's difficult to overemphasize the importance of the selected, specific detail in any area of fiction. When you watch the news, which
incident would trouble you more: to hear that twenty-two people had
died in a freeway pileup in the fog? Or that among them was a three-
year-old girl named Rachel Horner, found dead with her Cabbage
Patch Kid clutched in her arms?

Readers are individuals. Each of us responds more strongly, iden-
tifies more easily with another individual, not crowds of nameless,
faceless people. The writer makes the reader respond to a character
by depicting that character as a memorable, interesting, flesh-and-
blood person—by the use of specific detail, specific traits.

It may be accomplished by a sympathetic gesture within the first
one hundred words of the piece. We don't know the character yet but
we sympathize. He or she stops to speak to a small child—or a cat or
dog. Cliché, but still effective, especially if it's an unattractive child or
animal. An unsympathetic gesture may be just as effective. This time,
the character pitches a stone at the cat or dog, snarls at the kid.

Writers may build with a bit of puzzling but intriguing behavior:
The character who kicks the cat or dog, snarls at the kid, but goes out
of his way to help the blind man. He's this kind of person but a sucker
for someone who's helpless, vulnerable—in a specific way. The ges-

tures may convince the reader far more successfully than merely telling him about the complicated traits.

Do you see a woman clearly when the writer has described her as a blue-eyed blonde? What if you made her Scarlett O'Hara with a curly blond wig and with blue eyes, but they're just as arrogant if she doesn't see you watching her?

"A tall man" doesn't give the reader a clear picture. A man who is bone thin and six feet four is easier to see. The klutz is a klutz, all right, if you read that he can't even close his desk drawer without getting his tie caught in it. Almost everyone will have a better idea of a dishonest politician if it is stated specifically *how* he's been dishonest.

In describing a character, think what you can do with one detail about, let's say, the jewelry worn by this person. A gem-encrusted cross. Or a pendant that signifies a certain astrological sign. A pin designating membership in some organization. The reader would know a great deal about a man or woman who is forty and still wearing a high-school class ring. Or the character who prominently displays a Phi Beta Kappa key.

Character tags are specific details fine-tuned to create story people who are easy for the reader to remember, a device especially useful in the case of minor characters. Someone who bobs up once for a brief turn and then reappears much later in the story will be easier to recall by way of one of those carefully selected details. Perhaps he clears his throat frequently, a nervous tic. Maybe it's a woman who uses a perfume which precedes her everywhere. Or it could be someone who drives a car that seems out-of-character somehow: a minister or an elderly librarian in a racy sports car; a wealthy man in a clunker. Almost always, the reader will remember the character at the mention of the irritating throat-clearing, the overpowering perfume, or the particular car.

Let's say your character is at a cocktail party, and she admires a woman's earrings. The woman is plump and blonde and pretty and possibly in her forties. She's also a woman who can't accept a compliment gracefully. She gets flustered at the comment about her earrings and protests that they're just little cheapies. She picked them up at the local Pic-n-Save. Okay. Twenty pages later when she appears in the story again, is your reader likely to recall her by name? Possibly not. Maybe not even when you refer to a plump, pretty, fortyish blonde. But if you mention the Pic-n-Save earings, chances are your reader will be right with you.

If you say a woman is wearing "the perfect dress to attend a funeral," you don't have to add another word. If you want to play around with a detail like that, she'd be wearing "the perfect dress to attend a funeral—if it happened to be that of the woman who stole her job, the man she loved, and even her hairdresser, in the space of six weeks." *That* dress you'd describe, perhaps in parallel terms to the emotions she's feeling.

Make your settings easier to remember, too, with specific tags. The ones that work best are those that appeal to the senses, a vivid color, a distinctive fragrance, a unique sound.

When a writer fails to be specific about a setting, it's sometimes called "soft writing." A character walks down a street and there are no visual clues. He gets into a car, and that isn't described, either. What we have is someone moving in space with nothing—no word, no phrase—to delineate that space. The reader wants at least a brief sense of the surroundings: a noisy city street during the rush hour, cracked sidewalks reflecting a glaring midday sun, trash blowing along the gutter.

And of course every car has a personality, some of them so colorful, they cry out for a name. ("My first car was an ancient Plymouth we called the Blue Goose. Why? Well, it was blue, and my son, teasing me because I'm a mechanical moron, used to say, 'whenever anything goes wrong, you think all you have to do is give it a little gas. Goose her, and she'll get going.' He had stated the case so accurately, the car remained the Blue Goose until the day it went to that old junkyard in the sky.") Does this give you a good picture of the lady in question?

It is possible to attain realism and win your reader's total belief by way of a few judicious details. A character who has a certain way of buttering bread or cutting meat. Nutty superstitions, especially if they're made up by the character.

Say you want to describe a family sitting for a portrait, the kind where Pop props the camera on a tripod, sets the timer and leaps into the picture himself. He fixes his small son's hair. Mom doesn't like it. She whips out a comb and styles it herself. When they turn away, Sonny gives his head a tremendous shake, and the hair goes back to the way it looked originally. Such a scene presses buttons. This is Bombeck's forte, hitting the universal note, the one all readers recognize.

I wrote a novel once about a burned-out college English teacher, who signs on as helper to a handyman. She's the daughter of a carpenter, she's good with her hands. She has to prove that to her boss—also to the reader. Several people said one detail accomplished that. On her first day on the job, the handyman looks her over and notes she's brought her own tools. He asks her how she sharpened the hoe. She says matter-of-factly, "With a file."

It is worth endless effort to find the *exact* word: Is the lady thin, slender, scrawny, willowy, or fragile? Small-boned or large-boned? If you read that a character is thin, don't you get a bony picture? If she's small-boned and elegant, there's a totally different image. A detail (this one's overused because it's good) may say volumes: "a bracelet too large for her fragile wrist." If you want to use thin in a more attractive sense, your heroine might have eyes too large for her thin face. (Few women have eyes that are too large to be attractive!) She's a gamine, but appealing.

How do you describe hands? Thin, scrawny, clawlike? Long slender fingers, fine. Small hands? Or hands like a child's? Childlike hands. Plump hands, or fat hands, or chubby hands? A subtle difference there. A small plump hand is lovely if you're describing a child or perhaps a sweet little old lady, but a man with small plump hands is not likely to be a winsome character.

Think what you can do with fingernails, describing the shape, their condition. See what one or two details can accomplish. Dirty broken nails, bitten nails, long tapering nails. The color of the polish tells a lot—is she a woman who wears colorless polish or shades of scarlet, blue, silver, green? If a man wears polish, it really doesn't make any difference what the color might be, because there's a powerful reader's conception at work about a man who wears polish on his nails. Not what you're thinking, perhaps—it might be a clue to his profession as well as to his personality.

Beginning writers often err in the use of detail in two ways. The first is by overkill, using too many adjectives and adverbs. We've all read writers who never met a modifier they didn't like. But a meager style isn't effective, either, sometimes because it's unclear, nonvisual, and almost certainly, because it fails to stir our senses and emotions.

Writers learn eventually to be SELECTIVE. To take time to find the exactly right modifier, the one that carries the weight of three or four.

The use of selected detail is a hallmark of the writer of distinguished fiction. Such writers use details that convey in a few words what lesser mortals might take paragraphs to say.

Here's an anecdote to emphasize that message. The noted director Alan Pakula was once asked to describe his reaction to Marilyn Monroe. He stammered, smiled, gestured, and finally blurted: "She was so luscious, you just wanted to take a bite out of her!"

JOHN HERSEY

The Conference occasionally honors a particular writer for "A Life-time of Literary Excellence." Past recipients have included Eudora Welty, Irwin Shaw, Erskine Caldwell, William Saroyan, Clifton Fadi-man, John Sanford, Ross Macdonald, Margaret Millar, Ray Bradbury, Gore Vidal and Jerzy Kosinski.

Pulitzer Prize winner John Hersey was thus honored at our 1990 Conference for such enduring works as *A Bell For Adano*, *Hiroshima*, *The War Lover*, and his valuable book for all serious writers, *The Writer's Craft*.

I assume that it is not possible in formal classes to "teach" or to "learn" to write imaginative literature, not anyway beyond a primitive level of competence, but I believe that if a student has the needed gifts it may be possible for a tactful teacher to help, to set the gifts free to do their destined work. One desirable step in this freeing process may be for the young writer to come to understand, both through tentative experience of the craft and by learning about the experience of others in it, what it means to live by and for writing. Thus writing may move beyond the naive stage of self-expression and be seen and felt, or at least tasted, as the central activity of a way of life. The student can begin to sense what attitudes writers take toward their work, how they go about it, what they think they are doing when they write, the obscure sources of the materials of their art, their methods of shaping and revising, their crises of confidence, their artistic goals and beliefs, their rituals, their pains and disappointments, their rewards; and so may be able to integrate these discoveries into his or her own ways of making and doing.

If a young writer can manage this, there is nothing more to do but to write and to read, to read and to write. Only the masters, finally, can teach writing; only the student herself or himself, by doing, by trial and error, can learn, can find his or her appropriate and uniquely personal voice in words. In the meantime, this writer will have found out how to read in two ways—for pleasure in the work itself, and also constantly watching the author's hand, trying to see how the master's effects, large and small have been crafted. . . .

Every serious new writer must firmly place himself or herself in relation to the tradition that has been handed down. The writer's craft, immensely supple though it is, and capable to change, neverthe-less cannot be invented in a vacuum: like any other, it is handed on.

Perhaps more than any other, because it is the craft of life. Our own year, our fashion, our time is only one flutter of the wing in the long flight of the word.

Point of View

*A*ll right, class, trivia time!

Name me a story, a great short story by an American writer, wherein the author goes into the point of view of a lion.

Right!

"The Short Happy Life of Francis Macomber" by Ernest Hemingway:

A breeze was blowing toward them and the grass rippled gently in the wind. He looked at the gun-bearer and he could see the gun-bearer was suffering too with fear.

Thirty-five yards into the grass the big lion lay flattened out along the ground. His ears were back and his only movement was a slight twitching up and down of his long, black-tufted tail. He had turned at bay as soon as he had reached this cover and he was sick with the wound through his full belly, and weakening with the wound through his lungs that brought a thin foamy red to his mouth each time he breathed. His flanks were wet and hot and flies were on the little openings the solid bullets had made in his tawny hide, and his big yellow eyes, narrowed with hate, looked straight ahead, only blinking when the pain came as he breathed, and his claws dug in the soft baked earth. All of him, pain, sickness, hatred and all of his remaining strength, was tightening into an absolute concentration for a rush. He could hear the men talking and he waited, gathering all of himself into this preparation for a charge as soon as the men would come into the grass. As he heard their voices his tail stiffened to twitch up and down, and, as they came into the edge of the grass, he made a coughing grunt and charged.

Point of view simply means who is observing the action and thinking about it or speaking about it at that point in the novel or short story. There are three basic points of view: omniscient, first person singular, or third person.

In the Macomber story, Hemingway has adopted the Godlike omniscient point of view; that is, he can, as he chooses, go into all three of the characters' minds, and even the lion's and know what they are thinking and relay that information to the reader.

In *The Sun Also Rises*, Hemingway chooses, for reasons of his own, to tell us the story strictly from the first-person-singular point of view. The "I" of the story in this case is Jake Barnes, who has suffered a genital wound in the first world war which makes it impossible for him to consummate his love for Lady Brett. All the action is seen through Jake's eyes which means that he can only know what is in his own mind and sight and must guess at what takes place "offstage," out of his sight, or rely on what other characters tell him.

In his novel *For Whom the Bell Tolls*, Hemingway writes in the third person; the action is seen, for the most part, through the persona of his young American hero Robert Jordan.

In *To Have and Have Not*, Hemingway does a unique thing: he takes the third-person viewpoint in the first third of the novel, the first-person narrator point of view in the second third, and the omniscient point of view in the third part.

The technique is not recommended. By and large, the beginning writer would be wise to stick to one point of view; a singleness of viewpoint intensifies the unity of your story, so for the time being, anyway, let's eliminate the omniscient point of view. That leaves us with the first person and the third. Which to use? Both have equally strong defenders and sometimes the subject matter, plot, or choice of protagonist will dictate which is the better. If, for example, you are writing a suspense story wherein the hero or heroine's life is constantly in danger, you might do well to avoid the "I" form so as not to lessen the suspense, since if "I" lived to tell the tale "I" didn't get killed. (Although I do know of one story where the narrator does get killed. In James M. Cain's gripping and durable novel, *Double Indemnity*, we learn on the last page that the "I" of the story has been poisoned and is writing the book as he dies.)

Some great books have been written in the first person: *David Copperfield, Huckleberry Finn, Moby Dick, The Great Gatsby, Rebecca, Catcher in the Rye*, to name a few. One of the advantages is the immediate intimacy one establishes, the credibility of the author's saying "look, I'm telling you this story personally, looking you right in the eye, it really happened, believe me, and it happened just this way, trust me. It all started when ... "

One of the drawbacks of the first person is in describing oneself, especially if one is the protagonist, handsome, or beautiful, and required to do heroic things; it is difficult to accomplish this without seeming vainglorious. Here's where minor characters can come into play and help tell the reader what our hero or heroine is like. Sometimes the narrator is not the protagonist of the story. This too lends a sense of verisimilitude. "Listen, I want to tell you about this incredible person I met, a captain named Ahab, an ancient mariner, a fellow named Gatsby, a runaway slave named Jim," or whomever. We'll listen. The narrator in that kind of a story generally states his credentials up front. Here is Pat Conroy's beginning for his spellbinding novel *The Prince of Tides*:

My wound is geography. It is also my anchorage, my port of call.

I grew up slowly beside the tides and marshes of Colleton; my arms were tawny and strong from working long days on the shrimp boat in the blazing South Carolina heat. Because I was a Wingo, I worked as soon as I could walk; I could pick a blue crab clean when I was five. I had killed my first deer by the age of seven, and at nine was regularly putting meat on my family's table. I was born and raised on a Carolina sea island and I carried the sunshine of the low-country; inked in dark gold, on my back and shoulders. As a boy I was happy above the channels, navigating a small boat between the sandbars with their quiet nation of oysters exposed on the brown flats at the low watermark. I knew every shrimper by name, and they knew me and sounded their horns when they passsed me fishing in the river.

When I was ten I killed a bald eagle for pleasure, for the singularity of the act, despite the divine, exhilarating beauty of its solitary flight over schools of whiting. It was the only thing I had ever killed that I had never seen before. After my father beat me for breaking the law and for killing the last eagle in Colleton County, he made me build a fire, dress the bird, and eat its flesh as tears rolled down my face. Then he turned me into Sheriff Benson, who locked me in a cell for over an hour. My father took the feathers and made a crude Indian headdress for me to wear to school. He believed in the expiation of sin. I wore the headdress for weeks, until it began to disintegrate feather by feather.

In her wonderful story *The Famous Toboggan of Laughter*, Ella Leffland lets us know immediately that the story is not to be about herself but about her eccentric, madcap, and sad friend Mayo. Look how much

the reader is given by the narrator in this opening that is a model of
how to start a story, introduce an individualized protagonist, and set
the scene:

"Whenever I see a picture of the Eiffel Tower, it always reminds
me of Paris."
   I didn't bother answering. I didn't like her. Anyway, she was
already past me, halfway down the boat deck. She was always in a
big hurry, Mayo, never waited for a response. She was reckless,
too. The first day out she climbed halfway up the ladder to the
pilothouse just for laughs, and having only one arm, she almost
fell off. Every night she drank with the drinkers or smoked pot
with the pot smokers, stumbling into our cabin at dawn and making extra noise for the benefit of our other cabinmate, a retired
missionary woman in her seventies. Mayo was my age, nineteen
or twenty. I made no pretense of liking her, but she seemed to be
the star of our student crowd even though, or maybe because, her
rudeness was breathtaking, the kind that hits you in the solar
plexus. There was always a lot of laughter and stomping of feet
around her.

Jay McInerney is a master of the first person singular. In this opening
of his novel, *Story of My Life*, notice how cleverly he lures us into this
vulnerable, angry girl's world, how much information he gives us in
a very short space, how well we know her already. At the very beginning of this tough and tender novel we know that the narrator, Alison,
is going to be the protagonist and that it is going to be a bumpy ride:

I'm like, I don't believe this shit.
   I'm totally pissed at my old man who's somewhere in the Virgin Islands, I don't know where. The check wasn't in the mailbox
today which means I can't go to school Monday morning. I'm on
the monthly payment program because Dad says wanting to be
an actress is some flaky whim and I never stick to anything—this
from a guy who's been married five times—and this way if I drop
out in the middle of the semester he won't get burned for the full
tuition. Meanwhile he buys his new bimbo Tanya who's a year
younger than me a 450 SL convertible—always gone for the
young ones, haven't we, Dad?—plus her own condo so she can
have some privacy to do her writing. Like she can even *read*. He
actually believes her when she says she's writing a novel but when
I want to spend eight hours a day busting ass at Lee Strasberg it's
like, *another one of Alison's crazy ideas*. Story of my life. My old man

is fifty-two going on twelve. And then there's Skip Pendleton, which is another reason I'm pissed.

So I'm on the phone screaming at my father's secretary when there's a call on my other line. I go hello and this guy goes, hi, I'm whatever-his-name-is, I'm a friend of Skip's and I say yeah? and he says, I thought maybe we could go out sometime.

And I say, what am I, dial-a-date?

Skip Pendleton's this jerk I was in lust with once for about three minutes. He hasn't called me in like three weeks which is fine, okay, I can deal with that, but suddenly I'm like a baseball card he trades with his friends? Give me a break. So I go to this guy, what makes you think I'd want to go out with you, I don't even know you? and he says, Skip told me about you. Right. So I'm like, what did he tell you? and the guy goes — Skip said you were hot. I say, great, I'm totally honored that the great Skip Pendleton thinks I'm hot. I'm just a jalapeño pepper waiting for some strange burrito, honey. I mean, *really*.

Many publishers say they find the third person the most satisfactory and commercial approach, and most novels on the best-seller list are written this way. For example, your Danielle Steels and Robert Ludlums and Sidney Sheldons are usually third person narratives. Here's the provocative opening of Mary Higgins Clark's 1989 novel *While My Pretty One Sleeps*:

He drove cautiously up the Thruway toward Morrison State Park. The thirty-five-mile trip from Manhattan to Rockland County had been a nightmare. Even though it was six o'clock, there was no sense of approaching dawn. The snow that had begun during the night had steadily increased until now it was beating relentlessly against the windshield. The overhead clouds, heavy and gray, were like enormous balloons pumped to the breaking point. The forecast had been for two inches, with "precipitation tapering off after midnight." As usual the weatherman had been wrong.

But he was near the entrance to the park, and, with the storm, there probably wouldn't be anyone hiking or jogging. He'd passed a State Trooper ten miles back, but the car had rushed past him, lights flashing, probably on the way to an accident somewhere. Certainly the cops had no reason to even think about the contents of his trunk, no reason to suspect that under a pile of luggage a plastic bag containing the body of a prominent sixty-one-year-old writer, Ethel Lambston, was wedged in a space-defying squeeze against the spare tire.

For pure adventure and action the third person seems to work out best. The author can describe things the narrator might not know or be able to see. It is simply not as constricting.

Here is how William Diehl starts his 1987 thriller *Thai Horse*, a sprawling novel which wouldn't have lent itself to the first person:

He hardly felt the hit, but he heard it. The muffled roar shook the stick slightly, and he looked out to see the end of his right wing shatter and flake away. A moment later the familiar and frightening sound of .50 caliber shells rattled the fuselage behind him as the bullets ripped the twin-engine OV-10. Suddenly the plane began to yaw, then it made a wrenching slip in the opposite direction. The plane dipped slightly toward the good wing and dropped a hundred feet. Cody was fighting the aircraft, trying to get it stable. He pressed the radio button: "Mayday ... Mayday ... this is Chilidog one to Corkscrew. I'm hit and out of control. ... "

The voice was remarkably calm, almost resigned. The only hint of trouble was in the timbre of his voice. It was shaking from the violent action of the plane, like a stereo with too much bass.

They were too low to bail out. Cody always played it like that, treetop-level stuff. "Get down where you can see the whites of their eyes," he would tell his men. From under the umbrella of green foliage, deadly ground fire chewed at the twin-engine assault plane. Fifty-calibers rattled the fuselage.

"Brace yourself," he told his gunner. There was no response. Cody turned in the cockpit and looked back. Rossiter was slumped in the seat, his canopy riddled, his face shot away. But Cody had no time to feel sorry for the youngster, he was losing the plane. The jungle catapulted toward him. Two hundred yards in front of him was the river and on the other side of the river was freedom. He knew he'd never make it.

In summing up the problem of which point of view to take, the only way to find out is to try it out first in third person; if you feel you *must* go into other characters' heads, do it. And if you feel you need the intimacy and credibility of first person, try that also. Or, if you feel daring, use all three methods. Remember that the first rule of writing is that, despite books like this, there are no rules.

MARTIN CRUZ SMITH

The author of *Nightwing*, *Gorky Park*, *Stallion Gate* and *Polar Star* told the Conference:

I have to love the characters I write about. And you should love the characters you write about. I say that because you're going to be stuck with these characters. If you write a novel you're going to be stuck with these characters for a couple of years. If you don't love them, you're going to grow to hate them. And the only way you'll really examine them and get to know them is by loving them for what they are. We know one can love a villain. In *Gorky Park* I love Osborn because he's such a glistening villain. And I certainly was deeply in love with Arkady and Irina.

I had finished *Gorky Park* at a time that I knew was supposed to be the worst time in American publishing in a hundred years. And what we did, my agent and I, we just said, we are going to be so outrageous and arrogant and confident that we are going to seize somebody's attention. Because they're scared. The editors are scared, the publishing houses are scared. We want to embolden them, and the only way we can do that is by being bold ourselves. It's the only way we can seize their attention.

My editor said, as good editors do, "If you don't want to change a word, we'll publish it and we'll be proud to publish it. But I am an editor and I am a good one, and if you allow me to, I think I can make the book if not a whole lot better a little better and a lot cleaner."

And he did.

I have worked with a lot of editors, and the good editors are not in there to reshape you. They're there to help you. And if you do get someone like that, prize, praise, and hold onto them.

The Obligatory Sex Scene

A nd now we come to what William F. Buckley called "the O.S.S." when he spoke of it at the Conference. He meant the scene or scenes in many of our modern novels where the reader watches the protagonists go to bed together: the obligatory sex scene.

Of course, it is not obligatory at all, it is only obligatory for certain writers. There are many successful modern novels which have no explicit sex; for example Amy Tan's *Joy Luck Club*, Mary Higgins Clark's 1989 best seller, *While My Pretty One Sleeps*, Tom Clancy's books, Harriet Doerr's *Stones of Ibarra*, Victoria Holt's books, and on and on.

But, facing reality, a glance at the best-seller fiction list shows that an inordinate number of titles contain at least one steamy scene; if the sex were cut from any of Judith Krantz's and Jackie Collins' novels, only a pamphlet would remain.

Bawdy scenes in literature have been around since Chaucer's day, but such novels as *Jane Eyre, Pride and Prejudice, Wuthering Heights, Of Human Bondage, A Farewell to Arms,* and *Gone with the Wind* are still around to remind us that sex can be subtle and unclinical and romantic.

If you do not plan to put explicit sex into your writings, you may find the following pages unnecessary and offensive and choose to skip this section. The selections I have chosen, while they would have sent our grandparents into orbit, are not nearly so bad as many of the scenes in such past and highly esteemed best sellers as, for example, Ken Follett's *Lie Down with Lions*, Judith Krantz's *Mistral's Daughter*, or Nancy Holmes' *Nobody's Fault*.

In the old days, the hero went into the bedroom with a female, the door would close, three asterisks would appear on the page, and nine months later she would have a baby. Today the reader follows them into the bedroom, helps them undress and anything goes. Gore Vidal, a guest at our 1990 Conference, says: "I suspect that one of the reasons we create fiction is to make sex exciting."

How to write it? What to put in? What to leave out? How to refer to the parts of the body—clinically or poetically?

The year he came to the Conference, Sloan Wilson, author of *The Man in the Gray Flannel Suit*, told students: "If the sex scene doesn't make you want to do it—whatever it is they're doing—it hasn't been written right."

Nothing is more personal in writing, nothing can be guided by less rules. My own feeling is that less is more.

One of the most erotic scenes in all literature describes no deep kissing, no cupping of breasts, no "dewey vales of enchantment," no *penetrazione*. It is the sexual climax of Emma Bovary and Léon, the younger clerk—their first sexual encounter after a long period of longing for each other. It is a masterpiece of indirection and a superb example of "leave something to the imagination and the power of suggestion."

An urchin was playing in the square:

"Go get me a cab!"

The youngster vanished like a shot up the Rue des Quatre-Vents, and for a few minutes they were left alone, face to face and a little embarrassed.

"Oh Léon! Really—I don't know whether I should . . .!" she said, a little coyly. Then, putting on a serious tone:

"It's very improper, you know."

"What's improper about it?" retorted the clerk. "Everybody does it in Paris!"

It was an irresistible and clinching argument.

But there was no sign of a cab. Léon was terrified that she'd retreat into the church. Finally the cab appeared.

"Drive past the north door, at least!" the verger called out from the entrance. "Take a look at the Resurrection, the Last Judgment, Paradise, King David, and the souls of the damned in the flames of hell!"

"Where does Monsieur wish to go?" asked the coachman.

"Anywhere!" said Léon, pushing Emma into the carriage.

And the lumbering contraption rolled away.

It went down the Rue Grand-Pont, crossed the Place des Arts, the Quai Napoléon and the Pont Neuf, and stopped in front of the statue of Pierre Corneille.

"Keep going!" called a voice from within.

It started off again, and gathering speed on the down grade beyond the Carrefour Lafayette it came galloping up to the railway station.

"No! Straight on!" gasped the same voice.

Rattling out through the station gates, the cab soon turned into the Boulevard, where it proceeded at a gentle trot between the double row of tall elms. The coachman wiped his brow, stowed his leather hat between his legs, and veered the cab off beyond the side lanes to the grass strip along the river front.

It continued along the river on the cobbled towing path for a long time in the direction of Oyssel, leaving the islands behind.

But suddenly it rushed off through Quatre-Mares, Sotteville, the Grande-Chaussée, the Rue d'Elbeuf, and made its third stop — this time at the Jardin des Plantes.

"Get going!" cried the voice, more furiously.

And starting off again it went through Saint-Sever, along the Quai des Curandiers and the Quai aux Meules, recrossed the bridge, crossed the Place du Champ-de-Mars and continued on behind the garden of the hospital, where old men in black jackets were strolling in the sun on a terrace green with ivy, it went up the Boulevard Bouvreuil, along the Boulevard Cauchoise, and traversed Mont-Riboudet as far as the hill at Deville.

There it turned back, and from then on it wandered at random, with no apparent goal. It was seen at Saint-Pol, at Lescure, at Mont-Gargan, at Rouge-Mare and the Place du Gaillardbois; in the Rue Maladrerie, the Rue Dinanderie, and in front of one church after another — Saint-Romain, Saint-Vivien, Saint-Maclou, Saint-Nicaise; in front of the customs house, at the Basse Vieille-Tour, at Trois-Pipes, and at the Cimetière Monumental. From his seat the coachman now and again cast longing glances at a café. He couldn't imagine what restless craving for movement was making these people persist in refusing to stop. He tried a few times, only to hear immediate angry exclamations from behind. So he lashed anew at his two sweating nags, and paid no attention whatever to bumps in the road; he ran into things right and left, past caring — demoralized, and almost weeping with thirst, fatigue, and despair.

Along the river from amidst the wagons and the barrels, along the streets, the bourgeois on the corners stared wide-eyed at this unheard of spectacle — a carriage with drawn blinds that kept appearing and reappearing, sealed tighter than a tomb and tossing like a ship.

At a certain moment in the early afternoon, when the sun was blazing down most fiercely on the old silver-plated lamps, a bare hand appeared from under the little yellow cloth curtains and threw out some torn scraps of paper. The wind caught them and scattered them, and they alighted at a distance, like white butterflies, on a field of flowering red clover.

Finally, at about six o'clock, the carriage stopped in a side street near the Place Beauvoisine. A woman got out and walked off, her veil down, without a backward glance.

(Interesting footnote: A year after the publication of the novel, cabs in Hamburg, Germany, could be rented for sexual dalliance; they were known as "Bovaries.")

Now, from that eloquent simplicity, let's go to the opposite extreme, baroque overkill. This extravagant sexual smorgasbord was written, or rather overwritten, by Anthony Burgess in his 1966 novel, *Tremor of Intent*. After reading it, it will be tough next time to write a sex scene with a straight face.

Hillier and the Indian woman Miss Devi are having their first sexual encounter aboard a ship, and after several wild pages of coupling they achieve nirvana:

He worked slowly, then faster, then let the cries of birds possess his ears — gannet, cormorant, bittern, ibis, spoonbill, flamingo, curassow, quail, rail, coot, trumpeter, bustard, plover, avocet, oystercatcher, curlew, oriole, crossbill, finch, shrike, godwit, wheatear, bluethroat. The cries condensed to a great roar of blood. The cabin soared, its ceiling blew off in the stratosphere and released them both. He clung, riding her, fearful of being dislodged, then, as the honeyed cantilena broke and flowed, he was ready to sink with her, she deflating herself to what she had been, her blown river of hair settling after the storm and flood.

But even now it was not all over. The last fit was in full awareness of time and place, the mole on the left shoulder noted, the close weave of the skin, the sweat that gummed body to body. The aim was to slice off the externals of the *jaghana* of each, so that viscera engaged, coiling, and knotting into one complex of snakes. Here nature must allow of total penetration, both bodies lingam and yoni. 'Now pain,' she said. Her talons attacked his back; it was as if she were nailing him to herself. When she perceived his sinking, she broke away — viscera of each retreating and coiling in again, each polished belly slamming to, a door with secret hinges. She gave his neck and chest the sounding touch, so that the hairs stood erect, passed on to the half-moon on the buttocks, then the tiger's claw, the peacock's foot, the hare's jump, the blue lotus-leaf.

And, by the way, it was Anthony Burgess who said in his autobiography: "Literature is all, or mostly, about sex."

He may be right. But take in consideration that while Chekhov constantly writes about sex, he never describes the sexual act.

To me, this sex scene by Larry McMurtry in *Moving On* is a perfect example of explicit sex that stops short of being clinical. It also has a larger reason than prurience for being in the book: conflict! The young protagonists' marriage is not going well; they are fond of each other but are drawing apart for reasons not entirely clear to either of them. As my old grandfather never said: "When a marriage goes on the rocks, the rocks can usually be found under the mattress." Here the author gets in the Obligatory Sex Scene while deriving the added benefits of advancing the story and exploring character, thus extracting far more than merely a romp in the hay from the encounter:

> Later, after she had dried and gone in and sat in the small warm bathroom awhile filing her nails, and was stretched on the bed in her green nightgown turning through an issue of *Vogue*, Jim left his pictures and came silently to the bed and began to rub her back. The ends of her hair were still damp. He folded her hair into two parts and tucked it around her throat, so her shoulders and the back of her neck were bare. "If you're through with your pictures turn off the overhead light, will you?" she said. He did and came back and massaged her shoulders and the base of her skull a bit. Tiring of that, he began a little timidly to move his hands under the loose straps of the gown, down her rib cage and around toward her breasts. Patsy knew she was being caressed but felt a slight catch of stubbornness in herself and kept reading the *Vogue* with concentration for a few minutes, until Jim's silent urging made her feel guilty. She turned on her side so he could reach a breast and then with a little excusing yawn dropped the *Vogue* off the bed and turned on her back acquiescently.
>
> She liked the way he massaged her neck and shoulders and had begun to feel genuinely acquiescent, but Jim didn't know it. He was never quite sure when she wanted him to go on and when she didn't. As it was, he felt his desire to be something of an intrusion and became hasty about it. "Hey," Patsy said. She sat up, shrugged her gown off, and threw it on the floor with a quick gesture of resolve. The green gown billowed as it settled and Jim saw the line of Patsy's ribs as she stretched an arm to turn off the bed light. When she turned back to him in the sudden darkness he was not quite where she thought he was and their heads bumped. It took them a moment to realign their bodies.
>
> "I'm sorry," Jim said, though it was just a slight bump. Patsy

was silent. It seemed always just at that moment, at the beginning of lovemaking, that she was most silent, most mysterious to him. At that moment he had no sense that he knew what she really wanted, or really liked, and she gave no clues at all. He could not even hear her breathing, and he felt, as he always felt, that he must hurry or she would cease to be interested — perhaps already had. So he did hurry, feeling himself an imposer until he reached a point where his own pleasure became stronger than any thought of Patsy.

Elmore Leonard's lean prose and realistic dialogue extends even to his sex scenes, which are always explicit but never clinical or embarrassing. Here is a typical one from his 1982 *Cat Chaser*. The last line is lovely, especially since this is their first encounter:

He caught the scent of her perfume, moved a cautious step and felt her hair brush his face. She was between his arms and he closed them around her now, feeling her hands slide up over his ribs.
    He said in almost a whisper, "You find the candle?"
    "No. It must be in the bathroom."
    He said, "Do we need it?"
    He felt her hands, her breath — this slim girl, not as tall as he'd remembered her, the image of her across a room. He felt the silky material covering her bare skin, the skin smoothly taut, her body delicate but firm pressing into him, their mouths brushing, finding the right place again, and this time drifting into a dreamlike kind of consciousness, Moran aware but not seeing himself, Mary moving against him, moving him, guiding gently, and Moran knew where they were going, feeling the foot of the bed against his leg and it was all the bearings he needed. They bailed out in the dark and fell into the double bed in the excitement of each other. She said, "You don't know how long . . ." He said, "I know." Barely moving their mouths apart to speak. She said, "God, I want you." He said, "How do you get this off?" He said, "Shit, I tore it." She said, "I don't care, tear it," pulling his belt apart. He said, "Can you wait just a second?" She said, "No." He said, "I can't either. Jesus." She said, "Don't talk." He said, "One second . . ." and got on his knees and pulled off her sandals and slacks and somehow got out of his pants, pausing then, catching his breath to pull his shirt over his head and when he sank down again into the bed they were naked, with nothing to make them hold back all that longing they could now release. The lights came on as they were making love, a soft bedroom glow that was just enough and

could have been cued as Moran said, "Oh, man," and had to smile
as he saw Mary smiling. Now they could see each other and it
wasn't simply an act of their bodies, they were identified to each
other, finally where they wanted to be more than anywhere.
Moran's urge raised him stiff-armed, raised his face to the head-
board, to the wall above them and he groaned, letting go that was
like, "Gaiiiyaaa!" and brought Mary's eyes open, but she closed
them again, murmuring, moving, and remained in iridescent
sparkling dark as he came back to her again, winding down, settling.

She felt moisture on his back, his shoulders. She said, "Oh,
God," as though it might be her last breath. Then opened her
eyes to study his face in repose, his eyelashes, his eyelids lightly
closed.

She said quietly, "Well . . . how have you been?"

Notice how sensual and tactile this scene is, appealing to all our
senses in order to put the reader into the act, into that bed:

*The scent of her perfume . . . felt her hair brush his face . . . feeling her hands
slide over his ribs . . . felt her hands, her breath . . . the silky material . . .*

About that last line from the scene, Elmore Leonard wrote me
recently that if he "were writing that today I'd leave out the adverb.
But 'quietly' is about the only adverb I ever use with 'said.'"

That's a good point. Most beginning writers can't just say "he
said" or "she said"—they have to tack on *ruthlessly, happily, sarcastically,
snidely, cruelly, lovingly,* and so forth, when all those characteristics
should be inherent and apparent in the situation, the characters, and
the dialogue itself. Someone recently handed me a story that contained the immortal line " 'Oh, yeah?' the thug asked sarcastically and
rhetorically, 'and so who am I — King Kong?' "

One of the most poignant love stories ever written is Turgenev's
First Love, a novella about a young man in love with his father's mis-
tress, which contains no explicit sex. And the steamiest novel about
pure, or rather, impure sex is still the tale of Constance Chatterly and
her randy gamekeeper, Mellors. I urge you to read both before writing of love and sex.

Viola, a wonderful cleaning woman I had years ago, once asked
to borrow *Lady Chatterly's Lover.* The next day I found the book on my
desk with this note: "Thanks! Missus Chatterly didn't know what she
wanted but she sure'n hell knew what she *needed!*"

Just possibly the most incisive review ever given of that controver-
sial book.

Sex is not a new invention, but writing about the subject honestly is relatively new. Flaubert in 1856 wrote unsentimentally and truly about sex in what has been called the first modern novel, *Madame Bovary*; he was pilloried for it and the book was suppressed. In 1852 he wrote to his friend Louise Colet indignantly about a current novel he'd read by Lamartine:

> And first of all, to put the matter bluntly, does he fuck her or doesn't he? The pair of them aren't human beings, they're mannequins. How beautiful these love stories are where the principal thing is so surrounded by mystery that one doesn't know what in the world is going on, sexual intercourse being systematically relegated to the shadow along with drinking, eating, pissing, etc! This partiality irritates me no end. Here's a strapping young fellow who is living with a woman who loves him and whom he loves, and never a desire! Not a single impure cloud ever appears to darken this pale blue lake! Had he told the real story, it would have been even more beautiful! But truth demands hairier males than Monsieur de Lamartine. It is easier in fact to draw an angel than a woman: the wings hide the hunched back.

And to that, novelist Mario Vargas Llosa adds in his book *The Perpetual Orgy*:

> I have very often had precisely the same reaction to a story: a novel that leaves out sexual experience annoys me as much as one that reduces life exclusively to sexual experience (although the latter irritates me less than the former; I have already said that among forms of unreality I prefer the most concrete one). I need to know whether the hero excites the heroine (and vice versa), and in order for these protagonists to seem lifelike to me, it is indispensable that I be caught up in their mutual excitement. The treatment of sex constitutes one of the most delicate problems in fiction; along with politics it is perhaps the most difficult subject of all to deal with.

Later, Flaubert wrote to Louise: "The good old sex organ is the basis of human affection; it is not itself affection, but rather its *substratum*, as philosophers would say. No woman has ever loved a eunuch."

Gore Vidal tells us that Tennessee Williams declared: "I cannot write any story unless there is at least one character for whom I have physical desire."

No matter how you write about sex, whether explicitly or

180 ■ *The Complete Guide to Writing Fiction*

obliquely, use all five of your senses. As a matter of fact, use them when writing about *anything*.

Marilyn Lowery writes under the name of Philippa Castle and came to the Conference as a teacher for several years. In her book *How to Write Romance Novels*, she urges writers to remember the senses when writing about sex, romance, or any other human experience:

> In describing the heroine's feelings, constantly remind yourself to appeal to the five senses. As the heroine tastes the food, the reader tastes the food. As the heroine feels the gorgeous brocades and velvets, so does the reader. Strange sounds attract, or sights astound. The more often you appeal to the senses, the more believable your story will be.

A good practice for such description is to actually use you own senses and write about the experience.

1. Taste. Try a lemon. What is the taste? How does it feel in your mouth? What is your tongue doing as you taste it? What is your mouth doing? Now try a persimmon. What is the taste? Astringent? Sweet? Add another sense. How does it *feel* on your tongue? Slippery? Slithery? How does your tongue feel after you have swallowed the bite of persimmon?

2. Touch. Describe the feel of a smooth piece of wood, of a rough eraser, of a strand of your hair. But do not take the easy adjectives. Have you written anything out of the ordinary?

3. Sight. In her poem "Aubade," Edith Sitwell says that the "morning light creaks." Light cannot creak. And yet we know what creaking light looks like. The sensation produced in one modality or point (in this case sound) when another has been stimulated (sight) is called *synesthesia*. Such a surprise can heighten your effect.

4. Hearing. Close your eyes and listen to the sounds around you. Alliteration can be an effective way to describe them. This technique is the repetition of a consonant sound such as, "*She* listened to the *s*oft *s*lapping of the waves on the *s*hore."

Henry Thoreau in *A Week on the Concord and Merrimack Rivers* describes sounds of dogs barking at night, "from the loudest and hoarsest bark to the faintest aerial palpitation under the eaves of heaven." He describes the bark of the terrier, "at first loud and rapid, then faint and slow, to be imitated only in a whisper; wow-wow-wow-wow — wo — wo — w — w." Here he has used *onomatopoeia*, suiting the sound to the meaning.

Can your reader hear the rustle of your heroine's gown or the tapping of her heels on the pavement? Do you prove that your characters exist through the sounds they make or the sounds they hear around them?

5. *Smell.* Don't reserve the use of this sense for food. A man's shaving lotion smells—tell how it smells. Hair has an odor. Skin has an odor. The smell of the hero to the heroine can be powerful in a love scene. Make the scene more potent. Tell us about the *taste* of his mouth on hers. Appeal to more than one sense at a time.

Sense impressions are vital in conveying subtle love scenes. The explicit in sex can be avoided if the senses are aroused— several at once. You want your scene to be both passionate and lifelike.

JACKIE COLLINS

Our longtime nonfiction workshop leader, Cork Millner, interviewed this popular novelist at the 1987 Conference:

CORK MILLNER: Do you start with one character and go on from there? Do you start with the whole book in mind?

JC: I start with one character. (Usually I start with the title.) I know in my future I'm going to do another book about Lucky, a heroine I like a lot. But I don't know what she's going to do next. I'm going to sit down with Lucky and she'll just take off. And she will do it as we write.

CM: So your plot evolves as you move with your character? Fitzgerald once said, "Character is action," and that's exactly what happens with your writing.

JC: I don't think I write too many characters. I love my characters. I love inventing new ones and putting them in situations where they mix and intermingle and perhaps come back in other books. I enjoy doing that.

CM: You said to me earlier that you write by hand.

JC: It's absolutely the best way to do it because then you can do it anywhere. And I think that's a great advantage and be able to sit on an airplane . . . I used to write my books when I was taking my kids to school. I would be writing them in the car, at a stoplight and then I would pull over to the side because I was in the midst of a particularly interesting bit. It's great to be able to type and it's great to be able to use the word processor, but you get a lot more done if you can just scribble wherever you are.

I'm a storyteller. I want to tell stories. And so I do it my way. You can't be frightened about what people are going to say about the fact that you do it your way. You have to just go for it in your own particular style.

I write a lot of raunchy language. But then I write a lot of raunchy characters. You can't sit down and think, "Oh, my God, my maiden aunt is going to read this book." You have to be completely free when you write to do what you want to do, for your characters to do what they want to do.

CM: Do you have a writing schedule?

JC: Yes, I write for about seven hours a day, seven days a week, which is too long. It's because I always get myself in a corner and I have to finish a book in time. I aim to do twenty pages of my handwriting a day, and I end up between ten and fifteen.

The best way to write is get straight out of bed without cleaning your teeth, go straight into the study, and stop about half an hour later and get dressed because you've already started the kind of rhythm so you're going to keep with it the rest of the day.

CM: You are amazingly successful. Why do you continue to write?

JC: I think the reason we all write is because we love to do it. I never did it for the money. The money and the success are wonderful, but I don't write for that. I love creating characters. I love telling stories, my kind of stories.

CM: How did you decide on which publisher to send your first book to?

JC: What I did, which I thought was quite smart at the time was I looked through my bookcase. And I looked for the publisher who had published most of the books I had bought and enjoyed. And I thought, if I like what he publishes, he might like what I write. So I sent the manuscript to him without an agent. It took about six months. Finally the managing director called me and said, "We want to publish your book." They didn't know at the time who I was.

CM: What are the elements for a best seller?

JC: The elements for a best seller: 1) Write about a subject that you really know about. 2) Don't be hesitant about what you write. Don't worry about what people are going to think about you. Just write what you want to write. 3) Write it in your own particular style. 4) Write. Don't talk about it. Write it.

CM: Do you feel the writer has a responsibility to the reader?

JC: I think all writers have a different role to play. I think that the role that I play is to write books that really entertain people and take them out of themselves. I also think that I write very strong women and that my women are positive role models, not all of them, because I write about women as we really are. But I have this one terrific woman in every book that women can look up to because I have a lot of young readers. I have a lot of girls of thirteeen, fourteen, fifteen who read me. I had a young woman come up to me in Bloomingdale's and say, "I just broke up with my boyfriend. And normally I would lie down on the floor and cry and scream and wait for the phone to ring. But I'm reading *Lucky* and I handled it in a whole different way." I am not writing great social messages, but I'm saying to women, "You can be stronger" and I'm saying it in an entertaining way.

SEVENTEEN

Flashbacks and Plants

I once asked Sinclair Lewis how best to handle flashbacks.
"Don't" was his complete reply.

Joan Oppenheimer has been one of the Conference's most popular teachers for years, and she provides a more helpful answer. In addition to teaching for the University of California, Joan has written more than twenty books for the young adult market. Here are some valuable hints from her on flashbacks and other facets of writing that we are constantly queried on at the Conference:

It is almost always best to tell a story in chronological sequence, making flashbacks as short as possible to fill the reader in on salient details. Flashbacks, however masterful, however intriguing, stop the story. Anything which does that is guaranteed to irritate the reader.

Yes, occasionally entire books are written within a frame, the whole story in flashback. It is a point that will be debated endlessly, whether a particular story might have been told better without the frame, without the need for flashback. Why take a chance? It means a lot of rewrite if the editor happens to be from the anti-flashback school. It's a decision you should make after you've considered all the alternatives.

Transitions into flashbacks must be smooth and natural so the reader won't be jolted or confused. A common transition makes use of a place or person or object that reminds a character of something in the past. A fragrance can be highly evocative. Music can take us instantly to a particular time and place when we heard it, usually under circumstances imbued with emotion.

The flashbacks that work best are little scenes, complete in themselves, appealing to all the senses. The writer sometimes uses one "had" to go into flashback, then runs the ensuing action as if it is a direct scene.

You may need one more "had" to emerge from flashback. In other words if you go into flashback by way of saying, "Bethany had never found Henry's sarcastic comments amusing," you may emerge from a scene (which gives the reader an example of Henry's wit) by picking up Bethany where we left her, thinking, "No, there's nothing remotely funny about vicious stories that hurt people."

Another method to come out of flashback is by way of a direct statement, "By Friday, however, the situation had changed. The dinner party which seemed on Monday so significant, no longer preoccupied him."

It may be tricky, entering and emerging from flashback, without unsettling or confusing the reader as to what is present and what is past. It's worth a lot of experimenting, a lot of practice, to perfect this bit of technique. Readers are endlessly curious about the background influences that may have shaped a leading character.

Flashbacks are especially valuable in novels, even those in which the character ages from child to adult, supplying little bits that remind the reader one hundred pages later about something that happened early on. If the character is grown when the novel begins, it will be necessary for several forays into childhood to show the reader how the character arrived at maturity as a certain kind of person.

A flashback may take several pages (be sure it sustains this length) or consist of a few lines:

She could see him clearly, aged five, head flung back, face flushed, eyes bright with anger. She'd said without thinking, "It'll never happen," and he had shouted at her, "Don't *ever* say never!"

It's a mistake to insert a flashback into the midst of fascinating action. Stay with the pilot of the plane in the midst of a storm, sweating over the instrument panel. Don't be tempted to make even a brief journey into the past to tell the reader what brought him to this predicament. Those details should be made clear either before the crisis or afterward—not in the middle.

Flashbacks. We need them, but the beginning writer will be wise to learn when to use them, how long they should be, and which details are vital for the reader to know. Study them in the professional writers' work that you most admire.

Another important device is the *plant*. You find plants in every kind of fiction. When the protagonist realizes somewhere along the line that good old Aunt Bella isn't crazy at all, merely pretending, it will be well along in the story. The plants that lead to the discovery will be fitted in here and there along the way. They'll add up to the assumption that Auntie's playing games.

None of the hints will be blatant. Each time the main character questions Bella's behavior, there will be a diversion so the reader will forget, or the question will be a casual one, not important enough to remember as the story goes on. The main character might ask herself with disgust, why would anybody fake being crazy?

Three laws for plants:

1. Make a plant before you need it.

2. Play fair; never cheat the reader.

3. To disguise it, place it alongside a dramatic moment.

To explain:

If the fact that a character is left-handed is vital to the plot, show the reader in Chapter one or possibly Chapter five or six, but well before Chapter thirteen when that fact becomes important.

Always play fair with your reader. If the protagonist is puzzled, mystified, the reader is too. That's okay. But if the protagonist has access to special information and you withhold that from the reader — or worse still, distort it — that's cheating. Readers resent cheating in fiction just as much as they dislike it in real life.

On the other hand, if the protagonist (detective, cop, or merely little Sally Jones who happens to stumble on an accident, murder, or puzzling problem) makes a guess about something, suspects something, it's perfectly okay if it turns out to be wrong. Protagonist and reader have been equally fooled. Perfectly acceptable.

What isn't okay is when the detective picks up something from the ground at the scene of the crime and at the end of the story, he produces the piece of evidence that nails down the killer. We all love to be fooled, fairly, but not when it involves cheating.

Here's an example of a plant early on and the way to disguise it:

The mail lay on the hall table. The moment Mary came in the door, she saw the letter on top addressed in Fran's familiar writing. A lot of left-handed people wrote with that distinctive slanted script.

As she reached for the stack of mail, the phone beside it shrilled. Mary winced and wished once more that she could convince Cora to adjust the sound. When she heard the voice on the line, she smiled into the mirror above the table. "Max! I'm so glad you called!"

Have we diverted your attention from the fact that Fran is left-handed? Yet, in the end, when we dredge up that vital fact, all we have to do is give Mary a vivid picture of that letter and rerun her thought about left-handed writers—and the reader will remember and be pleased that the writer played fair. Somehow the writer fooled him, diverted him, and he may never know how. It's not important. The best technique (as in all kinds of magic) never shows the bones, the building blocks, or the practice that leads to professional expertise.

Mary could have been diverted by a crash in the kitchen, and found her pet kitten happily lapping up the cream left out in the expensive china creamer, part of a set and a piece that Mary will never be able to replace. Shock! Irritation—with the kitten and with herself for being so careless. Would that be enough to disguise the fact that Mary's college roommate Fran is a leftie?

Plants are obviously most vital in the mystery or suspense story. Here's where the method of plotting comes in handy, because these stories are plotted backward. You, the writer, know what has happened, who the villain is, and why the crime has been committed. Working backward, you fit your plants in neatly to divert attention from the real culprit, possibly to direct suspicion to someone else. Protagonists are always wrong about who's guilty in the first chapters of these books. If they do wonder about the villain's guilt, it's only in a lineup of all the characters involved. Here again, when these questions are asked, there must be a diversion if only by way of bringing up quickly a far better possibility that someone else is the criminal.

Your plants have to be most subtle in this kind of story, sometimes merely a matter of having the baddie on the scene at the time of the crime—and capable of having committed it—and seeing that several other characters have also had opportunity to slip the poison in Great Uncle Otto's Ovaltine.

In one of my mysteries, the heroine discovered a dumbwaiter hidden behind a picture in Grandpa Luther von Weber's bedroom. If the panel were left open, she could hear the kitchen crew below quite clearly. Nobody who read the book picked up on the fact that the reverse would also be true. Someone down in the kitchen could hear the conversations in Grandpa's bedroom almost as clearly. Especially because the old man had a hearing loss, and people were apt to raise their voices when they spoke to him.

Plants may be valuable in describing settings, as well, beginning with the old cliché about the gun on the wall which will go off—which *has* to go off—before the end of the story.

JOSEPH WAMBAUGH

The author of such classic police oriented books as *The Onion Field, The Centurions, The Choir Boys,* and *The Blooding* told the 1989 audience:

I started with short stories and sent them everywhere. And everyone rejected them. One came back from *Playboy* and I waited about a year. Then I sent it back, and some cruel bastard of an editor returned it with a note saying "It's no better this time than it was last time!" I wish I'd saved his name; I'm powerful now and I could get revenge!

It takes me three to four months to write a book, any book, fiction, nonfiction.

My first books aren't very good, but they have a lot of energy which can make up for a lot. But remember, I was first of all a policeman and a part-time clothing salesman. Nobody knew I was a closet writer, nobody! Until the first book, *The Centurions,* became a Book-of-the-Month-Club main selection. Then I had to tell a few people. The short stories *never* sold. To this day! I did turn—expand—two of the short stories into novels: *The Blue Knight* and *The Choir Boys.*

I tried outlining, but it never worked for me. Create the character and let 'em take over, it's true.

If you'll just sit down and do four double-spaced typewritten pages a day, and you can do that, that's 1,000 words a day. You'll have a book in three or four months. That is, a rough draft. Then you've got rid of that terrible bugaboo—the blank page. Now you can fool around—have fun—you're looking at this big pile of stuff—and now you can embellish it any way you want.

When I'm writing a book, I write every day until I get tired. Then it's a seven-day-a-week job for me and I don't do anything else. I mean nothing else.

Did filing police reports help me with my writing? Yes, it helped me with my nonfiction writing. And my fiction writing!

I think Truman Capote's *In Cold Blood* is the best of the true crime writing. It opened the door. Generally most of the people involved in true crimes are dull—it takes the writer to find out why they're interesting, and especially the people around them.

Endings

*L*ongfellow said: "Great is the art of beginning, but greater the art of ending."

Someone else said, "Get the end right and the beginning right and the middle will take care of itself."

We all know what a good beginning is: start fast, hook the reader, set the scene, and so forth. Less clear is how and when to end a story or novel. Joseph Conrad said that no work is ever finished, it is only abandoned. (I have a director friend who says his first, and worst, film "wasn't released—it escaped!")

We can make many generalities about beginnings, fewer about endings. For example, where does the story end that climaxes in a man's suicide? Do we have to see the tying of the noose, the purchase of the cyanide, the actual firing of the gun? Or is it perhaps more subtle and effective to see him merely open the desk drawer where the gun lies? Perhaps it is more poignant to end the story when he takes a piece of paper and begins to write: "To my wife: When you read this note I shall be out of earshot of your nagging voice, beyond the pain that you know so well how to inflict," etcetera.

Hemingway maintains, in *Death in the Afternoon:* "Madame, all stories, if continued far enough, end in death, and he is no true-story teller who would keep that from you."

True, but of course most stories are not carried that far. Nor does the reader necessarily have to "see" that death.

In my novel *Dangerfield*, I planted the fact several times that although the great writer (based on Sinclair Lewis) had been sober for many years, if he were to drink again doctors said he would die. At the end of the book, his son finds the locked liquor cabinet smashed open and several bottles gone. That is all the reader needed to know about what was tantamount to a suicide.

In Luis Spota's powerful novel *The Wounds of Hunger,* his young bullfighter goes through hell all through the book in order to get a chance to fight in the big Mexico City arena. We know the character so well that we know, in spite of his weaknesses and past indecision, that if he puts his mind to it he will triumph and become a great matador. The big day comes and everything is riding on it: Will he find the determination and courage within himself to perform bravely in front of the lethal horns?

> He came out with his montera hat in his hands and the dress cape slung over his arm. The hotelkeeper, an old Spaniard, rasped with his stale cigar breath: "You better cut off the bull's ears or I'll cut yours off."
> "That," Luis replied very seriously, "is what I intend to do."
> He smiled and gave Luis a pat.
> The car that El Gallego had brought was waiting at the door of the hotel. From the windows of the neighboring houses there sprouted clusters of heads watching the torero. Luis waited until the belongings were packed in the car. As they started off, Camioneto whispered: "Matador, I've got only five pesos—enough to get us to the plaza but not enough to bring us back."
> Luis's eyes fixed on Insurgentes Avenue stretching out ahead of him.
> "We don't need any more," Luis Ortega said between clenched teeth. "They're either going to carry me back on their shoulders or they're bringing me back in an ambulance."
> Camioneto shuddered seeing his face when he said it.

Notice how Spota uses the secondary character's reaction to reinforce Luis Ortega's decision. We know, by previous scenes and episodes, that when Luis makes up his mind to do something it gets done. Therefore, we do not even have to see the bullfight. The novel ends on the next page in this fashion:

> Old Doctor Ibarra came around. He scratched his neck and smiled at him.
> "Go out there and really work close to the horns, lad. After all, you know you've got free medical service here."
> Strangely, the rough joke gave him courage and he was grateful.
> "Yes, Doctor."
> His heart stopped pounding for a second and then started again, harder, when they swung back the gate. Luis put on his

montera, shoving it down level with his eyebrows. He looked up at the stands. There wasn't a single vacant seat in the largest bull ring in all the world. Once I said I would fill this place up, he thought. And now by God I've done it and no one here is going to be sorry he came.

Someone shouted: "Get ready to go!"

Luis heard himself murmur. "Never a backward step!" as he and the other two matadors took their places at the head of their men. Then he remembered to take off his hat since he was making his first appearance in this plaza de toros.

At that moment, the chime of the clock of the Plaza México struck four times.

"The time!"

The band blared out suddenly and the crowd roared.

And Luis Ortega took his first step into the future.

The End

Very unusual, ending the book here, considering the entire novel has been pointing to this moment, this bullfight. Yet the author was right, we didn't need to see it. We know he will have a triumphant afternoon and will be launched as a great matador. It is a *satisfying* ending.

And that word is the key. The ending should *satisfy*. This doesn't mean that it be necessarily a "happy ending." *Hamlet* has a tragic ending with bodies stacked on bodies like logs in a log jam, yet it is a satisfying ending: characters acted out their destinies, villains got their comeuppances, and Hamlet paid for his previous indecisions.

Continuing in a taurine vein, in my novel *Matador* the protagonist dies, but it is a satisfying ending in that he achieves what he wanted to do; had he failed to prove he was better than the younger man or showed himself to be a coward that would have been an unsatisfactory ending and the reader would feel defrauded.

But how to end the ending? I felt the novel needed something more after the protagonist died, a glimpse of the reaction of his manager, the man who had made him famous, who truly loved him. What would Chaves do after his beloved friend and protégé died? He would want to get away from the scene, but then what? I could think of nothing appropriate till a student of mine made a good suggestion which I quickly worked into the end, a sad but satisfying end:

Cascabel came in. "I called your mother, Pacorro. She's on her way here."

"Gracias, Desperdicios. How she must be suffering." Suddenly he stiffened. "Doctor, I can't feel anything in my right leg."

"You're all right, Paco," said Doctor Quintana. "There's nothing to be worried about."

Pacote lay there breathing hard. Then he said: "Doctor, I can't feel anything in my left leg!"

"That's all right," said the doctor. "You'll be well in no time. You'll be walking around in a month."

"Doctor," said Pacote in a frightened voice. "Are my eyes open? I can't see!"

He half rose up on the table and then fell back.

The doctor examined him. He stayed there with his back to Pepe, and then he reached over and gently closed the dark eyes.

A great sob came from Chaves.

"More and more," said Cascabel dully, the tears spilling down his face. "They kept demanding more and more—and more was his life, so he gave it to them."

"We did everything possible," the doctor apologized. "But the size of the . . ."

"Sure, sure," said Chaves. There were tears in his mouth, and he spat them out on the floor. He backed away from the table and stumbled toward the door. He went out, lurching past the other, not seeing them. It was night now but not very dark yet. He went out into the quiet patio de caballos and through the gate. There was a silent crowd lounging there, and one person asked, "How is he?" But Chaves kept walking, not hearing. He was conscious of the American journalist walking along beside him saying: "Señor Chaves, I wondered if I could . . ."

Chaves shoved him aside and went down a narrow, crooked street, not knowing where he was going, just wanting to get away from the plaza de toros. He rounded a corner and was aware of someone way below him talking to him.

"Por Dios, caballero . . ."

He looked down and saw a truncated man riding on a coaster with children's skates underneath. The man smiled a toothless smile, dropping one of the leather-covered blocks with which he propelled himself and holding out his hand.

"Charity, for God, caballero, charity for the love of God, pity this wretched . . ."

"Holy Mother of Jesus!" Chaves croaked. He groped in his pockets frantically and threw all his coins and the gold money clip with Solórzano's torn bills in it, and a medallion and the keys attached to his lucky monkey's head and his wallet and his cigars and his address book and the comb he carried for Pacote to use in the ring and his wig—all of it he showered down over the half-man. Then blindly he staggered past him down the street.

"Heaven will repay you," the beggar mouthed happily as he gathered up the loot.

In certain stories even when the protagonist dies a violent death it can be termed a "happy" ending. In Jack London's astonishing story, "Lost Face," the hero cleverly tricks the cruel Indian chief into beheading him by claiming to have a magic potion which renders his neck invulnerable to his enemy's axe, thus avoiding the horribly prolonged torture death the rest of his men have endured. Because the hero succeeds in outwitting the Indian, making him the laughing stock of the tribe, he emerges victorious, albeit posthumously, so the ending is entirely satisfactory and not at all sad.

Hemingway's simple ending to *A Farewell to Arms* is sad, but it is the *right* ending. He was supposed to have rewritten it many—some say thirty-three—times to achieve the empty feeling of the protagonist's controlled anguish over the death of his love. I wonder if he had written it in the *third* person if the dialogue would have remained the same? Here the narrator is holding himself in.

The doctor speaks to him in the hospital:

"Good-night," he said. "I cannot take you to your hotel?"

"No, thank you."

"It was the only thing to do," he said. "The operation proved—"

"I do not want to talk about it," I said.

"I would like to take you to your hotel."

"No, thank you."

He went down the hall. I went to the door of the room.

"You can't come in now," one of the nurses said.

"Yes I can," I said.

"You can't come in yet."

"You get out," I said. "The other one too."

But after I had got them out and shut the door and turned off the light it wasn't any good. It was like saying good-by to a statue. After a while I went out and left the hospital and walked back to the hotel in the rain.

Some of the different endings to the novel can be seen in Boston's JFK Library. Many of them paint an even darker picture.

"That is all there is to the story," read one ending. "Catherine died and you will die and I will die and that is all I can promise you."

In another, he wallowed in bitterness. "See Naples and die is a fine idea: You will live to hate its guts if you live there. Perhaps there is no luck in a Peninsula."

Sometimes he was philosophical: "That is all there is to this story. There is supposed to be something which controls all these things and not one sparrow is forgotten before God."

Some endings were verbose:

"After people die you have to bury them but you do not have to write about it. You do not have to write about an undertaker. Nor the business of burial in a foreign country. Nor do you have to write about that day and the next night nor the day after nor the night after nor all the days after and all the nights after while numbness turns to snow and snow blunts with use. In writing you have a certain choice that you do not have in life."

It would appear the author ultimately picked the best and simplest ending.

Hemingway's novel, *For Whom the Bell Tolls,* begins this way:

He lay flat on the brown, pine-needled floor of the forest, his chin on his folded arms, and high overhead the wind blew in the tops of the pine trees.

The book ends, 470 pages later, with Robert Jordan lying again on pine needles, his hip broken, his submachine gun at the ready, awaiting certain death:

Lieutenant Berrendo, watching the trail, came riding up, his thin face serious and grave. His submachine gun lay across his saddle in the crook of his left arm. Robert Jordan lay behind the tree, holding onto himself very carefully and delicately to keep his hands steady. He was waiting until the officer reached the sunlit place where the first trees of the pine forest joined the green slope of the meadow. He could feel his heart beating against the pine needle floor of the forest.

Once again, it is a sad ending but a correct one, a *satisfying* one; Jordan was willing to give his young life for a cause he believed in. And the author doesn't have to spell out what is going to happen; we know Robert Jordan, his character and his skills. We know the end now.

William Saroyan saw the death of his young impoverished writer from the protagonist's eyes in *The Daring Young Man on the Flying Trapeze:*

He placed the shining penny on the table, looking upon it with the delight of a miser. How prettily it smiles, he said. Without reading them he looked at the words, *E Pluribus Unum One Cent United States of America,* and turning the penny over, he saw Lincoln and the words, *In God We Trust Liberty 1923.* How beautiful it is, he said.

He became drowsy and felt a ghastly illness coming over his blood, a feeling of nausea and disintegration. Bewildered, he stood beside his bed, thinking that there *is nothing to do but sleep.* Already he felt himself making great strides through the fluid of the earth, swimming away to the beginning. He fell face down upon the bed, saying, I ought first at least to give the coin to some child. A child could buy any number of things with a penny.

Then swiftly, neatly, with the grace of the young man on the trapeze, he was gone from his body. For an eternal moment he was all things at once: the bird, the fish, the rodent, the reptile, and man. An ocean of print undulated endlessly and darkly before him. The city burned. The herded crowd rioted. The earth circled away, and knowing that he did so, he turned his lost face to the empty sky and became dreamless, unalive, perfect.

Unalive is a haunting word, and pure Saroyan.

One of the most poignant deaths in literature is that of Peyton Farquhar, the young soldier in Ambrose Bierce's "Occurrence at Owl Creek Bridge." In the opening paragraph he is about to be hanged from the bridge. He thinks of escaping. It then appears that he does escape and makes his way down the river to his home and to his beloved wife:

He stands at the gate of his own home. All is as he left it, and all bright and beautiful in the morning sunshine. He must have traveled the entire night. As he pushes open the gate and passes up the wide white walk, he sees a flutter of female garments; his wife, looking fresh and cool and sweet, steps down the veranda to meet him. At the bottom of the steps she stands waiting, with a smile of ineffable joy, an attitude of matchless grace and dignity. Ah, how beautiful she is! He springs forward with extended arms. As he is about to clasp her he feels a stunning blow upon the back of the neck; a blinding white light blazes all about him with a sound like the shock of a cannon—then all is darkness and silence!

Peyton Farquhar was dead; his body, with a broken neck, swung gently from side to side beneath the timbers of the Owl Creek Bridge.

The reader then realizes that the escape was all in his mind, that there was no escape from death for many of the young men in the Civil War, and that war is hell. And that Bierce was a great writer.

This story, as well as Faulkner's classic "A Rose For Emily," seems a valid use of a surprise ending, but in general "trick" endings—such as in W.W. Jacobs' classic "The Monkey's Paw," where the third wish that the old couple makes to restore their son to them results in his almost returning in his decayed dead state; and in Frank Stockton's "The Lady or the Tiger?" where the reader has to decide whether death or happiness will emerge from a coliseum tunnel; and in most of O. Henry's stories—have fallen out of favor. I still enjoy reading that type of story and you can find them in some of the mystery and suspense magazines. But this type of ending will not be found in the so-called "slice-of-life" stories in *The New Yorker* and *The Atlantic Monthly*.

Anton Chekhov once declared: "My own experience is that once a story has been written, one has to cross out the beginning and the end. It is there that we authors do most of our lying."

He also said: "My instinct tells me that at the end of a story or a novel I must artfully concentrate for the reader an impression of the entire work, and therefore must casually mention something about those whom I have already presented."

In D.H. Lawrence's sensual novel *Lady Chatterly's Lover*, he "artfully concentrates for the reader an impression of the entire work." Here are the very last paragraphs of gamekeeper Mellors' heartfelt, summing-up letter to Constance Chatterly ("John Thomas" and "Lady Jane" being petnames for their respective genitalia):

> Now I can't even leave off writing to you.
>
> But a great deal of us is together, and we can but abide by it, and steer our courses to meet soon. John Thomas says good night to Lady Jane, a little droopingly, but with a hopeful heart.

I wonder if there is a more chilling ending to a piece of writing than Jonathan Swift's ironic "A Modest Proposal" in which he suggests that Ireland's hunger problem be solved by buying and serving up one-year-old children at the tables of "people of quality":

> I profess, in the sincerity of my heart, that I have not the least personal interest in endeavouring to promote this necessary work, having no other motive than the public good of my country, by advancing our trade, providing for infants, relieving the poor, and giving some pleasure to the rich. I have no children by which I

can propose to get a single penny, the youngest being nine years old, and my wife past childbearing.

Horrible, but appropriate and in keeping with the rest of the piece.

"Things have a way of turning out so badly," Amanda Wingate says to her daughter Laura in *The Glass Menagerie.*

But they don't have to in fiction, always. There are many happy endings in great literature. Or at least satisfying ones. Alice returns safe and sound from Wonderland, "and she would remember the happy summer days." We know Scarlett O'Hara is going to make it somehow, Huck Finn and Jim end up just fine after their hegira, Don Quixote gets back to La Mancha in one piece, Ulysses makes it home and slays his wife's suitors, Captain Queeg receives his comeuppance, Tom Jones ends up with the girl and the money, the Prisoner of Zenda escapes, and Elizabeth nabs Darcy in *Pride and Prejudice.*

You will find that most good stories end the way that they *must* end, that the characters of the protagonists or antagonists dictate the outcome, and in this way the endings satisfy the reader. Many beginning writers, instead of having the characters decide the outcome, bring in Mother Nature to help them wind up things tidily: a nice earthquake, for example, or a flood, storm, or forest fire. The gods stepping in, *Deus ex machina,* rarely satisfies, except, perhaps, on the wide, wide silver screen.

Joseph Conrad was a master of the ending, as Clifton Fadiman, famous essayist and a long time participant in our Conference, pointed out in his book *Enter, Conversing:*

> This, cunning in its use of rhythm to hypnotize the reader, is from *Youth,* the tale of the romantic East that Marlow evokes out of his radiant young manhood and tells in late middle age to a group of lifeworn contemporaries:

> And we all nodded at him: the man of finance, the man of accounts, the man of law, we all nodded at him over the polished table that like a still sheet of brown water reflected our faces, lined, wrinkled; our faces marked by toil, by deceptions, by success, by love; our weary eyes looking still, looking always, looking anxiously for something out of life, that while it is expected is already gone—has passed unseen, in a sigh, in a flash—together with the youth, with the strength, with the romance of illusions.

Here the effect is achieved not by statement but by incantation.

Note that it is all one long sentence, developing inexorably like the slow decay of our lives, but that its incremental effect depends on the careful handling of five related series of short phrases set off by commas: the group beginning with "the man of finance"; that beginning "by toil"; that beginning with "looking still"; that beginning with "unseen"; that beginning with "with the youth." It is impossible to read this crafty sentence aloud without making the pauses Conrad wishes you to make; his marks of punctuation exert on you precisely the influence that the conductor's baton wields over his orchestra. The magical result is that a platitude (for all that Conrad is saying is that we cannot retain the illusion of youth) moves us like a revelation. It's all done with a few commas and a few ordinary words. If you care to note how literature differs from mere writing, there you have it.

Hemingway loved *Huckleberry Finn,* saying that "all American writing comes from that. There was nothing before. There has been nothing as good since." Yet he hated the ending. "If you read it you must stop where the Nigger Jim is stolen from the boys. That is the real end. The rest is just cheating."

Some stories would be nothing without their endings, such as Anatole France's famous story "The Procurator of Judea." In his latter years Pontius Pilate is being idly questioned about certain events that had occurred during his reign:

> Pontius Pilate contracted his brows, and his hand rose to his forehead in the attitude of one who probes the deeps of memory. Then after a silence of some seconds—
>
> "Jesus?" he murmured, "Jesus—of Nazareth? I cannot call him to mind."

One story which I admire but whose ending has never entirely satisfied me, is John Cheever's "The Five-Forty-Eight." Miss Dent is an unstable, rather pathetic, young secretary in New York. Her boss, Blake, seduces her one night, then has her fired the next day. She has a breakdown. She begs him for help, but he ignores her notes. Months go by. Then one day she follows him aboard the commuter train on his smug way to his fancy home and family in Connecticut. She sits next to him, holds a gun on him, and tells him of the suffering she has gone through because of him. At his stop she follows him off the train, the pistol hidden but aimed. In a dark area beside the station she forces him to grovel and put his face in the dirt. Then, satisfied, she leaves to catch a train back to New York.

Although I think this is a fine story with superb characterization, I have never felt fully happy with that ending. Blake is so despicable that I felt he should suffer more, much more. In literature we do not like to see villains get away with their skullduggery. Last year at the Conference, I read the story at one of my workshops, up to the last page, up to where Blake and Miss Dent get off the train. Then, without telling how Cheever ended his story, I invited participants to write their own endings in a half-hour exercise. There were several excellent submissions, but one young student, Tony Haskett, came up with what I consider the perfect ending. So, with our apologies to the late, great John Cheever, I reprint it here:

Suddenly Blake wished he had read the note she had sent him so long before. It might have contained a clue or warning. How could he have known? He wasn't clairvoyant as she claimed to be. Her expression reminded him of the face she had worn that night when she had returned from the bathroom wearing her thin nylon nightgown and a fresh spray of perfume behind her ears. Then there had been a glow in her eyes like a candle through the holes in a jack-o-lantern. But now all the self-doubt was gone.

"Take off your clothes," she said.

Blake hesitated. Her hand moved, and he saw the gun for the first time. It was small and blue and ugly. The hole at the end of the barrel gaped at him like an open manhole, though it was really less than half the diameter of a dime. A twenty-two, he realized. He began to undress.

"Your underwear, too."

"Please," he whispered.

"Your underwear."

Blake complied. Now his clothes lay in a ragged bundle at his feet. The whistle of the six-fifteen express sounded in the distance. He wondered how he would look to those passengers who lined the train windows as they glanced out as the train rolled by.

"Pick them up."

He did.

She gestured with the gun at the tracks. "Over there."

Blake walked to the edge of the concrete platform. The gravel bit into his naked feet. He waited for the bullet to pierce his back.

"Throw them over."

"Please," he said.

"Now."

He threw his clothes down onto the steel rails and oily cross ties. He could feel the six-fifteen coming.

"Kneel."

He did. The train thundered past. He was surprised to see no faces looking out at him. He was alone. He heard the shot and he fell forward, surprised that there was no pain. Slowly Blake got to his knees again, put his hand behind his back and felt. No blood. He turned. Miss Dent lay there on the cement, the gun still in her hand, her leg twisted in an impossible angle. There was a small hole beneath her jaw and a pool of red spread slowly out from beneath her dark hair. When the train finally passed, Blake looked down to see his clothes were gone. He stood on the cold concrete until he heard the low whistle of the six-twenty-eight coming to him through the night. Then he turned and walked naked and alone back to the station.

DOMINICK DUNNE

These were some of the valuable words offered to us in 1989 by Dominick Dunne, author of the huge best seller *The Two Mrs. Grenvilles* and *An Inconvenient Woman*.

Get that first draft down on paper! If you are stuck in some section just put in a page with "here so-and-so somehow finds out where the key was hidden," or "here there's a scene where they fall in love," or "I don't know exactly what goes on right here," and then plunge on! Get it all down! Finish the book! Then go back and fill in or ask for help from an editor.

I'm a late-life writer—I didn't *start* writing until I was fifty years old. So take heart some of you! When I was graduated from Williams College the first job I had was stage manager of the "Howdy Doody Show." From there I went to some of the great live TV shows of that period. Then I produced a lot of movies, *The Boys in the Band, Panic in Needle Park, Play It as It Lays* and so forth. Exciting times, but I had the feeling this wasn't *it*. I got more and more discontented.

Finally, I walked away from Hollywood and I went to Oregon, a cabin in the woods, and began to write my first novel. You know, it's one thing to say you're going to write a novel and it sounds so wonderful when you tell your friends about this wonderful Hollywood scandal you're going to write about and they say "oh that's fabulous" but then you get there in the cabin all by yourself and you get to the typewriter and it never sounds the same way when you get it down on paper. *If* you get it down on paper. And if any of you are having that problem I want to tell you what you have to do: set a certain time each day and that is to be your writing time and nothing—*nothing*—must interfere with that time. That is *Your Writing Time,* in capital letters.

I worked hard on that book. It was based on a true case about a famous Hollywood producer who stole some money from an actor and it got published and it was such a flop, a real bomb. It was called *The Winners.* And it got the worst review imaginable in *The New York Times;* they just savaged it.

I've always been very sensitive and I'd worked hard on that book—it's just as hard to write a bad book as a good one, you know. But let me tell you how I took that terrible criticism.

I said to myself, "Listen, I'm fifty-three years old and I wrote a book and I got a book published by Simon and Schuster and by God it got reviewed in *The New York Times!*"

So I didn't give up, and Michael Korda, the editor, believed in me, and he said, "Listen, Dominick, you know all these fancy people and there's nothing that the public likes to read more than about the rich and the powerful in a criminal situation." And let me tell you, I heard those words and a bell went off! I thought *that's it!*

You see, I'd seen this famous showgirl in the Stork Club one night—she was married to this guy from one of the most prominent Long Island families. She was just a knockout, this lady, and they got up to dance and when she stood up—she was in a strapless evening dress, and in the fifties when ladies wore strapless dresses they had one of the great gestures of all times—and that was when they did this [demonstrates on one side of his chest] and they did this [demonstrates on the other side], and I was just dazzled by this woman, and when she walked out to the dance floor it was like out-of-my-way-everybody! She started to dance with this guy and she had her lips right at his ear and she sang to him the whole time and I said this is *it,* this is how I want to live! I want to be with these people like this always! A year later she shot and killed that man. I told the story to Korda and he said, "That's the novel you're going to write."

And that's how *The Two Mrs. Grenvilles* came into being.

Revision

A Hollywood producer handed Gore Vidal a screenplay of one of his books and asked him to revise it. After reading it, Gore said: "This screenplay doesn't need a revision—it needs a trip to Lourdes."

You've heard it before; you'll hear it again and again: *Books and stories aren't written—they are rewritten!*

Professional writers know this. Beginning writers don't. They groan and moan and whimper and scream a lot when advised "to run it through the typewriter again," or to "revise that beginning completely," or to take that gorgeous, detailed and totally unnecessary description of the donkey ride to the bottom of the Grand Canyon and throw it into the Canyon itself.

We never think about how *War and Peace* was written—we just assume it appeared as a full-blown masterpiece out of Tolstoy's forehead like Athena out of Zeus'; yet we know that Tolstoy rewrote the work many times and was still not satisfied with the many drafts.

Novelist Brian Moore says:

A lot of writers say writing is misery. You've heard all that. I don't believe that at all. I am not happy when I'm not writing, and I'm quite happy when I am writing, even if it's not going well. People say that I write quite simply, but they don't realize how much I rewrite.

I have never regretted rewriting a story or chapter or article even if I improved upon only a few words per page; they add up.

In writing the first draft of an article on the Thames for a national travel magazine, I first wrote this phrase: *Cows standing along the bank.*

Upon rereading, it struck me as nonvisual and passive, so in the second draft I changed it to:

Black and white cows along the bank, drinking.
On the third rewrite I added:
Black and white cows along the bank drinking their reflections.
The rewriting was rewarded by that phrase being chosen last year for *Reader's Digest* magazine's "Toward a More Picturesque Speech" section.

Cutting is an essential and often painful part of the act of revising. You must ask yourself: is this page of introspection or action or dialogue truly helping the story? Does it move the plot? Does it advance the action? Does it reveal motivation? Does it characterize my protagonist? Does it impart information vital to the reader's understanding of the story?

If not—take a deep breath and axe it. And next time you have to cut a paragraph, a page, or even a chapter, think of Thomas Wolfe as he revised the monumental manuscript of *Of Time and the River*:

> What I had written about the great train was really good. But what I had to face, the very bitter lesson that everyone who wants to write has got to learn, was that a thing may in itself be the finest piece of writing one has ever done, and yet have absolutely no place in the manuscript one hopes to publish. This is a hard thing, but it must be faced, and so we faced it.
>
> My spirit quivered at the bloody execution. My soul recoiled before the carnage of so many lovely things cut out upon which my heart was set. But it had to be done, and we did it . . .
>
> Now in the original version, the manuscript which described the journey of the train across Virginia at night was considerably longer than the average novel. What was needed was just an introductory chapter or two, and what I had written was over 100,000 words in length, and this same difficulty, this lack of proportion, was also evident in other parts of the manuscript.

After I write an article, a chapter, or story, I read it through several times, looking for specific things each time. First, I look for clichés and ways to enliven the images. Then I read it looking only at the verbs—can I get a stronger, more apt verb in each sentence? Next, the adjectives: Do I really need them all? The same with adverbs—do I need *any* of them? Then I read the dialogue aloud, trying to make it sound more natural and colloquial, seeking to eliminate the words we do in real life. ("Forget something?" instead of "Did you forget something?" for instance.)

No one speaks in perfect sentences except when making a speech. Even Winston Churchill probably spoke in disjointed, ungrammatical phrases when in private; perhaps even like this:

"Morning, Clemmie dear. Bad night, terrible night. I dreamt that—ah, scones, I do love hot scones—that Hitler had invaded—just a touch of marmalade, there's a dear—had invaded England at the height of his power. Now, now, don't scold—a tiny bit of brandy in m'coffee, won't hurt a thing. And there I was all alone on the beach, yes—face to face with Herr Schickelgruber—he with a machine gun and I with only a bent saber and —just a bit more brandy, there's my good girl, so I said *Mister* Hitler, called him mister (should have seen his mustache twitch at that), said, so Mister Hitler, we meet at last! 'Bout to run him through with my saber, skewer him, en brochette, when you called for breakfast, 'm'love. Delicious, that brandy from De Gaulle, delicious!"

Of course it is possible that you *want* a character to emerge as stuffy or pedantic or pretentious, in which case, in contrast to the other characters in revising the dialogue you would have him or her talk in a stilted fashion:

"I do so love the opera, but one does become *très fatigué* with the bourgeois ones like *Bohème* and *Butterfly,* especially having been exposed, as I have, to the more recondite ones of, say, Amico Fritz and the Pearl Fishers, which, of course, one never hears of, except among a few of the cognoscenti."

Revise, revise, and, even when not actually writing, be thinking of your story and how you can make it better.

Flaubert, a great one for rewriting and rewriting again and never being satisfied, once wailed to his friend Louise Colet:

What a beastly thing prose is! It's never finished; there is always something to do over. A good prose sentence must be like a good line of verse, *unchangeable,* as rhythmic and as sonorous.

The humorist S. J. Perelman once answered an interviewer who asked how many drafts of a story he did:

Thirty-seven. I once tried doing thirty-three, but something was lacking, a certain—how shall I say?—*je ne sais quoi.* On another occasion, I tried forty-two versions, but the final effect was too lapidary—you know what I mean, Jack? What the hell are you trying to extort—my trade secrets?

No writer believed in rewriting more than Hemingway. (See *Endings* for his dozens of rewrites of *Farewell to Arms.*) Here he is in *By Line: Ernest Hemingway:*

You must be prepared to work always without applause. When you are excited about something is when the first draft is done. But no one can see it until you have gone over it again and again until you have communicated the emotion, the sights and the sounds to the reader, and by the time you have completed this the words, sometimes, will not make sense to you as you read them, so many times have you reread them. By the time the book comes out you will have started something else and it is all behind you and you do not want to hear about it.

But having said all that about revision, listen to this:

I write five pages a day, every day, and these are finished pages. I make a few pencil changes while the page is on the typewriter roller, but I don't revise and I don't retype anything. Essentially what you see is my first draft. Sometimes the five pages will take an hour, sometimes six, but I won't leave until they're done. If it's a scene full of dialogue, it may go like hell, and the five pages just shoot by.

These sacrilegious words were spoken by Robert Parker, the highly successful mystery writer, creator of the Spenser novels. It proves that all writers work differently. My advice is adopt Parker's work habits—but don't stop rewriting!

Anita Clay Kornfeld, author of such best sellers as *Vintage*, is one of the Conference's most popular teachers. Here she talks of revision and how to write so that it sounds *not* like writing:

Sometimes when I begin reading a student's manuscript I find myself wanting to reach for the telephone and call the writer and say, "Let's *talk*." Even the most articulate person, when he sits down to write, too often trips over his own profundity. The "storytelling" slides into the ditch while the writer strides ahead spewing out obscure, stilted words, or making pronouncements to the world under the guise of fiction.

I often think of writing as that wonderful opportunity to talk—without interruption—with the privilege of revision.

Having come from Tennessee, from an era when people gathered routinely on front porches at sunsets, fanned away gnats, and let the night put even the fastest talkers in perspective, one learned quickly, if unconsciously, what storytelling was all about.

Think back a moment: How many times have you heard from a

regular flow of conversation the natural beginnings to stories?

One that comes immediately to my mind, for example, goes back to when I was about ten years old and eager to learn about anything "adult."

Our nextdoor neighbor, Marybelle Hembree, used to join our front-porch gatherings, and usually managed to dominate the conversation with her latest gossip. I can still see her pulling herself up, taking a deep breath, narrowing her eyes, and beginning: "You won't *believe* what happened to me yesterday on my way to the Company Store!"

Even if most of the listeners didn't really believe much of what she said, everyone listened. The question hung in the air. "So, *what* happened, Marybelle?"

As I look back, I can see the basic ingredients of her storytelling unfolding: "Well, I no sooner slammed the front gate shut when I saw him. Why, I nearly dropped dead on the spot! It was like seeing a ghost all bent over, the shape of a beanpole caught in a cyclone."

"Who in this wide world was it?" everyone wanted to know.

"Remember that man who got sent to the penitentiary? That one-eyed Revellet boy they called Shug? The one who killed that woman after he did *you-know-what* that we can't say out loud when little girls with big ears are hanging on to every word. Things little girls don't need to know about until they're grown women and know how to steer clear of one-eyed devils like Shug Revellet . . ."

How many times have you heard someone say, "That reminds *me* of the time when . . ."?

Try the game of front-porch storytelling. Coerce your memory for a moment. Forget all about stern English professors or grade school teachers pounding out the rules and rigors of correct sentence structure. Forget, if you will, those deeply felt philosophical beliefs, those political slogans your hero will make in your next story. Forget the dream, for a moment, of yourself on TV talk shows, of your name riding the best-seller list, of those meetings you will be having in New York with your publisher, or those animated telephone conversations with your agent, calling about negotiating your TV contracts, once you've written the great American novel.

Take out a pen and paper, or sit down at your typewriter or word processor. Remember, this is a *game*. You're not going to be graded. You're not going to worry right now about spelling or punctuation or double spacing or a faded typewriter ribbon. You won't be counting out how much postage it will cost to send it out to your favorite magazine. This is an exercise in "talking on paper."

It involves a trip—a trip to the attic of your memory, where all kinds of dark, musty corners and carefully stashed-away containers hold fabulous story beginnings. Open the doors! Let them come tumbling out, willy nilly—these fragments from our secret passions, embarrassments, our shames, loves, and sorrows.

Just the other day, I read a manuscript from a student who has been learning to play the attic game and "talk on paper." This year marks his third year at the Santa Barbara Writers' Conference. For the first time, he was comfortably telling a story. There was no more of the verbal pomposity, that *rigor mortis* in characters that used to seem more like paper dolls than real people. I could *see* them, *hear* them, even sense the colors and odors, the texture of the setting, and those people caught in the conflict that made it a marvelous story. I kept eagerly turning each page of his manuscript, wanting to know what happened next.

Never forget, something must happen! A lot of beginning writers—and too many advanced ones—often forget that there is no drama without conflict. A hero or heroine is at a starting point, is a definite age, at a specific time and in a specific place. It isn't enough, however, to establish the who, what, when and where. There is a big "why." And there are sounds, colors, smells, touch and tone to weave into this fabric of storytelling. There are themes, and there should be tension. And, inevitably, there will be dialogue.

I've heard so many writers complain, "I have such a hard time with dialogue."

Front-porch story tellers rarely do. Most people in normal conversation rarely do. All around us we hear people freely expressing what is on their minds—and all too often without the need of revision!

The best story tellers are generally the best listeners. If you listen carefully to conversations taking place around you, you will hear dialogue spoken in fragments. There will be constant interruptions. I doubt that you will hear many people speaking perfectly constructed sentences. Yet, so many beginning writers will sit down to write dialogue that would turn any character into a stick figure.

I like to remind writers to take stock of their tool kits, periodically. After all, sculptors and painters must replenish their paints, their supply of clay, adjust easels, sharpen chisels and such. Unlike the visual artists', however, many of the writer's tools are invisible. It is hard even to keep track of the ghosts in the attic of our memories—those story ideas that play hide-and-seek with us. We work with the most common tools known: *words*. This is, one might think, the easiest craft of all, if that is the case.

It is the easiest, and it is the most difficult. At every turn, someone is saying, "One of these days *I'm* going to write a book. Boy, do *I* have a story to tell!"

Most people do indeed have a story—many stories—to tell. Yet, few find the tenacity, along with the opportunity, or whatever their reasons, to actually write that story.

Sometimes writers begin but give up the attempt when the going gets rough. There are many reasons why. But one I find that causes most to stop is an innate fear of rejection. There are plenty of critics out there! One's husband, wife, mother, or roommate—anyone handed the manuscript to read—all too often turns suddenly into a self-appointed *New York Times* book reviewer. Rejections don't always come in the form of little slips of paper, the beginning writer soon discovers. One must reach into the tool kit again and again and take out that most valuable tool of all: *selectivity*—especially when it comes to who gets hold of your manuscripts.

Selectivity has been called one of the great arts of living. I believe that learning what is workable in living isn't all that different from what is workable in writing. Indeed, I see *writing* as a mirror image of living.

I see writing (I prefer *"talking on paper,"* since it takes away some of the intimidation without reducing the craft) basically as sharing. If the stories the writer tells are to be significant, inevitably that writer has had to reach deeply inside; he or she has had to dare open doors to painful memories as well as those where hope and triumph abide.

We are told there is nothing new in this world. I don't argue with that. But there is always that wonderfully unique variation on a universal theme. There is always that chance that a writer will give us a very separate point of view, as oblique as it may seem, which will set it distinctly apart from other stories about the same subject matter.

So if intimidation has kept your writing from finding its way to the publishing world, try "talking on paper." Believe in your own vision. You are enough. You don't have to be Virginia Woolf or Faulkner or Hemingway or Proust. You don't have to please your mother, spouse, lover or friend. You don't have to get elected President of the United States or prove to the world through *The New York Times Book Review* that you are Nobel-prize material.

Just tell us your stories! Tell them out of that fabric woven by the ragtag elements of your own life experiences, of your secret hopes and dreams, your hurts, your embarrassments, your laughter and your tears. If it has meant something to you, most likely it is going to mean something to others out there.

It isn't really all that difficult. Remember, you are already carrying around your tool kit. You have a vast attic of memories to explore for story ideas. All you have to do is "talk" on paper, and then use those splendid tools we call selectivity and revision!

DANIELLE STEEL

She is considered to be the best-selling woman novelist of all time. She told our Conference in part:

I block out days of time for writing and nothing else. If you let anything infringe on your writing time, it will. And you won't get the writing done. Taking one day off can cost me five days of getting back in the mood. Going out to lunch can cost me anywhere from five hours to three days. And for me it's not worth it. For my own sense of well-being I have to finish my work before I can play.

The essential for me in writing is discipline. Discipline keeps me sitting there, no matter what.

That's how I write my book, but the real issue here is how you write yours. I write twenty hours a day; maybe you only write two or four or six. There are writers who write from nine till one every day. Or ten till noon and then out to lunch with their friends. Some people produce ten pages a day; others only write one or two.

We all write differently and we work differently and we live differently. I used to think when I had children that somebody else had the rule book and they hadn't given it to me, and everybody else knew how to do it right except me. I find the same thing in writing: you think that everybody knows what they're doing and that you don't.

Your way is just as right as my way. You have to find what you want to write. Apply yourself to it. And when you've finished, find an agent, pray for a publisher, and then you've made it.

The truth is you've made it the day you've finished writing your first book, whether it's ever published or not because that's the real accomplishment.

It used to make me mad as hell when people asked me what I did, and I said I was a writer. "Oh, have you published?" What difference does it make? Being a writer means you've written something. It doesn't necessarily mean you've published anything. There are no guarantees that you'll be published. When I was writing my first book I found an article in *The New York Times* about a lady who was ninety-one and had just published her first book after seventy years of trying to get published.

You are just as much a writer as I am. I happen to be a lucky writer, but I was just as much a writer twelve years ago as I am now. After I first got published I wrote five books that never got published and still live in my basement.

There are always people who will put you down. The main thing is you're doing what you want to do, which is writing. Work hard. Enjoy yourself. And don't look over your shoulder at what the other guy is doing.

It isn't easy and it isn't quick. The money isn't instant or even very much at first. It's a wonderful way to make a living, but it's an odd life, this solitary life of a writer. A life of intense involvement and caring, of endless hours clacking along in the silence of the night. But there are moments when it all goes well, as if you are doing an elegant slalom down a grand mountain . . . and then that final moment, that incredible, wonderful pinpoint of light and time when everything is perfect: you've done it, and it's over!

TWENTY

Mystery Writing

In the march up the heights of fame there comes a spot close to the summit in which man reads nothing but detective stories.
— Heywood Hale Broun

*W*hen I lived and worked for six fascinating months with Sinclair Lewis in Massachusetts in 1947, one of my duties was to drive down biweekly to the little college town of Williamstown five miles away to pick up "some good mysteries" for him. He wasn't very particular; he just wanted a "good mystery" to get him through the night. All morning he'd been writing, from 6:00 A.M. until noon. In the afternoon he'd been reading serious books, usually something to do with what he was working on, biography, autobiography, history, Plato's *Republic*, Flaubert, something important.

But come nightfall, he wanted *mysteries*!

And nothing too cerebral. I have the feeling that he wouldn't have liked *Fifth Business* by Robertson Davies—to me one of the greatest mysteries of modern times—if indeed it is a "mystery novel." Much as he liked Ross Macdonald (Ken Millar) personally, he found his books "too serious, too good" for his purpose. He wouldn't have liked the mathematical and intricate *The Gold Bug* of Poe. Nor Willkie Collins. But failing James M. Cain and Dashiell Hammett and Raymond Chandler, he would take just about anything written by a professional mystery writer. He wanted something to go to sleep by, but not to be *put* to sleep by. He wanted formulae, yes, but with a flair. No dangling murders or murderers, except at the end of a rope; he wanted solutions and conclusions and no continued-tomorrows and, please, no Freudian rationalizations. What he wanted was neat and tidy *nepenthe*, another world.

Franklin Roosevelt had the same addiction.

How do the mystery writers do it? Here's the Conference mystery-guru Leonard Tourney, to tell us something about the genre "the craftiness of mystery writers." He's written several fine mysteries, including the acclaimed *Old Saxon Blood*, and knows whereof he speaks.

I have chosen "craftiness" for my title rather than the more predictable and innocuous "craft." It has always seemed to me that mystery writers are both more manipulative than other writers and more devious. Their plots seem more premeditated; their effects more the result of a strong will to achieve absolute power over the reader's imagination. But if you want to write a novel of mystery or suspense, you must first understand that many of the qualities of this popular type of fiction are shared by all stories. All fiction has character, conflict, plot, description, theme—all the elements you have read about elsewhere in this book. All good stories are suspenseful, and some may deal with horrific events such as death, deception, and crime without bearing the label "mystery." But mysteries contain these elements in concentrated doses, and while there is no exact formula for concocting a good one, I'll leave you with some practical suggestions.

There are nine "tips," but please don't confuse them with commandments. They're only tips. Take them for what they're worth:

1. Know what kind of book you're writing

So far I've used the term "mystery" in a dangerously vague way. We are really talking here not about a single kind of book but a whole family. There are, for example, the detective novel and its blood brothers the police-procedural and spy thriller; the novel of psychological suspense and its distant cousin the novel of Gothic terror. Critics, with academician's enthusiasm for classifying, sometimes enjoy drawing fine lines between these "kinds" of books, even though they share an interest in moral disorder, induce anxiety about what will happen next, and feature protagonists whose investigations or experience are the means by which concealed facts are revealed to the curious reader. Editors often join in the schematizing for marketing purposes, convinced (and sometimes rightly) that the readers of one species of "mystery" will not necessarily be the reader of another.

Because there's undoubtedly much truth in this belief, you would be wise to begin your efforts by reading around in the mystery genres and noticing the differences. Even the detective novel, a clearly defined subspecies, has its own varieties. There's the hard-boiled detective story with its typically urban setting and generous helping of physical violence. There's the "cozy" mystery so popular in the British tradition where the murder is more likely to be committed at the vicarage than in a back alley and the detective is a polite, cerebral type.

Your choice of *kind* will depend largely on your own background, temperament, and literary taste. But do make your choice an informed one. Read books of the kind you want to write. Find out what the successful writers do and do not include. Imitation may not be the sincerest form of flattery but it is the quickest way to learn. Once you know your way around the genre you have chosen you will be in position to achieve the originality all writers strive for.

2. Make it new!

Mysteries are books about crime and its detection. Neither takes place in a vacuum. Having chosen what kind of mystery you want to write, you must now select the criminal act that will give rise to the plot. And you must locate the action in a particular place, a setting conducive to the atmosphere you wish to create.

It is an advantage, given the great number of mysteries around, to try to be original in both these decisions. Of course it's possible to write yet another novel about murder on the back streets of New York or in the staid environment of a country estate. But this is familiar stuff, and beginners are more likely to get published if they can offer editors and readers something new, either in the way of criminal conspiracy, or setting, or both.

This does not mean, however, that you should set your novel in Fargo, North Dakota, or Ely, Nevada, just because both towns have been slighted as scenes of crimes. Nor should you invent improbable criminal conspiracies just to avoid the ancient verities like greed, suppression of evidence, jealousy, and revenge. Novelty and originality are not always the same thing. But do try to avoid the clichés. They turn editors off and are less fun to write.

3. Research!

Having chosen your crime and its scene, now get to know both. If you have decided to write about a group of counterfeiters who have a falling-out, learn something about how counterfeiters operate. You may have to do some reading in your local library, make friends with a police officer or deputy D.A., or extend your social acquaintances. If a psychotic murderer is your cup of tea, start a newspaper file, take a course in abnormal psychology, or interview that weird second cousin of yours. Do not depend on television or even other novels for your information about the darker side of human personality. I would even advise you to "look into your heart and write," as the poet Sir Philip Sidney once advised himself in a sonnet, did I not know what gentle and law-abiding hearts resided in those who pick up the pen to write of crime and violence.

What is true of the crime is equally true of its setting. Know your terrain. It is certainly helpful to live in the place you write about—or at least to have been there. But if that has not been possible, or if your setting is a historical period and you find yourself regrettably without a time machine, you may have to resort to books, road maps, or an inspired imagination. Remember that giving the reader a firm sense of place is as important in mysteries as it is in fiction in general.

4. Make your characters real people

You've heard this advice before, I know. I urge it upon you again only to dispel the common misconception that mysteries, being essentially intellectual puzzles, are quite properly populated by characters with all the personality and depth of pawns on a chess board. Mysteries are not merely intellectual puzzles, and shallow characters are boring, no matter what genre they populate.

The characters of mystery fiction are typically ordinary people in extraordinary situations. The laws of psychological realism all apply. They have personal histories, likes and dislikes, complex motives, and, perhaps most important, flaws. "Of course villains have flaws," you say. "If they didn't, they wouldn't be villains."

Yes, but they must not be totally flawed. My favorite villains — *antagonists* is a better word — are not without their virtues. They are no less complex than the rest of us, and generally only a little worse. They may want power, money, or revenge compulsively, but those negative drives do not absolutely exclude positive feelings that anchor the most devious and desperate of characters in psychological reality.

Likewise for the hero, protagonist, or "detective," of the mystery. Characters with too much personal beauty, supercharged sexuality according to Hollywood formulas, or idealized lifestyles may achieve an imaginative perfection, but they are less credible and frequently tedious. The best detectives are vulnerable — psychologically and often physically. In the struggle with evil they too are at risk, and as they sift and probe the clues in the case, they do so in the complete humanity of a flawed nature.

5. Get off to a fast start

Readers of mysteries are impatient folks — and editors are worse. While neither absolutely requires blood and gore in the first paragraph neither will they tolerate a leisurely opening that merely introduces characters and setting and hints at foul play in the offing. So plan to get off the block on the first page, if not the first sentence. Hook the reader's imagination. Make it impossible for him or her to keep from reading on. Consider this opening from *Odds Against* by Dick Frances, one of Britain's most successful mystery novelists:

> I was never particularly keen on my job before the day I got shot and nearly lost it, along with my life. But the .38 slug of lead which made a pepper shaker out of my intestines left me with fire in my

belly in more ways than one. Otherwise I should never have met Zanna Martin, and would still be held fast in the spider threads of departed joys, of no use to anyone, least of all myself.

Now here is an opening paragraph that arrests the imagination by posing questions the reader will certainly read on to answer. Who is the narrator and what is the job he is so keen on now—now that he nearly lost his life from a gunshot wound? Who shot him and why? And who is the mysterious Zanna Martin and the departed joys that held him like a spider web?

In his novel *Minnesota Strip*, Michael Collins follows a similar strategy in an initial action sequence that is sure to intrigue lovers of the more viseral type of mystery novel:

The girl ran among the shadows near the river on the first cold night of a New York September. She looked behind her through the light of a solitary street lamp. A street of dark tenements and windowless warehouses. She stumbled as she ran, her ankles turning in black high-heeled pumps.

The girl in the passage is obviously not running for aerobic exercise. She is fleeing something—or someone. The area of the city through which she runs is obviously not safe and her stumbling and impractical shoes do not abode well for a successful escape. The brief beginning is pregnant with danger for an as yet unidentified character who nonetheless manages to invite our sympathy and concern.

This is what I mean by getting off to a fast start. Engage the reader's curiosity immediately. A dead body need not sprawl upon the floor, bullets need not shatter the stillness of a summer night, but something must happen—and soon—or the reader will go on to another book, or turn on the TV.

What is a "twist?" It is a sudden turn in the course of events, a defeat of the reader's expectations. Sometimes the twist is a mere veering from the set course. For example, in pursuit of X as the primary suspect in a murder case, the detective now determines that it is Y who is more likely to be the guilty party.

But the twist may be even more wrenching. It can be an actual reversal in expectation: The same detective in the example above now concludes that it is not X who is guilty, but the heretofore presumed victim of X's alleged crime. In P. D. James' intriguing little mystery, *An Unsuitable Job for a Woman*, the guilty party turns out to be the very person who has hired Cordelia Gray, James' detective, in the first place!

216 ■ *The Complete Guide to Writing Fiction*

Plots can be twisted by the sudden introduction of new elements —
like a piece of fresh evidence or the reappearance of a character
thought to be dead, or an abrupt confession by a character the reader
feels is innocent, or the sudden death of the most likely suspect. The
strategy is to keep the poor reader constantly off guard.

But in plotting, as in many things, moderation is a good rule.
While it is true that a plot too simple is a dull read, it is equally true that
too convoluted or intricate a plot has its own problems. Somewhere
between excessive simplicity and the other extreme is a happy medium. I would tell you where the fine line between the extremes was
drawn if I knew myself. Getting it right is often a matter of trial and
error. Testing the waters of reader satisfaction can often be accomplished by having a friend or colleague whose opinion you regard give
your manuscript a look. But never be satisfied with a single opinion.
Different readers have different tolerances for plot complexity.

I will strongly suggest, however, that you don't undermine a
strong story line with too many subplots — or with even a single sub-
plot that is too involved. Successful storytelling is largely a matter of
disciplining the reader's imagination, and too many stories distract
both from the central line of events and from whatever atmosphere,
mood, or effect you are trying to achieve there.

6. Build suspense

Suspense is a quality of all fiction. Why read on except to find out
what will happen next? Of course in a successful mystery suspense
occurs in a more concentrated dose. The trick is to know the formula
and how to administer it so that the suspense intensifies as the plot
unfolds. A truly gripping novel — a real "page turner" — builds suspense by creating in the reader's mind ever more intense waves of
curiosity and anxiety. A dull mystery is one where suspense is either
intermittent or nonexistent.

Suspense is possible in fiction because of two human traits: the
first is curiosity; the second is the capacity we all share of being able
to experience vicariously the predicaments and states of mind of imag-
inary persons. Successful writers understand these principles and cap-
italize on them.

Suspense is a state of anxious uncertainty. As a writer you create
it in the reader's mind by deferring the answer to a question to a point
where the reader's initial curiosity is intensified. If the question is
answered too soon, no anxious uncertainty results. The same is true
if the question is too mundane or trivial. Will X take a taxi or limousine
to the airport? Only a few readers will care, and perhaps none will
care enough to become nervous as to the outcome.

At the same time, if the answer to a compelling question is suspended too long, the reader may find the suspense either intolerable or walk away in despair of ever having his or her curiosity gratified. Like plot-twisting then, creating suspense is a matter of finding a happy medium between too much and too little. There are a few rules of thumb:

Create characters the readers care about.

Place the characters in risky situations.

Never gratify a reader's curiosity on one point without piquing it on another.

Build suspense.

As the story or novel progresses the suspense should intensify. That means that questions of greater magnitude (e.g., Who killed Y? What will happen to X? And what were Z's real motives?) are answered last, thereby producing a crescendo of concern and a strong reader commitment to keep turning the pages.

Nothing is more gratifying to a mystery writer than to be told a reader "couldn't put the book down."

7. Give the reader a clue

Mysteries, unlike novels of raw, physical adventure, are intellectual exercises, even when the protagonist is a belligerent hunk from the American "hard-boiled" school of detective fiction. There may be bullets flying and fists too, but there is also a steady progress toward knowledge as the protagonist infers from discovered facts the scope and source of the criminal enterprise.

These facts are called "clues," and their selection and placement in the plot is one of the skills peculiar to the writer of mysteries.

Some clues provide direct evidence: that old standby, a fingerprint for example, or a signature on a letter. A witness's testimony that such a person was in the right place at the right time. And, of course, a smoking gun in the chief suspect's hand. Other clues communicate more subtly and require high probability inferences, such as the aroma of a rare type of perfume at the scene of the crime, a discovered relationship between victim and suspect, or a pawn ticket in a coat pocket. Thus in planting clues you create a fictional world of signs, not all of which are relevant to the matter at hand.

In the traditional whodunit (that is, a plot in which the protagonist's goal is the identification of the antagonist), a premium is placed on clues that are out of the ordinary. While there is nothing wrong with fingerprints on a glass or a glove dropped in the hall, these "signs" of criminal involvement are too tried-and-true to distinguish either the detective's powers of discernment or demonstrate the writer's capacity for originality. A good clue is one that is difficult to decipher either because it is an object or item of information that is not normally thought of as incriminating, or that which the clue signifies is something other than the ordinary person might have supposed. In *The Sign of Four*, Conan Doyle has Sherlock Holmes describe the three qualities of the ideal detective as knowledge, the powers of observation, and detection. Clearly, this implies that the role of the detective is that of a reader of signs, but since part of the reader's pleasure in a mystery is witnessing the skill displayed by the detective, this pleasure will only be given if the clues are difficult to decipher.

Just as it is important to select interesting, and perhaps even novel clues, it is also important to place them strategically. In a mystery, the truth sits in magnificent obscurity like the center of a maze, surrounded by trails false and true. As the detective, or whoever functions as such, moves closer to the center, the clues should increase in subtlety, for although any clumsy amateur might enter the maze and grope forward in the darkness, only the protagonist is able to discover the heart of the mystery by interpreting every sign properly.

Just as suspense should build toward a climax, each clue should be more difficult than the last until the detective has assembled all and discerned the true significance of the pattern.

8. Tie up loose ends

In fiction, the denouement is the outcome, or clarification, of the plot. The mystery writer seems under a heavier obligation than most writers to ensure that no significant questions remain unanswered or significant persons unaccounted for. Red herrings may entice the detective at one point or another into dead-end streets, but as the plot winds up you should present the truth of the matter in a neat package.

Accomplishing this is a matter of careful revision and self-discipline.

Revision, because it is easy to leave characters behind or important facts unexplained by sheer oversight. Every published author will admit to the mortifying discovery (after the book is in print) that a character has been left in Los Angeles without a way to get home, or the protagonist never explained what happened to the victim's Aunt Sally although a great to-do was made of her disappearance in Chapter Seven. To err in such ways is undeniably human, but writers try to avoid such gaffes all the same.

But what does self-discipline have to do with loose ends, you ask? The brain of an imaginative writer is like a cluttered attic. There are many stories up there, and each is clamoring to be told. They should not be told all at once, however. Save some of your material for the next book. You're more likely to have one if you concentrate your attention on the particular story at hand.

9. *Write frugally*

Some mysteries are written in so spare a style they seem to have no style at all. In fact, all writing has style. The question is what sort?

I recommend a spare style in mysteries, a transparent style that communicates the scenes, characters, and atmosphere without calling the reader's attention to the writer. Because mysteries often feature scenes of bloodcurdling danger and horror, depict characters in agonizing pain, and strive for terrifying effects, some writers — and especially beginners — suppose that a lavish helping of "fine writing" will enable the scene or effect to be realized. In fact, such overwriting usually kills the effect desired, for the reader's attention is so focused on the writer's skill as a writer (or lack of it) that *what* has been said takes second place to *how*. Style should always be an asset to the action, never a distraction.

A writer, therefore, should also be a merciless editor, willing to sacrifice that delightfully self-indulgent passage of purple prose to the good of the story no matter how painful the sacrifice. For writing is hard work — only the writer knows how hard. And a good novel of mystery or suspense requires as much revision and pruning as any so-called mainstream novel.

K E Y N O T E R

MARTIN CRUZ SMITH

The author of the classic *Gorky Park* and *Polar Star* spoke to the Conference in 1984:

I wrote every page of *Gorky Park* an average of three times. I wrote the first page about thirty times, and it was the very last page I wrote because I had so much difficulty with it. And after I had finished the last page — I had never been able to tackle successfully the first page — and I wrote the last page and I wrote the last image of the sables and I was coming out of my chair with excitement and with a power and a clarity of writing that I had never known before in my life. And then, while I was still levitating, took that out, took the first two pages and rewrote them.

We have come out of the genre and come alive as writers. Writers have a particular kind of power: I could give up, I could starve, but I couldn't get fired.

But after six years of going to *Gorky Park* and then quitting because I would run out of money, and then writing Jake Logan westerns and

Nick Carter mysteries and Simon Quinn mysteries and adventures of the Wilderness family and finally *Nightwing*, I had enough money to finally do nothing but finish *Gorky Park*. And by that time a great favor had been done for me by the man who wouldn't give me my book. Because by that time I was a far better writer than I was when I had walked out of his office. I had five years and eleven more books I had written in the meantime. And all the time I was . . . I was learning how to write, by God.

We are dealing with a man of enormous integrity in a dishonest society — and that is, of course, the tension of the book. The tension is not the bodies in the park, the tension is not the sables. And when you write, I hope you learn the lesson it took me a terribly long time to learn — which is the tension is not the bodies in the snow and it is not the bodies in the closet, the body in the car trunk; the tension is the character of the person who wants to know the truth. If you have the character, and you have that sense of integrity to pursue yourself, that's all the tension you need.

It is worth it to take time to do the research, not for the reader's benefit, but for your benefit. I can't write well at all unless I'm interested in what I'm writing about. And it takes research sometimes to find that . . . I spend an enormous amount of time on research because (of course you don't have to write) it provides your interest.

I wrote *Nightwing*, which deals with Hopi mysticism. I did very nice research but with one terrible flaw. The flaw was I ran out of money, and I did not have the money to go to Arizona to really walk around, to really just know the atmosphere and see the plants, get some dust on my shoes. And I wrote the book and all kinds of paper research was great but it lacked that. A flawed book for that reason.

I have the writing schedule that happens to a man who has no discipline. Which means I am always at or near the typewriter. And this is a very dumb thing, and I do not urge it. But because good ideas happen to me infrequently, I want to be there when it happens. So I will start at about ten in the morning and I will off and on work until ten or eleven at night. And if I am writing well I desperately want to be there. You know that wonderful rush when you are writing well and it is so exciting and you are the most brilliant man on earth. And I covet those moments. And I stretch them out. So I always find an excuse to be near the typewriter.

The sojourn into the country where Arkady Renko is being questioned is my favorite part of the book [*Gorky Park*]. It seems to be a somewhat inexplicable pause in the action of the book because he is not just questioned; there is a point there where suddenly we spend thirty pages away from the action of the book.

It was going to be very small but something disturbed me about the book and what disturbed me was the character of Pribluda. I had gone to enormous care to make all my characters real characters. And yet I had coming through this book a cardboard character in the form of Pribluda, who was a KGB major who was an adversary of Arkady Renko. But he was such a cardboard character, and I was displeased with myself and unhappy with him and then suddenly when I was there Pribluda started growing and Pribluda started turning from cardboard to flesh. Seeing that happen I was determined not to rush the story on to the plot, but I was going to stay there and see what happened if I gave Pribluda a chance to breathe.

I can only tell you that if you ever see a character starting to breathe, you do not shut him up, you do not sit on him, and you do not ship him out. You stay with him.

The Right-Brain Experience in Fiction Writing

*M*any people come to the Conference wanting to write but unable to free themselves from inhibition enough to write to their
full potential. That's where Marilee Zdenek comes in.

An innovative mainstay of the Conference for many years, Marilee
is the author of six books, including *Inventing the Future* and the best
seller, *Right Brain Experience: An Intimate Program to Free the Powers of
Your Imagination.* She has also written for the theater and reviewed
books for the *L.A. Times.* Founder of Right Brain Resources, she frequently leads seminars in Europe and the U.S. on techniques for stim-
ulating creative ideas.

Try some of her suggestions—she has helped a great many writers
become more creative than they could have imagined.

What you can do, or dream you can, begin it; Boldness has genius,
power and magic in it.

Goethe

Something magical seems to be happening when you are writing
at your best. In your mind's eye, you can see the characters before
you, watch them move, smell the scent of their bodies; you can hear
the sound of their voices as they suddenly take on a life of their own—
often saying things you had no idea they were thinking. You can see
the colors in the room, the texture of clothing, and soon you may feel
that all you need to do is record what is happening in this dreamscape
that is your novel. You may be so close to someone in your story that
you feel her tears on your cheeks and at night you may actually dream
your character's dream.

At those times, you may experience certain physiological changes.

Colors appear more vivid than usual; feelings are more accessible; familiar music is suddenly more exquisite, and you can work long hours without fatigue.

Most good writers (including many outstanding members of the literary community) have the ability to enter this state of mind but are not consciously aware of how they get there. Obviously their imaginations serve them well, but often they don't feel in control of the process. It is as if they are dependent upon the generosity of a capricious Muse, who comes bringing brilliant insights and rich metaphors or else sits tauntingly out of reach.

Joseph Heller said, "I don't understand the process of imagination though I know that I am very much at its mercy. I feel like these ideas are floating around in the air and they pick me to settle upon." James Dickey said, "It's really a kind of madness I feel when I'm writing . . . I don't know what it is . . ." Erica Jong said, "I don't know where the first line comes from and I don't know who says it to me. It may be the Muse (I really believe in the Muse, by the way)."

Many other fine writers have had no explanation for their intense periods of creativity or for the devastating periods of blocked imaginings. At lunch one day, some years ago, Irwin Shaw told me that he was terrified of the blank page. He would start each writing day in a state of high anxiety, feeling that the magic was gone, doubting his own creative powers, and hoping that somehow the words would start to flow and the characters come to life.

Not everyone feels so vulnerable. In fact, there are writers who know how to consciously invoke these exquisite periods of creative intensity at times of their own choosing. Without the use of alcohol or drugs, they can spend a few minutes in mental preparation and then enter a state of consciousness which intensifies their powers of imagination, of recall, and of sensual awareness.

For a study of highly successful creative thinkers, I interviewed many professional writers, including Ray Bradbury, Charles Schulz, Stirling Silliphant, and Barbara Goldsmith, who indicated that their work was enhanced by certain types of mental, and sometimes physical, activities. Experiences that were reported as most beneficial to the creative process include deep relaxation techniques, vivid mental imagery experiences induced by fantasy during a waking-dream state, intense sensory stimulation, dream programming, free-associations that often invoke childhood experiences, and even "programmed affirmations" that provide a way to build and sustain confidence during the writing and publishing process.

These activities are commonly referred to as "right-brain" experiences. Although both hemispheres of the brain are active in almost every activity, each has its own area of specialization and each processes information differently. This emphasis on the value of right-brain stimulation in no way underestimates the participation and contributions of the left hemisphere. The left brain—with its externally focused, analytical, verbal, linear mode of processing information—has its own essential role in the creative process. But when you need to be internally focused, to be sensitive to the intonations of your character's voice and body language, to comprehend symbols and metaphors, to think visually and holistically, or to enhance imaginative thinking, it is vitally important to know how to gain access to the right hemisphere, which is specialized for these functions. Emotions, although seated in the temporal-limbic system of the brain and realized in both hemispheres, are more correctly perceived in the right brain than in the left. The ability to stimulate these right-brain specializations is obviously of great benefit to anyone interested in creative thinking and internal focusing.

Not all of the people interviewed in the survey were aware of the connection between these modalities and their creative work until they were prompted to evaluate them during the interview. However, those who were cognizant of their own procedures reflected confidence in their ability to initiate periods of intense creativity at times of their own choosing.

Whether these techniques are used consciously and ritualistically or intuitively and sporadically, most good writers cultivate enough of them to open channels of communication between the unconscious mind and conscious awareness. Those who know how to invoke the dreamstate at will, know that the Muse doesn't live off in the heavens somewhere; she lounges over on the intuitive, sensual, metaphoric side of the brain and is more than happy to cooperate in the creative process whenever they relax and invite her to help.

Internally focused mental exercises (such as the guided imagery experience that will be described later in this chapter) are also valuable for helping writers discover the stories that are central to their lives. Although some writers use the actual events from their personal experiences as cornerstones for their novels, others prefer to embrace the *emotional* truth of their lives and discover the metaphors that bring their own fears and longings into fiction. For example, a writer who was abandoned as a child could write with authenticity about other types of losses; the circumstances might have nothing to do with childhood, but his personal experiences would become grist for the mill of fiction.

In your own life, events have occurred that prepared you to write best about certain types of emotional responses. You have been told, no doubt, to "write what you know"; I would encourage you even more to write what you feel. And to write from the vulnerable places at the very core of your being, using feelings that may have been experienced long ago but that resonate in your life, even now.

Years ago, Michelangelo was carving a statue in a courtyard and a small boy asked him why he was hitting at that rock. The great sculptor answered: "Because there's an angel inside and it wants to come out." As a writer, your finest work will emerge when you free the angels (and the dragons) that exist within you. Set them free and give them names. Disguise them in any way you choose and put them in hundreds of scenarios that may have nothing to do with the facts of your life. Just let these characters confront situations that evoke your own passions and they will live on the page with greater power and authenticity than you may have dared imagine.

"Right-brain" experiences provide you with a way to enliven your imagination and to stay centered in your work. They do not, however, replace the value of other writer's skills—those logical, analytical "left-brain" contributions to your book that make up the writer's craft and which will be described in any good book on writing fiction. The experiential tack will not make a great writer out of someone who has no sense of the traditional skills; it will however, make a better writer out of a good one, and at the very least, it will bring greater joy to the writing process.

If you want to enhance your ability to create vivid images in the dreamstate, to experience the "waking dream" or, if you will, the "*working* dream," you can easily learn specific mental exercises that can set you on your way. If you want to experience that now, to determine if this is a helpful approach to your work as a novelist, you can begin by experiencing one of the techniques that will be suggested here. Try it for yourself and see if you find it helpful. When you finish the upcoming guided imagery section, The Working Dream, you may want to begin writing a scene for your novel while you are still in the mood of the dream. See what happens. In a very short period of time you'll know if this is right for you.

The guided imagery that is suggested here is designed to stimulate all of your senses as you experience the traditional progressive-relaxation exercise; this creates alpha waves in both hemispheres of the brain and will help you relax and intensify your concentration. Then the suggestion of a "magical train" will enable you to gain distance from the perceptions of your usual waking state and allow your imagination to play with new possibilities suggested by your preconscious or unconscious mind. Then, when you are led to the house in the meadow, you may discover that your internal dream-maker creates characters and situations that invoke intense feelings and new observations.

A word of caution: Never use any right-brain exercises when your attention is required by small children or others who are dependent upon your alertness. It should not be used in a location that could be dangerous. A person who is emotionally disturbed should not use this, or any other technique of dealing with unconscious material, except with the help of a professional therapist. The exercise is very simple; for some people the power of it exceeds their expectations.

In preparation for The Working Dream, you'll need to find a quiet place, a comfortable chair, and have your pen and notebook within easy reach. You may want to have some gentle, nondirective music playing softly (you may enjoy music by Steve Halpern, Brian Eno, or Rob Whitesides-Woo) or you may prefer a tape of ocean sounds that helps you create the mood. Read through the scenario for The Working Dream and then recreate the scene in your mind's eye, moving *very* slowly, allowing the images to emerge in their own way. (If you haven't used imagery techniques before, you may want to put the suggestions on tape, or ask a friend to lead you through this. The Working Dream usually takes about twenty or thirty minutes.)

Most people find it helpful to use a *mandala* before beginning The Working Dream.

This type of simple design has been used for thousands of years by meditators to intensify concentration and reduce the frequency of intrusive thoughts. Since it is the right side of the brain that is specialized for spacial relationships, you can stimulate this hemisphere by staring at the center of the design for three or four minutes. You can let go of all intrusive thoughts and fix your attention on the very center of the mandala. (Of course, your left brain may want to count the squares or triangles but if you resist that temptation and allow your right hemisphere to dominate the exercise, you will find that it is quite easy to become relaxed during this experience.)

During The Working Dream, if any image is suggested that is not pleasing to you, adjust the suggestions to meet your personal needs. If distracting thoughts come into your awareness, accept them and let them pass through your mind without drawing your attention from this experience. You will decide how relaxed you want to be and how intensely you will experience the dream. As each of the images are suggested, allow yourself to concentrate on that image, focus your attention on the colors, the shapes . . . be aware of the smells and the sensations against your skin. Listen to the changing sounds . . . let all of your senses be aroused. *The more you are able to concentrate on the suggestions, the more vivid your experience will be.*

Now close your eyes and begin your journey. There is nothing you have to take with you; everything you need has been prepared for you.

The Working Dream

First, create these images in your mind:

A long, private, deserted beach with golden sand . . .

An ocean with gentle waves . . .

A single set of train tracks running parallel with the shore, only a short walk from the ocean's edge.

Beside the tracks, there's a wooden platform containing a wide bench, a comfortable chair . . . between the tracks and the sea, a blanket is spread out on the sand.

In your fantasy, imagine yourself into this scene. You are waiting for the train that will take you on a magical journey. You have arrived early and may choose to wait on the platform or on the blanket in the sand. You have plenty of time. Use this time of waiting to let go of the concerns of your daily life.

First, take a deep breath . . . and release it slowly. And then another, releasing all tension. Exhale any hurtful feelings, any anxieties or tensions, any negative attitudes, for they are of no use to you here.

Feel the warmth of the sun against your skin and the gentle touch of a summer breeze against your body. Be aware of the sand as it responds to your movement.

Can you hear the sea? The sound of a gull in the distance? Listen to the waves. Take your time. Smell the air, and taste the salt on your lips.

Watch the clouds, the changing forms. Notice the colors of the sea. Follow the movement of one wave; watch it build and break on the shore.

Lie back and take a deep breath . . . imagine that the warmth and healing power of the golden light fills your lungs. Then that warm, soothing light moves up to your shoulders, relaxing you, comforting you . . . And the golden light moves up into your neck, up into your brain and mind, your thoughts and feelings. Slowly, gently, the light moves down your body, into your arms, your hands, your fingertips. It circles back to the very top of your spine and slowly moves down your back, relaxing you, comforting you. And the golden light moves down your body, touching your hips and thighs, touching your calves, your feet, and becoming a positive energy that flows through your body, creating within you the perfect mood for the journey . . . for the train . . . for the Dream.

In the distance, you hear your train approaching. You have plenty of time. The train will stop and wait until you're ready to leave. It is your train and it will be as short or as long as you want it to be and it will look any way that you have chosen for it to look. It is coming here just for you and you can hear the distant whistle. Feel the vibrations in your body as it comes closer, and as it approaches it begins to slow down. Hear the sounds of it as it gradually comes to a stop and waits for you. Take your time.

Notice the color of your train, and the style. Notice the texture. Be aware that there is a special place for you to ride in this train, a place that will be just right for you. There is an observation compartment above one of the cars, there is a special car, perhaps, and there are other places you could ride. Take time to experience the train as being your own. Remember that it will adapt to your needs in any way that is right for you.

Be aware of the seat beneath you; the colors, the textures, the smells. Your train begins to move and you feel the gentle rocking movement. Listen to the rhythm of the sound of the wheels moving on the steel tracks.

Your train is a magical train and it can move on invisible tracks that spread out across the earth, lacing the mountains and the deserts and the plains. Your train can cross continents, skim across lakes and seas to distant lands. It can travel as high as you want to go, moving at any speed that is right for you. Your train can go where it wants to go and do what it wants to do — moving forward in time and backward in time, bringing you to a place where you will discover something important for you to know.

Gradually, your train begins its descent to the place that is special for you. Soon it moves in slow motion as in a dream . . . And now a soft fog is pressing against the window for you are entering the Dream.

The train stops and you make your way to the steps, and down to the deserted platform, down to the path that is right for you to take. And you follow the path that leads you through the fog into the sunlight. And you are in a lush meadow. Soon you approach a house and you look carefully at this house, observing the color, the style, the windows, and the door.

It is all right for you to enter this house so now you move toward it. You put your hand on the knob and feel the cool metal against your touch. Walk in and look at the room and see that you are alone there. Run your fingers along the walls and feel the texture. Find a place in the corner of the room where you can wait, where you can observe the room and all that will happen there, without being seen. Take time to notice the furniture, the colors, the style. Perhaps there is a scent in the room and you can identify the smell. Wait in the stillness. Listen.

Now you see someone enter the room, someone you have known in life, or in your book, or in a dream. Notice how this person moves, how gently or heavily the feet touch the surface of the floor. Observe the hair and notice the color and texture and the style. Study the face, noticing how the skin is smooth or wrinkled, how the brows form above the eyes. Look at the shape of the nose, and the mouth. What is revealed about the character that you didn't notice before?

Perhaps someone else enters the room, and you observe carefully how this character walks and looks. Notice the details, the smells, the sounds. The characters begin to talk and you may hear, or think you hear, what they are saying. You may hear only the tone of the voice or you may hear the words and you wait and listen. You can imagine what they are saying even if you cannot hear the words.

Did someone just say, "Why did you come?" Perhaps you heard something else. What do you hear now? What is happening now, in this room? And what is happening in some other room in the house? There may be something you want to say, or to ask. Remember, anything is possible in a dream.

There are other rooms in this house and you may want to see them. What has happened in these rooms? Is something happening now? Take your time.

Before you leave, notice that a book is lying on the table to your left. What color is the jacket of the book? Do you know what the book is about? Pick it up and see if there is something about this book that could be important to you.

Soon the Dream will end. Let your thoughts lead you out of the house and down the path, through time and space. You can return to your workroom using any means of transport you choose. You can even float back as you would in a sleeping dream. Now be aware of your room, the chair, the pen and paper that are before you.

Retaining as much of the mood of the Dream as possible, write what you experienced, using the present tense. Write in fragments or passages, working backward in memory from the book . . . to the house . . . to the train . . . and the beach. Or you may want to go directly to the part of the Dream that was the most vivid or important to you.

If you want to intensify this experience, you could reenter the Dream, and this time, while riding the train, you could observe your shoes very carefully. Then imagine other shoes that you have worn — dancing shoes or tennis shoes or loafers. Discover that you are now wearing a pair of shoes that you remember from the distant past, and then discover that your feet have become much smaller in size and your legs are shorter and you are, in fantasy, once again that child that you were long ago. When you get off the train, experience the feeling of those shoes on your feet and let them lead you into the house and into a memory you want to experience.

In this exercise, people often discover memories that are quite moving. Choose wisely when you select the shoes you will wear and the age you will be in this Dream. Always protect yourself from memories that are too intense and hurtful; know that you can always exit the Dream when you want to, or you can let a healing fantasy rework the reality of the past. Know yourself and choose wisely — using both hemispheres of your brain!

In libraries and bookstores, there are scores of books containing other scenarios for imagery experiences. Many fine writers/performers have produced right-brain techniques and, if you want to go more deeply into this type of work you can find books and tapes that will help you. You will find them filed under Psychology or Self-help, Reference or New Age. You can create your own scenarios, if you choose to. After you have mastered the skill of entering a vivid fantasy at will, it will only take you a few minutes to enter the scene when you are working on your novel. Once you begin to experience your Dream at this level, you will feel new boldness and power in your work. With a little imagination, the whole process suddenly begins to feel like magic.

TOM McGUANE

Here he is again, by popular demand. Rodeo rider, novelist, short story writer, and screenplay writer, Tom McGuane told the Conference students to believe in themselves, to go for it:

Every writer with a good idea for a book has this same terrified subdued feeling, which is the reluctant desire to step up to the plate for better or worse. That, coupled with being utterly willing to make a fool of themselves, can sometimes be the driving wedge required to hit upon original material, which is always surprising. It can start absolutely anywhere.

Just begin talking to yourself—on paper. Robert Stone said, "When you've written a draft or something and you read part of it and you think it's wrong, it is wrong." That's the rule.

At that point you know all that anyone knows about revision. If you say, "Well gee, who am I to know?" Well, you wrote it! You have to take that chance. That is the opportunity and the holy terror of making yourself ridiculous that every writer has to know to approach his own personal truth.

Once you reach that stage, you should have a kind of liberation about drafting material, finding the shapes of material. Everybody has to be able to cartoon, has to know what things are. We have had writers, Henry James, William Styron, who have these wonderful great yeasty brains which enable them to design things entirely and then commit them in an increasingly perfected form to the page— men like Hemingway who would draft something in a month and then spend years concealing the fact of how quickly it came to him. I think very few writers work that way.

You can't fear speed. You can't fear a side to your voice that you've never heard before. You can't fear disgrace. You have to pick a point, however small part of yourself, that you absolutely believe in. There is no such thing as unsuitable material in serious fiction. The idea that we have to go out and commit experience as though it were a kind of Martian world we were going to launch ourselves into and there gather material that we don't currently have, but material that would be dignified enough to practice literature, is crazy.

As a practitioner of literature for the last twenty years, the thing that most frustrates me in being around arriving writers of whatever age is my inability or anyone else's inability to make them understand how those wonderful things are always there, are always in your life. Any writer who has written six or eight or ten books looks to see these undisclosed treasures, and wonders why don't these people know they have this in their hand, locked in their lives, locked in their family lives, in the daily routine of their maybe awful jobs. It's there. It's not on the Siberian frontier.

There is no such thing as a holy experience for writers. You don't have to go on the rodeo circuit or fight bulls, or go to war. You just have to write well and truly understand what your subject is. People recognize it the instant you recognize it. That's the fabulous thing that is never described correctly about the literary experience, which is: When *you* touch it right everybody gets it.

Block That Block!

O kay, so one morning you sit down at the old Olivetti or computer or pencil-cum-legal pad and stare at that blank page and nothing, but nothing, comes to mind. *Nada!*

What to do?

Some people rewrite the last page of the previous day's work. Not just reread it; write again. This works for me most of the time—it's like limbering-up exercises before tennis. Besides, I've never rewritten any page that I haven't improved in the process, even by a word or two.

Sinclair Lewis once told me that when he came to a place in his story where it just wouldn't budge no matter how hard he tried, he *introduced a new character.*

"Have the doorbell ring," he suggested. "My God, there's Uncle Fred! What's he doing here from England? What does he want? Dreadful Uncle Fred! Meddling Uncle Fred! Dangerous Uncle Fred! The rest of the characters *have* to react to him in different ways and a bunch of new conflicts arise and all of a sudden the story gets going again."

Good advice. Or try having a letter arrive. Maybe you don't even know yourself what's in it, until your character opens it. But it's something that affects your protagonist in some way. Your character *must* react to it and *do* something. The moment your main character *does* something, watch how easy it is to start writing your story again— especially if something stands in his or her way. (That ol' devil conflict again.)

Bill Downey is one of our most valued workshop leaders and has been part of every Santa Barbara Writers' Conference since the first one, way back in 1972. Newspaperman, novelist, essayist, biographer, autobiographer, right-brain expert, and teacher, he has experienced the dreaded jabberwocky of blockage in most of its myriad manifestations, and vanquished it with his vorpal sword:

"What *is* this writer's block business?" I am often asked at the Conference. Is it something that only afflicts writers? Does it occur in any other form?. Can it be prevented? Or, if you have it, is there a cure?

As a writing teacher and manuscript consultant I am expected to have easy answers to tough questions. But after years of study, shared experiences, observation, trial and error, a general consensus has evolved and high-percentage answers are showing an encouraging rate of accuracy.

In answer to the first question: Writer's block is a glitch in the creative process. A whole array of personality quirks are relative to the problem, but generally, writer's block means the writer can't get into the creative mode.

In answer to the remaining three questions, "yes" will suffice for the moment. The block appears in a number of ways, invading all forms of artistic expression. It can be overcome, but the best cure is prevention.

To understand writer's block more clearly, let's take a brief foray into the human brain: a three-pound miracle everyone has, an organ one scientist said would require a building a hundred stories tall—the size of the state of Texas—to duplicate in present technology.

Yet, this monolithic Texas-sized building in each of our skulls is where we live. No wonder we get lost, confused, and blocked. Most of us can't find our socks in a small apartment.

Yet our existence from one second to the next relies on a perfect performance from the brain's intricately designed complexity. The average human brain makes fifteen billion transactions every second, according to Dr. Richard Restak, a neurologist and brain authority.

Structurally, the brain is shaped like the halves of an English walnut. Each brain half has its own autonomy and the interchange between left-half and right is the basis for Dr. Restak's staggering statistic above. Therefore it's not difficult to see that the brain is quite busy, but mostly with its own business. It never sleeps. The conscious demands we make on it require a fractional amount of this vast, cerebral computer.

Serious competition exists between the left brain half and the right. This in itself causes much of the block under discussion. Each half, or hemisphere, has its own autonomy. Each has its own specialization and the subsequent competition can create writer's block.

We are born with an equitable access to either hemisphere, but due to education, social and traditional influence, all predominantly left-brain, we are bent to those expectations and the logical, linear thinking they represent. The left hemisphere is favored in most cultures. It specializes in logic, rules, obedience, analysis, and time awareness. Left-brain people are not particularly entertaining but they are reliable. They cut their grass regularly, wash their cars every week and worry about infringement on others.

Right-brain people, the creative force, generally are the opposite. We are less predictable and love to freelance and break the rules. We are more vulnerable because, to us, creativity and feelings are almost synonymous. We are softer, less territorial and great neighbors if you, too, are an artist. We are more likely to say "yes" than our left-brain counterpart, which is inherently distrustful.

Since our Western culture is so intensely left-brain, it should be obvious that shifting from the left side to the creative side would meet some resistance. The left brain feeds negativity into the artistic process: Why don't you do something sensible? Who cares what you create? You're getting to be like those bums you lunch with on Wednesdays.

The left brain is quite good at what it does. Even those artists who overcome its negativity work far below their potential when the critic contaminates their process.

Just knowing these things will provide a leg-up into the process for some writers. At last they can relax because: No, you are not insane. There is a negative factor which threatens everyone's creativity. In some it's worse than in others.

One of the simplest strategies for breaking free is to *write your way out of it.*

How can I write if I'm blocked, you wonder? Try this. Being blocked doesn't mean you can't hold a pencil. The exercise is called automatic writing. It can help.

Some writers spend five or ten minutes at this exercise before they even start their day's assignment. Automatic writing is nothing more than a warming-up activity very similar to the stretching athletes use before an event. It does warm up the creative mode.

Automatic writing requires that you make a list of random subjects that come to mind. Select the one that seems to catch your attention and start writing about it. Write anything that comes to mind. Write drivel. Write to see what you have to say. If the writing slows, repeat the last sentence until something new appears.

The exercise establishes the creative mode or brain shift which we

236 ■ *The Complete Guide to Writing Fiction*

connect with in order to write. The specialties of right brain are the key to creativity.

Writer's block might mean you should do more research in that place that won't budge. Perhaps it's telling you there's a thin place in the structure. Further research in the troubled area might recharge the creative force and set progress surging ahead better than ever.

As a writing instructor dealing with a lot of young writers, I have found that another common form of the block is the writer who is writing the wrong story, article, novel, or screenplay. One of my colleagues put it most succinctly: "I'm afraid," he explained to an aspiring novelist, "that you are not yet good enough to write this story."

Writing is a learning/growing experience. After a time the writer learns to listen to his feelings and instincts, then takes notice when something clicks or feels good. Sometimes a certain task in writing will come easily and be thoroughly enjoyable to perform. The brain is making a statement. Listen. This is the direction of your strength. To best avoid the block, write toward your strength.

Still, blocked writers should not panic. A piece of work becomes difficult for a reason. Sometimes there is an element of painful restimulation in a given topic or its related material. Try a page of automatic writing on the material causing the trouble. Maybe more research on the subject is necessary. Maybe it's not just your area of specialization. A real excitement must exist in every serious writing project. For some writers it's the money that brings this motivating energy. Wherever it comes from, the writer needs this energy, this excitement, to continue and especially to avoid the block.

Newspaper reporters merely sit down and write. Intrusions, telephones, cigar smoke, are pushed aside. There's no time for writer's block at deadline. Creative writers must acquire this same mental toughness. Know that as long as you are writing you are not blocked. Novelists for too long have been considered prima donnas who need cloistered villas in color-coordinated surroundings in order to write. What a fallacy. But the point is well made. Writers need a singlemindedness with which to push aside intrusions, distractions, and temptations.

Of course, there is the example of a successful colleague I once found at a bar with a voluptuous female on either side. The bartender was mixing margaritas as fast as he could.

"How's the old novel coming?" I asked my friend, at a loss for something more intelligent to say.

"I'm so damned blocked you can't believe it," he complained. The leggy companion at his right solicitously pecked his cheek. "Poor baby," she said.

I trudged home to my Underwood.

I rarely suffer from the blockage Bill Downey has been talking about, but just recently I found myself suffering from a tremendous and unexpected block. I was as blocked as Portnoy's father. There was no way that I could write a whole chapter of a book. So I bargained with myself.

"Write just one page," I told myself, "just one lousy page — not even a legal-pad size page, just a little shortie with lots of skimpy dialogue — and then you can go to that movie you've been wanting to see. Just one page!" As I often do, I told myself to remember Betty Smith. She only had time to write one page a day in her grubby New York apartment, but at the end of a year she had 365 of them, she called it *A Tree Grows in Brooklyn,* garnered critical acclaim, and made a fortune.

Well, I wrote that page, and it wasn't so bad, so I kept going and ended up with ten pages, a good day for me.

All writers, I find, play tricks on themselves to get themselves to the typewriter.

Newspapermen cannot indulge in the luxury of writer's block. For the last word on the subject, plus some other tips, here is journalist Roger Simon. The style is tongue-in-cheek, but there are also some nuggets contained in his *How to Become a Famous Author in Five Easy Steps:*

By the end of this little piece you will know how to write a book. I know you want to do this, because you write and tell me so.

"I have been a baker for forty-seven years," your letters say, "and the stories I could tell! We will split fifty-fifty. The book will be called: 'Rolling in Dough: The Marvin Shimkiss Story.' Please start writing 'Chapter One: The Early Years.' "

I turn down all such requests. But not because I think the books would be bad. Actually, forty-seven years of baking might make a very good book. But you don't need (or even "knead," ha-ha) me to write it.

You can do it yourself! I have learned this because I am currently writing a book. All journalists want to be authors. (Why more authors don't want to be journalists, I don't know. But they might have heard something about the hours.)

The first thing publishers tell journalists, however, is that journalism is not literature. And they are correct. Oscar Wilde said it best: "The difference between journalism and literature is that journalism is unreadable and literature is not read."

238 ■ *The Complete Guide to Writing Fiction*

So the first book I did was a collection of columns. And the first thing my friends said to me after it was published was: "When are you going to write a *real* book?"

And they had me. So I had to write a real book. With a beginning and a middle and an end. The whole schmeer.

But I learned a few things in the process, which I am going to share with you.

The first step in writing a book is writing a proposal. This is a lengthy, detailed outline of everything you are going to write and how you are going to organize it. It should be well written, to prove to the publisher that you can actually write, which the publisher doesn't believe for a second.

I found I am very bad at writing proposals. That's because a proposal is an outline of something that hasn't happened yet. But my agent has good advice for me.

"Fake it," he said.

"I'm a newspaperman," I said, "I can't fake things."

"So pretend you're an author," he said, "and then fake it all you want."

Secret No. 1: After the book is done, nobody goes back and reads the proposal. Which is why authors promise all kinds of wild things in their proposals. ("I will live with Barbara and George Bush for the next six months, recording their every conversation, fist-fight and kissy-faced interlude. This should make a good book. Please give me a lot of money to write it.") Try to stay close to reality in your proposal, but don't let it slow you down.

Okay, so your proposal is sold and you are goofy with delight. You are breaking out the champagne, calling up friends and buying the kids a Nintendo with the first part of your advance. That's the good news: The publisher gives you some money, called an advance, up front. But soon you will know the meaning of the old proverb: "Be careful what you wish for because you may get what you wish."

Because now *you have to write the book!*

This you never counted on. As an author once said, it's hard to type a book, let alone write one.

First, you have to pick a style. This was very difficult for me, until I came upon a wonderful quote:

Secret No. 2: "Many intelligent people, when about to write books, force on their minds a certain notion about style, just as they screw up their faces when they sit for their portraits."

This was said by Georg Christopher Lichtenberg, about whom I know nothing. (No, I don't have time to look him up, I'm writing a book, for cripes' sake!)

Okay, so now you have a style. You know not to "screw up your face" but to write naturally. So the next thing you do is . . . get writer's block!

Secret No. 3: There is no such thing as writer's block. My father drove a truck for forty years. And never once did he wake up in the morning and say: "I have truck driver's block today. I am not going to work."

Writer's block is a self-indulgence invented by authors who want to pretend they are "artistes" instead of wage earners.

If you want to cure writer's block real fast, just imagine having to give the advance back.

Secret No. 4: Here's the big one. I could probably patent this and make a fortune. But you are my readers and I love you, so here it is for free:

Write just six pages a day and you will have a book in three months. I am not kidding.

Write just six, double-spaced pages a day and at the end of five days, you will have a chapter. (And you get two days off for good behavior.) At the end of twelve weeks, you will have a book.

That's it. That's all it takes.

Now, your book is done. But you are wondering, who will buy my book? That is simple.

Secret No. 5: Be sure to have lots of relatives.

DANIELLE STEEL

More from one of the best-selling authors of all time:

I write books. What happens to them after that has always been magical and mysterious to me. I think that if any successful author is honest with you, they will tell you they have no idea why their books are best sellers. You write what you write, and what happens after that is up to the public.

There is no set formula, no guarantee for success, no surefire way to write a best seller. All you can do is write a book and hope for the best.

For myself, each time I write a book, I'm afraid it will never get through the necessary barbed wire. First, it has to meet my agent's approval, which is not always easy. If my agent doesn't like it, she won't even send it to my publisher. Then after my agent grudgingly admits that it didn't put her to sleep, it goes to my editor, and she has to like it. Then she passes it around to two or three anonymous people at the publisher's, and finally I'm told it's accepted. Except that usually they forget to call me, and I sit there for four weeks, holding my breath.

That's only the beginning of the process. After that the book has to be rewritten, edited, sometimes rewritten again, corrected, corrected in galley, approved all over again, and finally a year and a half or so after I write it, it goes to the public. Then there is the whole terror of how they will respond to it.

As soon as it is obvious that the book is a success comes the next wave of terror: can I do it again? Can I even think up a new concept? Will anyone like it? Can I get it past my agent? Will my editor approve it, my publisher buy it, my public read it and like it as well as the last one? And each time the tension is a little bit greater.

This business is fraught with uncertainty. Anyone who tells you how to write best sellers is a sham and a liar. I can tell you how I write books. I write them with fear, excitement, discipline, and a lot of hard work. It takes me six months to write the outline, and about a month to write the first draft. For me that's the shortest part of the process. But that's a matter of twenty-hour days, of not leaving my house, of not speaking to my friends, or speaking to anyone other than my husband and children. All I do is write. And the cleaning up process on a book after that is roughly another six months. So the whole process takes me about a year.

Where the ideas come from I don't know. There are concepts and themes that intrigue me, amuse me, trouble me. At one time ten years ago prison reform was interesting to me, and as a result I wrote *Passion's Promise* and *Now and Forever*. Like everyone, I cared about different themes at different times, and the books reflect that. Sometimes they are written to unburden my soul, sometimes they are written for fun.

Some books come easily. Some are a struggle from beginning to end. *The Ring* is the easiest book I ever wrote; *Remembrance* was the hardest book I ever wrote. And *Crossings* is my favorite.

Where do the ideas come from? I don't really know. I've always had a deeply religious feeling about my writing. I feel very unimportant in the scheme of it all. I pray a lot before I start a book and as I work through it. And the less important I feel the better the book goes.

The story comes from somewhere and seems to flow through me until it's finished. And I myself am in awe of the finished product as it sits there, 700 pages high on my desk. But I don't feel personally responsible for it. I never feel entirely sure I did it. I just seem to be part of the process.

The only part of the process I am absolutely sure of is the discipline involved. For me writing is a job, a career. It has been for twelve years. It is not an artistic pastime. I don't wait for inspiration to come at three in the morning. I sit down with my notebook and my pen at nine in the morning and force myself to sit there, working on an idea for an hour.

I work and I think and I push and I scribble until something comes. When I actually get something to work on, I sit at my typewriter and type until I ache so badly I can't get up. After twelve or fourteen hours, you feel as if your whole body is going to break in half. Everything hurts, your arms, your eyes, your shoulders, your neck, your hands. I've had cramps so badly when I sat typing that I couldn't move my hands for a couple hours, but I usually keep sitting there and push through it for another five or six hours.

And after a while my whole body goes numb and all I'm aware of is the story I'm writing. I hear it in my head. I see it in front of me like a film and I type what I see and hear.

I have often typed so long that I saw double. I have had to close my eyes to keep typing because vision was so blurred. I have fainted when I stood up and fallen asleep face first in my typewriter and woken up the next morning with the keyboard marks on my face.

But the aches and the agonies no longer matter. It feels wonderful. The feeling of accomplishment, of victory, of survival is overwhelming. It's a little bit like a marathon or climbing a mountain.

Short Story Versus the Novel

*I*s the novel merely a long short story? Most writers would say no, they are two different things, as "different as lightning from the lightning bug," as Mark Twain said about words. Theoretically they should be much alike since the same elements are involved in each, yet many great short-story writers were not good novelists and vice versa.

V.S. Pritchett, a master of the short story, once wrote: "The masters of the short story have rarely been good novelists." Yet he himself wrote several good novels.

The short story has recently come to the fore after a decline of many years. In the twenties, thirties, and forties, there were many more slick magazine markets for stories than there are now, yet in the last few years many collections of short stories have appeared. One I've especially enjoyed is Frederick Forsyth's *No Comebacks*, old-fashioned, well written, suspenseful stories with beginnings, middles, and ends. Plus there are hundreds of literary magazines looking for good material.

The short-story form seems to have come back strong and all beginning writers should rejoice, for what better way to practice the craft of writing? For years it has been easier to get a novel published than a short story, but apparently that is no longer the case. For example, Jonathan Winters, the eminent comedian, told me at the 1986 Conference that he was compiling a group of short stories, and I have the distinction of having told him I thought, without even reading them, they would never find a publisher. A couple of years later Random House published them under the title *Winters' Tales* and, astoundingly, the book has sold some 220,000 copies.

What exactly is a short story? Edgar Allan Poe defined it as a tale "no longer than can be read in a single sitting."

Editor Amy Kaufman has said: "The difference between novels and short stories: the story is a song, the novel is an opera."

Virtually everything said in this book about writing the novel can be applied to the short story except length, which *ipso facto* dictates a few restrictions.

One of its greatest practitioners, Poe spoke of the short story as providing "a single and unique effect" toward which every word contributes: "If his [the writer's] very initial sentence tend not to the outbringing of this effect, then he has failed in this first step. In the whole composition there should be no word written, of which the tendency, direct or indirect, is not to the one pre-established design."

In a novel, the writer may sprawl, may change points of view, may tell us about whaling or microbes or raising orchids, may develop minor characters, may show the fine qualities of the villain, or the villainous qualities of the hero, but there isn't *room* in a short story to deviate from one central idea. The story should be tightly and economically told. It can only tell of one central action and one major change in the life of the main character or characters. It should strive for a single emotional impact. It should have structure.

As Somerset Maugham has written:

The story an author has to tell should be coherent and persuasive; it should have a beginning, a middle and an end, and the end should be the natural consequence of the beginning. The episodes should have probability and should not only develop the theme, but grow out of the story. The creatures of the author's invention should be observed with individuality, and their actions should proceed from their characters; the reader must never be allowed to say: "So and so would never behave like that"; on the contrary, he should be obliged to say: "That's exactly how I should have expected so and so to behave."

And, *mirabile dictu*, a short story should be short: If your story runs over thirty pages, you're getting into the dangerous area of the novella. The novella lies in between novel length and short-story length and is a difficult form to sell. Book publishers don't like to publish novellas (unless you have a famous name) and only some of the women's magazines will look at them. About twenty pages (5,000 words) is the maximum short-story length.

How to start a short story? Pretty much the same as a novel.

Here is John Leggett on that point:

Knowing where to start a story — whether or not to tell it in a straightforward way, as clock and calendar follow us through the months and years—is bewildering.

If we imagine telling the story of a great general's life, we could probably make a good case for *not* beginning with his grandparents or even with his own birth and early schooling. It certainly sounds more interesting to start the story on the night before Antietam, with the boys in blue gathered around their campfires cleaning their rifles and exchanging pictures of the loved ones back in Philadelphia.

There are very few stories that don't benefit from starting as close as possible to the climax. That means an unchronological telling and so to get to the general's important boyhood and love life we will have to use the flashback. No great problem there in finding the trigger within the general's pre-battle reflections, and in pulling it.

The narrative techniques of the short story are the same as the narrative elements of the novel. Conceive of your story in scenes, draw individualized, appealing characters, put them in an interesting situation full of conflict, and show them changed at the end of whatever transpires in the story.

John Leggett again:

There is no better mark of a well-told story than that sense of secret understanding, an emotion defined, shared, yet still a very private matter between the teller and the told. The story may have originated at another time, in another place, but it seems to have been made for this moment, this listener alone, and ironically, it is a secret which he, or she, can hardly wait to share with someone. That secret sharing is the story's joy.

Budd Schulberg, who came to the Conference in 1975, is a master of the story teller's art. Here's how his stories germinate:

A great blue heron just flew by my window. Where was it going, in the dead of winter? The germ of a story, or a tale. That's how they begin. Of course a large bird flying by your window is simply a fact. An odd or interesting fact. A paragraph for *Audubon* magazine. What would make it a story? Well, if this large pale-blue bird is an anthropomorphic creature, he could be a symbol of a lost soul in a changing world. Why hasn't he gone south to the warmer climes self-respecting blue herons expect and deserve? Is he a symbol of the greenhouse effect: He thinks or senses that our

winters are getting warmer? Is he a metaphor for climatic aberra-
tion leading to social alienation? Or could this be the story of a
bird whose mate has been killed by man or some other marauder?
Many birds, from racing pigeons to swans, mate for life. Will this
one continue to search for his lost mate until he freezes or starves
to death? Or will a human sympathizer get involved? Will he or
she try to get to the bottom of this mystery of the great blue heron
who chose to stay, or simply was left behind? How does the human
character we've brought into the story cope with this problem?
Do the intervention and the coping change it from a fleeting event
to a story? The possibilities, we begin to see, are limitless. A story
is not an event, but a series of related events, one drawing on the
previous one, and building to a climax. It doesn't have to be a big
payoff climax like a smoochy clinch or a screeching car-chase at
the end of a movie. It can be quiet and almost deceptively unevent-
ful. Chekhov comes to mind as the master of such an ending, and
so does Hemingway, whose novels may date a little but whose
short stories are still wonderful on rereading. Any student of the
short story would do well to study their endings.

Ray Bradbury told us at the Conference that he frequently will
take a single word, perhaps the first word that comes to him in the
morning, sit back in his office and free-associate with that word, going
with it wherever it takes him, then form a short story from that.

At the Conference I use a similar trick in my workshops, a teaching
device I learned from the renowned Max Steele of the University of
North Carolina. It's called the 1,000-word sentence. I give the workshop the start of a sentence — something like "When I was young" —
and they have twenty minutes to finish it using *no punctuation whatsoever*. For some reason it is a very freeing, creative experience that has
produced the nucleus for some fine short stories.

Here's the beginning of an unusually good one written by Selden
Edwards, a school teacher and headmaster from Chicago. (He added
some punctuation afterwards for publication.)

I can tell you about Larry now because he's moved on to tinker
with other lives and with other men's wives and because in the
quiet loneliness of the past few months, rattling through the routine — thrashing sleeplessly in my half-empty bed — I approach the
perspective that has been eluding me all these years, perspective
on Mary's reasons and my own — Jesus, my own — for doing what
we did even though we knew we were dissolving a marriage that
ten years ago across wine glasses and candles looked like one of
the best that man, or at least two people, could come up with; but

we did what we did and decided on principle—vile principle—
and now Larry and Mary are gone, Larry to New York to tinker,
and Mary to lord-knows-where, which is the very pith of my loneliness and exasperation since I don't know where to begin looking,
though I guess I could try her only living relative, her father in
Chicago, but I don't know, and it's the not knowing that outstings
the not having because you can drown the not having in drink,
or other women, or the neatly rolled joints Larry left behind as
consolation, but the not knowing eats at my soul, at my very core,
and won't be neutralized by all the conventional balms, and
through it all I ask myself why I forced the issue, why I saw the
infidelity, why I called it infidelity, anything more than innocent
restlessness, something in the air of a bored and pill-weary subur-
ban community, where I'd forced her to settle, something I didn't
have to see and something I certainly didn't have to call her on,
and why I thought my manhood—manhood, that's it: "If all else
fails," I'd said back then, a fat bank vice presidency just around
the corner, "At least I can keep her happy"—my manhood more
important than those ten years of security, and why I thought my
wife in bed with a man I'd taken care to introduce her to—round
out her character and all that—was such an earth-shattering
event, when, in actuality, other marriages in these fashionable
pockets of Marin County bury similar offenses quietly without
ceremony each year, each month, each day, but Larry was my
friend, in my house where we usually saw Mary's friends, and
I just didn't expect my innocent—ludicrously innocent—needle-
pointing, rose dusting, carpool-driving, church-going little wife
falling for such transparent charm as "You're an oasis to a man
who's walked the desert of humanity for more years than he'd like
to think"—ridiculous you say, ridiculous I say—but I heard him
say it, right here in front of me that first night. . . .

This method has worked for so many people you might want to
try it. Let us say that you are writing a story about a failing marriage.
Try clearing your mind, then write the words:

"When I was first married I . . . ," then start writing at white heat,
feeling instead of *thinking*, and just let it flow *with no punctuation* for as
long as the words spill out. And you *will* find the words gushing out
once they are freed of the straitjacket of punctuation. What you will
end up with might amaze you; it won't be a finished story, of course,
but you will surely surprise yourself by what emerges, and you can
use it as a springboard, a nucleus, for your story.

Writing short stories is a valuable training ground, even if your ultimate goal is to be a novelist. As novelist-poet-teacher Janet Burroway says:

> It is a good idea to learn to write short stories before you attempt the scope of a novel, just as it is good to learn to write a lyric before you attempt an epic or to learn to draw an apple before you paint a god.

CHECKLIST FOR YOUR STORY

When you finish your story you might want to run through this list of basic ingredients and check them against your story:

1. In one simple sentence sum up to yourself what the story is about (viz: It's about a mousy woman, seduced and dumped by her employer, who gains revenge and redemption by making him grovel in the dirt at gunpoint). If you can't do it in one long sentence maybe you have problems; maybe it's not yet clear in your mind.

2. Do you have your principal characters wanting something, something very important to them? Is that aim made apparent to the reader?

3. Do you indicate to the reader what the main character's basic problem is — or at least foreshadow it — very early in the story? Is there a hook in the first paragraph to get the reader's attention? Do formidable obstacles stand in the way of the protagonist's aim? If there is an antagonist, is he or she a worthy one?

4. Is it clear for whom the reader should pull? Do we know whom or what we're against?

5. Does the dialogue propel the plot forward? Does the conversation reveal character and motivation? Or is it merely talk?

6. Does the story unfold in scenes? Or is there too much telling and not enough showing?

7. Is there inherent conflict, expressed or implied, on every page, in every scene?

8. Does the story grow and grow in tension until the resolution?

9. Is the ending, sad or happy, a satisfying one? Is it consistent with what we know about the protagonist's character? Is it brought about by the characters' actions?

10. Has the reader seen a change occur in the characters and their situation? Are things different than they were at the beginning of the story?

You may want to break some or all of these rules. But be aware of them. They work for most novels too.

The best way to learn how to write a short story is to read the enduring ones. There are some classic stories you *must* read simply because they have become a genre in themselves. ("What you've written here is sort of a 'Monkey's Paw.' " Or "We aren't looking for O. Henry or 'Lady and the Tiger' endings." Or "We like deductive Sherlock Holmes-type stories." Or "This has a shock ending like 'The Lottery'. " Or "Strive for a Cheever-Updike atmosphere" and so forth.)

Let me jot down a smattering of arbitrary, purely subjective choice of stories that will surely help you with your own, and which you will enjoy if you haven't read. Most are in easily obtainable collections.

"The Monkey's Paw," W.W. Jacobs
"The Gold Bug," "The Tell-Tale Heart," Edgar Allan Poe
"The Legacy," "The Necklace," Guy de Maupassant
"The Gift of the Magi," "The Ransom of Red Chief," O. Henry
"The Man Who Would Be King," Rudyard Kipling
"The Open Window," "Tobermory," Saki
"To Build a Fire," Jack London
"The Lady with the Toy Dog," Chekhov
"Champion," Ring Lardner
"Silent Snow, Secret Snow," Conrad Aiken
"Metamorphosis," Franz Kafka
"Big Blonde," Dorothy Parker
"Babylon Revisited," "The Rich Boy," F. Scott Fitzgerald
"Maria Concepción," "Noon Wine," Katherine Anne Porter
"The Snows of Kilimanjaro," "The Short Happy Life of Francis
    Macomber," Ernest Hemingway
"Rain," "The Treasure," Somerset Maugham
"The Lady or the Tiger," Frank Stockton
"The Open Boat," Stephen Crane
"A Good Man Is Hard to Find," Flannery O'Connor
"The Secret Life of Walter Mitty," "The Catbird Seat," James Thurber
"The Swimmer," "The Five-Forty-Eight," John Cheever
"A Face In The Crowd," Budd Schulberg
"A and P," John Updike
"Uncle Wiggily in Connecticut," J.D. Salinger
"Johnny Bear," "The Red Pony," John Steinbeck

"Act of Faith," "Girls in Their Summer Dresses," Irwin Shaw
"A Rose for Emily," "The Bear," William Faulkner
"Powerhouse," "Why I Live at the P.O.," Eudora Welty
"The Lottery," Shirley Jackson
"The Occurrence at Owl Creek Bridge," Ambrose Bierce
"The Basement Room," Graham Greene
"Mr. Morgan," James Michener
"Wet Saturday," John Collier
"Lamb to the Slaughter," Roald Dahl
"The Illustrated Man," "The Lake," Ray Bradbury
"Handcarved Coffins," Truman Capote
"Odour of Chrysanthemums," D.H. Lawrence

The list could go on and on.
    If I have left out your favorite story or your favorite writer, forgive me.
    The above are classic short stories; in a more modern vein here are a few suggestions:

"Shiloh," Bobbie Ann Mason
"Broken Homes," William Trevor
"Revenge," Jim Harrison
"Red Fish," Rick Bass
"The Emperor of the Air," Elias Canin
"What We Talk About When We Talk About Love," Raymond Carver
"The Linden Tree," Ella Lefland
"How to Skin a Cat," Thomas McGuane
"A River Runs Through It," Norman McLean
"A Vintage Thunderbird," Ann Beattie
"Idaho," Barry Hannah
"Engagements," Tama Janowitz
"Bluebeard's Egg," Margaret Atwood
"Coming Attractions," Tobias Wolff
"The Rake People," Judith Freeman
"Victory Over Japan," Ellen Gillchrist
"The River is Whiskey," T. Coraghessan Boyle
"Superior Women," Alice Adams
"Happy Families Are All Alike," Peter Taylor
"Him With His Foot in His Mouth," Saul Bellow
"The Trick of It," Michael Frayn
"Eleven Kinds of Loneliness," Richard Yates
"No Comebacks," Frederic Forsyth

ROBERT BLOCH

The author of *Psycho* was asked after his lecture how he begins a story:

When I write something, I always start with my last line so my only problem is how to get there.

Question: How do you take a really repulsive character and make him or her the sort of character readers or viewers will stay with?

Answer: By giving such characters certain attributes common to us all. By making those characters a little bit pathetic, with aspirations that they can't realize, with frustrations that some of us share but to a lesser degree and we don't solve in that fashion. I try very hard to humanize them.

Question: Do you find it easier to write a book from a screenplay or from your own ideas?

Answer: I have done only two script-into-novel adaptations. I find it much easier to work from my own material than to do an adaptation. I think that's true of most people because a screenplay as such should be only a guide for a writer, just as it is in many cases a guide for a director.

Question: What is your work schedule?

Answer: I sit down at nine o'clock. And I will write until I notice that the wastebasket is full of popcorn balls. I know that if I crumple up enough sheets of paper I must be getting tired, and I better quit for the day and then return to it when I'm fresh. And so the schedule generally runs from 9 to about 1. I do try to keep a regular schedule, five days a week. I feel that writing is a habit, and it must be enforced by self-discipline.

That is why so many people whom I've known, who are brilliant, who have fine minds, who have great creative talent, have never made it as writers because they don't have that self-discipline. They are not able to force themselves to do something that is less agreeable than going out and enjoying themselves and living it up a little.

I've always felt that people who have had an easy time in actual life are less prone to do anything in the creative arts because they have less need to.

Rejection – and Dejection

I recently came across a cartoon in a magazine with which I really identified. The drawing showed a matador in his suit of lights talking to a group of reporters outside the arena.

"I took up bullfighting," he says serenely, "because of the uncertainty of being a writer."

More truth than poetry in that statement; the bulls just wound your body. How about the mental *cornadas* one receives from editors and publishers and friends and family during the long *corrida* along the way to best-sellerdom?

We've all read about books and stories being rejected and then going on to fame and fortune. Nearly every successful writer has a horror tale of rejection to tell.

Face it: You are going to get rejections, and lots of them, if you are like the rest of us. Even great and famous writers like Ray Bradbury *still* have stories rejected. (And remember, he writes about twenty a year.)

I sold my first piece, an article, to *Esquire* when I was twenty-three years old, for $350. Can any excitement equal that first sale? Hey, this was easy. All you have to do is arrange a few words on a blank page and some nice people pay you a lot of money for it.

Then came reality. I didn't sell a thing for three years; I literally papered an entire bathroom with rejection letters. I almost quit a lot of times and only managed to support myself by teaching and painting portraits and playing the piano in a Peruvian nightclub. Then came the second sale, a short story to *Esquire*, which was maybe even more exciting than the first since I'd learned what a tough racket I was in. From then on there was no looking back, and little by little the rejections became fewer.

But I'd come *so* close to quitting!

How long can you keep banging your head against a wall?

How many potential Hemingways and Kafkas and James Joyces have not been able to survive the hurts of constant rejection and have quit? How many have, like the writer in *La Boheme*, burned the manuscript of what might have been a great play to keep the stove stoked? Or, less dramatically, have put it away in a trunk to be forgotten forever?

At one of his many appearances at the Conference Alex Haley told us:

> As a writer, you're rejected so often that you have to develop resilience. So when I'm down it rarely lasts more than twenty-four hours . . . I search around until I find something to be excited about.

The amazing thing is that any writers survive at all, considering the bewildering case histories of some of our most dazzling literary successes. Notice I do not use the word "achievement," but rather "successes," that crass commodity which Fitzgerald claimed nothing fails like. For the moment we will not consider artistic merit, being not so much concerned here with Euterpe, the Muse of Lyric Poetry, as with Mazuma, the Bitch Goddess.

For example, if we tell you that, way back when, Grace Metalious's *Peyton Place* was turned down by Houghton Mifflin as "just another junky sex novel," do not one-up us by retorting "bully for them," because regardless of its literary shortcomings and the fact that it was turned down by two other publishers, the novel was finally launched in the fall of 1956, sold 300,000 hardbound copies, 7,000,000 paper to-date, went to Hollywood, and its title has become sort of a generic term, like Sinclair Lewis' *Main Street*.

At a recent cocktail party I saw The Man Who Turned Down *Auntie Mame*. Poor devil, I suppose he has another name, but that's the handle he's gone by for many years now. He used to be robust and outgoing; now he's pale, furtive, and has developed an annoying little breathy laugh at everything anyone says, funny or not.

Actually, he shouldn't feel too bad, because at least six other publishers turned it down before Vanguard published it and put it on the best-seller list for two years. And these days, nearly everyone in the publishing game flaunts a story of a horrendous rejection; it has become sort of a badge of honor. ("Have I read *Catcher in the Rye*? My dear fellow, I turned it down!")

Sherwood Anderson, hailed by many as the greatest writer of his generation, was not able to get his first novel published until after he was forty.

Thirteen — count 'em — publishers turned down William Kennedy's best-selling Pulitzer Prize-winning novel *Ironweed*. When success finally came to him in 1980, he had been writing for thirty years and was fifty-nine years old.

Sidney Sheldon told us when he lectured at our Conference that his first novel, *The Naked Face*, was turned down by five publishers before William Morrow published it, and then it won an Edgar, mystery writing's highest accolade.

Alex Haley told us that he wrote every day, seven days a week, for eight years before his first piece was bought by a small magazine.

I think the editors' psychology in boasting about their turndowns is simply to show their basic contempt for writers, that one book isn't *really* better than another, it is only the publisher who makes it so. Many editors have dined out for years on their boasts that they indeed were one of the scapegoats who turned down *The Caine Mutiny*. (In fact, only one publisher, Alfred A. Knopf, rejected that spectacular best seller, and they did so on the basis that too large an advance was asked for the fragment of the manuscript that was shown them.)

In a similar fashion, a good number of the other cliché versions of famous rejections don't bear scrutiny, because one often finds that either the manuscript was not turned down or what was rejected was a version vastly different from what was finally published. An authentic case, however, was *Moby Dick*. It was published in 1851 to resounding apathy. Those who took any notice at all generally condemned it.

Moby Dick would be rediscovered in the 1920s and acclaimed a masterpiece, but when it was first published, poor Herman Melville had to cringe under such reviews as this one in the *New Monthly Magazine*: "Maniacal — mad as a March Hare — moving, gibbering, screaming like an incurable Bedlamite, reckless of keeper or strait-waistcoat."

Oh, the lovely destructive way with vitriol the reviewers had in those days, whether right or wrong! Take what the London *Daily Telegraph* wrote about Ibsen's now-classic *Ghosts* back in 1881: "Positively abominable — an open drain; a loathsome sore unbandaged, a dirty act done publicly; candid foulness — absolutely loathsome and fetid — literary carrion, crapulous stuff."

It is difficult now to see how Thoreau's *Walden* could have been bypassed, but it was, so much so that when the publisher returned all the unsold copies of the first small edition to the author, Thoreau claimed that he had become the owner of a library containing 800 volumns, 600 of which were his own. Of course, over the years *Walden* has grown so much in stature that no library can be called complete without it, yet think of the damage to Thoreau's psyche, spending his life unappreciated as a writer.

254 ■ *The Complete Guide to Writing Fiction*

But there have been many others equally as unappreciated and it seems to be the mark of a great writer that he or she continues to write in spite of a lack of commercial success. Proust, after having been turned down by many publishers and editors, had to resort to publishing *Swann's Way* at his own expense.

To jump from a permanent classic to a forgotten best seller, Kathleen Norris' first novel, *Mother*, was turned down by eighteen publishers before being published in 1911 and becoming one of the first novels ever to sell a million copies.

What writers of the present can learn from the successful writers of the past is not to give up no matter how many slips come in or how bad the situation seems to be. Even in prison, they should not stop writing and hoping. John Bunyan wrote *Pilgrim's Progress* and Oscar Wilde wrote *The Ballad of Reading Gaol* while in the pokey. O. Henry wrote many of his stories while doing time for forgery, and Verlaine, Dostoevsky, Thomas Moore, Leigh Hunt and Cervantes wrote their best behind bars.

How in heaven's name could any publisher in his right mind turn down *All Quiet on the Western Front, A Tree Grows in Brooklyn, Lust for Life,* and *Anne Frank: Diary of a Young Girl*? All of them were rejected not once, but many times.

"If they turn *them* down," moans the beginning writer, "what chance has the little novel I'm working on?" But there is also consolation for the writer in these rejection stories: "No wonder they turned down my novel," you can say, "if several of them are dumb enough to turn down a gold mine like *Exodus* or reject the late Erskine Caldwell's stuff for seven years as they did."

The trick is not to give up, *ever*. Supposing the late Erskine Caldwell had been able to stand only *six* years of soul-battering rejections. Instead of going on to write some forty books, he would have been a failure, like Victor Borge's uncle who unsuccessfully tried to market a variety of soft drinks called from 1-Up to 6-Up—and then quit. The late Dr. Laurence Peter's book, *The Peter Principle*, was rejected by thirteen publishers before it was finally accepted in 1969—and became part of the English language.

My own second novel, *Matador,* was turned down by Random House, publishers of my first book; taken by Houghton Mifflin, it went on to sell some 3,000,000 copies.

Experience and editorial talent seem to be no guarantee for spotting winners. The Boston firm of Little, Brown has been in business for 150 years, and you'd think that a group who could publish everything from *Quo Vadis* to *Franny and Zooey* would be able to spot a publishable book. Yet they turned down *Anatomy of a Murder* and *The*

Naked and the Dead, which became two of the best sellers of modern times. Publication, of course, does not guarantee any protection from slings and arrows; *The New Republic's* critic, for example, wrote haughtily of Mailer and his book: "If he has a taste for transcribing banalities, he also has a talent for it." But, then, Aristophanes wrote of Euripides: "cliché-anthologist . . . and maker of ragamuffin manikins," and Lord Byron dismissed The Bard airily with: "Shakespeare's name, you may depend upon it, stands absurdly too high and will go down . . . He took all his plots from old novels . . ."

Even the children's classic *And to Think That I Saw It on Mulberry Street* had a tough time making it. Here's how Clifton Fadiman described Dr. Seuss's trials with that book, his first:

"It was rejected by twenty-seven publishers, on four grounds:

1. Fantasy doesn't sell.

2. Verse doesn't sell.

3. It had no "pattern," whatever that meant.

4. It wasn't "practical," that is, it didn't teach the child how to become a better child, or grownup, or mortician.

"The twenty-eighth publisher was densely ignorant of the juvenile market. He published the book for a fantastic reason. He liked it." Since then Dr. Seuss's books have sold millions of copies. His *The Cat in the Hat* is probably the most influential first-grade reader since McGuffey's.

The list of near-misses goes on and on. *Sister Carrie* by Theodore Dreiser is now required reading in many English courses, but it took the author seven years to find a publisher for it. *This Side of Paradise*, the 1920 novel which created a sensation and rocketed F. Scott Fitzgerald to fame, was turned down by Scribner's and several other publishers before being revised and finally accepted by Scribner's. Even then there were many doubts. The galley proofs were hidden as long as possible, and Roger Burlingame, in his book *Of Making Many Books*, tells of the reaction at an important meeting in the sales department when Scribner introduced the book:

Often mistrusting his own judgment, he spoke about many books and asked to take them home to an erudite sister to read. His sister was supposed to be infallible, and it was true that many of the novels she had "cried over" sold prodigiously. So when it was known that he had taken *This Side of Paradise* home for the weekend, his colleagues were all agog on Monday morning. "And what did your sister say?" they asked in chorus. "She picked it up with the tongs," he replied, "because she wouldn't touch it with her hands after reading it, and put it into the fire."

Although the book was a great success and followed by enough others to make F. Scott Fitzgerald the most popular of American writers, he was a has-been by the age of forty, and his great novel *Tender Is the Night* sold less than 10,000 copies. (After going out of print, it was revived, now sells around a million copies a year, and is considered a classic.)

That is the chilling fear of writers—the ephemeral quality of success in this country. William Faulkner died in 1962 with all the literary laurels the world has to award, including the Nobel Prize, but in 1945 there was not a single one of his many books in print in this country. His *The Sound and the Fury* suffered thirteen rejections before the battered manuscript pleased a publisher.

If life is precarious and uncertain in the literary sphere, it is even more ulcer-making in the theater world. Elmer Rice's *Street Scene* was turned down many times before it was produced and won a Pulitzer Prize. Marc Connelly's *Green Pastures* was refused repeatedly because its central character was God, and Enid Bagnold's *Chalk Garden* was rejected throughout London. After its success in New York, it became an even greater success in London. *Uncle Tom's Cabin*, though at first a failure, became one of the most popular plays in history in subsequent versions after 1853.

Erskine Caldwell, the first writer to recieve the Santa Barbara Writers' Conference Lifetime Achievement Award, told us that the play from his novel *Tobacco Road* had savagely bad reviews, and the management was ready to cry quits at the end of the fifth week. Then, miraculously, business began to build, the play ran for seven years, wore out five Jeeter Lesters, and became one of the longest running plays of all time with 3,182 performances.

The third longest-run play, at the time, *Abie's Irish Rose*, was unmercifully panned by the first-night critics, and no one liked it except the people who attended the 2,326 subsequent performances.

William Goldman's screenplay of *Butch Cassidy and the Sundance Kid* was turned down by twenty-two producing companies before being made into a hit film by 20th Century Fox.

So why list all these depressing statistics? To hammer home the fact that *you must not quit*! Keep sending out your material, over and over.

Now: That doesn't mean you shouldn't listen to the reasons that your material has been rejected. If, for example, three people tell you, independently, that your beginning is slow, take another hard look at that beginning.

But remember, almost no writers had it easy when starting out. If they did, everyone would be a best-selling author. The ones who make it are the stubborn, persistent people who develop a thick skin, defy the rejection, and keep the material out there, trolling.

And in the words of that great author, Snoopy, typing away on top of his doghouse: "I reject your rejection!"

K E Y N O T E R

COLLEEN McCULLOUGH

The Thornbirds was still number one on the best-seller list when she came to the Conference on her way to Australia.

I worked on it for five years. I rewrote the whole thing ten times from beginning to end. Whole chapters were added and dropped, new characters were created, and others were unborn. I stayed up for four or five days in a row sometimes without sleeping at all. Now I hate the book. I'm not just saying that—I hate it with a passion. I think it's flat, dull, uninteresting, ghastly and a complete embarrassment to me. I can't see any virtue in it at all. Now, my book *Tim* I still like and wrote from the heart.

Tim is the poignant story of a middle-aged woman's consuming love for a retarded young man of great beauty and nobility of soul. (See *Characterization* for an excerpt.)

Criticism

*W*e write a story, we put our heart, soul, and a lot of adrenaline, hemoglobin, and stardust into it, and then—ah, then—it comes time for the moment of truth. Someone has to read the darned thing! Spouse? Friend? Agent? Editor? Publisher? Someone has to evaluate that combination of words you have transferred from your brain to paper. Otherwise it's a tree that falls unheard in the middle of a forest.

Then, after the reading, how to accept what they say? Almost no response to one's work is equal to the hoped-for one. Even a large check isn't quite good enough: "But what did you really *think* of it? How did it stack up with *War and Peace* and *Madame Bovary?*"

Mark Twain once said, "I'm always embarrassed when someone compliments me, because they never say enough."

As Franklin Jones says:

Honest criticism is hard to take, particularly from a relative, a friend, an acquaintance, or a stranger.

Perhaps feeble compliments are worse than no comments at all. Take, for example, Charlotte Brontë's almost begging for praise about her new book from a less than empathetic father. Rebecca Fraser quotes from a contemporary account of the scene where young Charlotte breaks the news to her father that she is at last the author of a published book:

Three months after its publication she promised her sisters one day at dinner she would tell him before tea. So she marched into his study with a copy wrapped up and the reviews. She said (I think I can remember the exact words)—"Papa, I've been writing a book." "Have you, my dear?" and he went on reading. "But papa, I want you to look at it." "I can't be troubled to read manuscripts." "But it is printed." "I hope you have not been involving yourself in any silly expense." "I think I shall gain some money by it. May I read you some reviews?" so she read them; and then she asked him if he would read the book. He said she might leave it and he would see . . .

In his usual teasing way, Mr. Brontë delayed his pronouncement till the end of tea. Then he said: "Children, Charlotte has been writing a book—and I think it is a better one than I expected." That was all that he had to say on the subject, which he didn't mention again until two years afterwards.

Oh, just incidentally, the book was one of the enduring classics of all time: *Jane Eyre*.

My own father was not really very impressed with the success of my novel *Matador* until one year after publication; my mother was doing her favorite crossword puzzle in *The New York Times* and suddenly exlaimed: "Fifty-three down! Fifty-three down!" The puzzle's clue for that line was "author of *Matador*." My father was finally impressed; it *must* be a good book if it made *The Times* crossword puzzle.

Since my father had read little fiction other than Kipling and O. Henry, his opinion should not have been that important to me one way or another. At all times one must consider the source of the criticism, good or bad. Unless one's parent or spouse is Helen Gurley Brown or Edith Wharton or Max Perkins or Alistair Cook, one should generally look outside the family for a first read; hopefully, a gentle, knowledgeable first-read. Your critic need not be a writer. Max Perkins, for example, was not an author, just as Yale's greatest swimming coach, Bob Kiputh, couldn't swim, Caruso's teacher couldn't sing, and Manolete's mentor wasn't a good bullfighter. It is wonderful if you can come upon someone who consistently can give you good objective advice, encouragement, and head you in the right direction. But that person is a very *rara avis* indeed, and if you should find one, *breed him!*

Author Ann Beattie is lucky: "I have one friend in Boston to whom I send everything I write. It doesn't go out of the house until he passes approval or disapproval."

Phyllis Gebauer first came to the Conference as a student. She soon started selling, wrote a fine comic novel, *Pagan Blessing*, several short stories for national magazines, and ultimately became a workshop leader at the Conference. Her room is always overcrowded with eager students. She *knows* about giving and taking criticism. Here she is on the art of taking it:

Some years ago when I read a section of my then-unpublished novel in a workshop at the writers' conference, I had a shattering experience that almost ended my career as a writer.

I can still remember that room, where I sat, and what I was wearing. But most of all I remember the comments: dogmatic, judgmental, and personal. Then a barrage of questions. Why had I done *this*? Why hadn't I done *that*?

I answered as best I could; then, when the session was over, ran to my room, locked the door, and gave way to a mini-breakdown. This was it. The opinion of my peers. I was a failure.

Later that day I was pulling myself together out by the pool when one after another of the people who had been in that morning's workshop came up to express concern about the attacks I'd received, then to asure me my work was good, as doubtless I knew by all the compliments.

Compliments?

Yes. Hadn't I heard them?

No, I hadn't. But as those people gave me *their* version of that workshop, I realized I had a lot to learn about the art of giving and taking criticism.

Since then I've progressed from student to published writer to workshop leader myself. I've had criticism that really helped, some that really hurt, and along the way had a chance to observe and talk about the experiences of other writers. As a result, I'm convinced there are skills involved in giving and getting comments. Skills we writers have to learn as much as we have to learn how to write an effective lead, create a convincing character, or devise a metaphor.

First, let's talk about "taking it." Here are ten tips I give my students to help them keep their perspective, sort through what they get, then use it wisely:

1. *Be aware of your mind-state.* Whether you're used to getting comments or not, the entire process may make you feel ill at ease, anxious, and vulnerable. This is because your work in a sense is yourself, reflecting as it does your limitations and strengths as well as your worldview. And there you are, asking someone else to sit in judgment. That isn't easy, so if the comments you get are negative, don't be surprised if you feel hurt, angry, defensive, or resentful.

2. *Be aware of what you really want.* You may think you're asking only for comments, but what you really want are two things that may be incompatible: an honest opinion and affirmation. Chances are you'll get the former more often than you will the latter, but if

the response has been negative, just knowing that any resultant depression may be caused partly by the denial of your human need to get approval may help you fight the mood off and get back to your keyboard.

3. *Be aware that you may not hear right.* When the comments you get are verbal, some masochistic urge we all seem to share may keep you from hearing all but the "bad stuff." Equally destructive (to your work if not your spirit) is the screening that lets you hear only the "good," thereby avoiding rewrites. Maybe it's our Puritan culture, but the latter kind of faulty hearing doesn't come into play all that often. The solution in both cases is easy: take notes or, whenever possible, use a tape recorder.

4. *Take care whom you ask.* If your friends or relatives haven't read fiction in years, why give them Chapter One of your experimental novel? Or show an article about computers to someone who reads only fantasy? Better to be considered a reclusive eccentric, or if you feel *compelled* to let these people know what you're up to, resolve in advance not to let their comments (good or bad) make any difference. The best rule of all though, is to show your work only to people whose opinion you're going to trust, or who you know aren't for some reason out to get you.

5. *Don't take it personally.* Hard as it is to accept, you can make mistakes in your writing and still be a decent human being. When people pan what you've done, remind yourself that while, yes, in a sense your writing is you, in another sense it's just a product you want to make marketable. The trick is to keep the criticism focused where it belongs: on the work, not on the person who produced it. That isn't easy if your commentators are careless about the way they express themselves. Which leads to the next point.

6. *Learn to recognize a personal attack and rise above it.* What does a personal attack sound like? It's usually emotional and accusative. "You have a genius for avoiding conflict and confrontation." "You didn't build up any suspense." "You didn't give me any descriptions." See the implications? It's not the work that's at fault, it's *you.* You did something wrong. Were remiss. Naughty. A question of semantics? Partly, but what those rebuking words do is zap you right back to early childhood. That's Daddy talking, hear him? So what do you do? The same things you did when you were a kid. Argue. Defend yourself. Feel rebellious and angry. All of which takes your attention away from improving your work and puts it right onto protecting your ego. So what's the solution? Well, you can't change your commentators' phrasing any more than you

262 ■ *The Complete Guide to Writing Fiction*

can change the attitudes that made them express themselves like that in the first place. But you *can* zap yourself back to being a grown-up. Meaning, you can identify the attack for what it is, then gird your emotional loins, hear what the person has to say, and see what you can learn from it.

7. *Look where it's coming from.* This I learned from actress-writer Brett Somers soon after the workshop that so upset me. She told me that if I read a scene where a middle-aged man makes love to his wife on a cold stone floor, and when I finish, three gray-haired men tell me the action in that scene is implausible, I should consider that it may not be my writing those men are reacting to, but a threat they see in my subject matter. All of which is another way of saying you've got to look beyond your commentators' words to any possible moods, blind spots, or prejudices that may have led those people to say what they did to you. This doesn't mean their negative comments aren't going to hurt. It's just that by considering their source, you force yourself to stay more objective.

8. *Don't waste time and energy trying to defend yourself.* In the first place, it's useless to argue with a person's reaction. And in the second, your goal is to find out what may be wrong with your work, not to justify what you've already put down there. What I do to avoid defensive confrontations in my workshops is to forbid authors to say a word after they've read aloud until all the comments, including mine, have been duly noted. By then, having been forced to listen, the authors have usually discerned a thread running through the remarks and instead of issuing a challenge, merely thank the group for having been helpful.

9. *If the response is negative, remind yourself you can't please everyone.* Self-evident, true, but worth mentioning because we all need approval. What you have to do, then, is admit this need exists, then remind yourself that just as you can't expect to be universally loved and esteemed, neither can you expect your work to be. Which is why there are so many different agents, editors, and publishers.

10. *Sort through what you get, then apply with caution.* Not all criticism is created equal. Some you'll reject because you know the commentator hasn't understood you. Or listened, or read right, or has no taste in truly great literature!!

That's what I always tell myself. Try doing the same is my advice to you.

JESSAMYN WEST

The author of *Friendly Persuasion* spoke to the Conference in 1978 and charmed the audience.

"Ladies and gentlemen and writers," she began. "Speeches are made by persons with deep feeling for their subject and themselves. Have you ever seen a volume of collected speeches? Why are there so few collections of speeches? Whatever is composed to please an audience, whether listening or written, will never be a *Wuthering Heights* or a *War and Peace*. Those were written to release something in the writer. Does anyone remember as much as two lines of any speech you ever heard?"

Then she went on to show that she did remember part of one speech: Churchill's "their finest hour" speech. "I come to you without any fear of being remembered," she added.

She didn't start writing until she was forty-three years old. "Seeing the extremely young people here in the audience pleases me," Ms. West said. "You must be willing to stick your neck out, to take a chance, to risk making a fool of yourself and discovering you are a fool, if you want to write. I was afraid to write, so I did what many people do. I went to University of California to work for a doctorate in English to work with words and be near what produced writing."

This was interrupted by a two-year bout with tuberculosis, and then Ms. West started writing. She told her husband, "I will write twelve stories and send each one to a different magazine and they will all be turned down. Then will you let me write in peace?"

The first letter back from a magazine informed her that her story was great, but their magazine was for Armenians. By any chance was she an Armenian using a pseudonym?

"Was I going to let this closeness to fame escape? Certainly not!" Ms. West said. "I went through the Napa phone book, but couldn't find an Armenian name. Finally I wrote and told them the truth. For years that editor wrote to me every time he saw a story of mine. He'd write, 'Still sorry you're not a young Armenian.'"

As to what characteristic is most helpful to a writer, she said the answer was not a love of people. "No, that could lead you to nursing, teaching, the ministry, or a massage parlor. What you need is a love of words." Pounding on the lectern, she said, "Pay attention to words!"

Her last words to the audience were: "I can't tell you how to write a great story or an immortal poem. If I could, I'd be home doing it myself right now!"

Reading and Writing

*H*emingway once said to a prospective biographer: "It's none of their business that you have to learn to write. Let them think you were born that way."

The only way to learn to write is by writing and reading, as Hemingway well knew. I am constantly amazed by students who come to the Conference wanting To Be Writers more than wanting to write, and not truly realizing that, along with writing, they must also read if they want to learn to write. I meet writers who are trying to write Robert Ludlum-like suspense stories, Danielle Steel-like love stories, or Ray Bradbury-like fantasy tales who haven't read those authors. Similarly, they often send stories or articles to magazines without studying the market and wonder why the submissions boomerang; you don't send a story on abortion to *Field and Stream* nor one on bass fishing in Peru to *The New Yorker*. Students will turn in a story about a valuable-necklace-that-turns-out-to-be-false or vice versa without realizing that Maugham and de Maupassant got there first, or about a preacher-who-turns-out-to-be-a-lech without seeing how the same material was treated in *The Scarlet Letter, Rain,* and *Elmer Gantry*.

Ask around, find out who is considered the best author in the area you want to write in and then read all you can of his or her works. Take a book of that writer that you admire and analyze it, inch by inch: How many pages is it, how many chapters? Does it start with action? How soon is the protagonist introduced? How soon is the problem revealed and how? By dialogue? By a minor character? At what point is the climax reached? What is the balance between dialogue and exposition and is this typical of most of the books of the genre? Does the story take place in one day or over three generations? Does this writer use metaphors and similes lavishly or sparingly? How detailed are the scenic and weather paragraphs?

Elmore Leonard came to the Conference in 1983 just about the time his great talent was being discovered by the American public (after plugging away in semi-obscurity for about thirty years!). He advocated not only analyzing the works of a writer you admire but even copying out several pages from a favorite book. Yes, typing them out word by word, the better to feel the mechanics and the rhythms of the style.

It is not all that easy being a writer, and if you haven't read much in your life it is going to be tougher. You must read constantly as well as write. Lawrence Kasdan, who wrote *Raiders of the Lost Ark*, has said that a career in writing "is like having homework for the rest of your life."

And why shouldn't it take as much preparation as being a plumber or even a doctor? A student lawyer has to read a lot of books; why not a writer?

Faulkner advises us:

Read everything—trash, classics, good and bad, and see how they do it. Just like an apprentice studying the master. Read! You'll absorb it. Then write. If it is good, you'll find out. If it's not, throw it out the window.

Whoever told you it was going to be easy? Certainly not the Irish playwright Brendan Behan. He used to come into the bar I owned in San Francisco, El Matador, and bemoan the hard life of a writer.

"Never take up the pen, m'lad," he'd advise anyone within earshot. "It'll suck you dry and ruin you."

Certainly not Harlan Ellison (*Star Trek*, etc.). He came to the Conference five years ago and laid it on the line:

Writing is the hardest work in the world.

I have been a bricklayer and a truck driver, and I tell you—as if you haven't been told a million times already—that writing is harder. Lonelier. And nobler and more enriching.

I agree with Hemingway that writers "have to learn to write." And one *can* learn to write. Here's what Harry Golden said about it:

Men are not born writers any more than they are born corporation presidents or curveball artists. If there is such a thing as a born writer then there must also be such a thing as a born bad writer and the metaphysical conditions attendant on this proposition are complex. It is much easier to see with Martial, the Latin poet, "He writes not whose poetry nobody reads."

If you can learn to tie your own shoelaces you can probably learn how to be a writer—with this difference: You have to tie your own shoelaces or you can't get into kindergarten! No one *has* to be a writer. What makes someone into a writer? Work. What kind of work? For the most part, reading other writers; particularly, reading good writers, reading writers who had something to say.

Nor do I insist here that every artist is explainable in specific human and psychological terms. I am at a loss to explain Shakespeare, at a loss to explain Mozart, nor can I explain exactly what the handle is that makes *Leaves of Grass* the best American poetry ever. But I do know this about most writers: They cannot be writers unless they are readers. For it is by reading that writers are able to relate to the past and it is only from a relation to the past that we achieve a sense of the present, and a sense of what is going to happen next.

Of course, it would be wonderful to have read all the great classics, *Moby Dick, Crime and Punishment, War and Peace*, etc. etc. But Time! Time!

I have just finished reading C.S. Forester's autobiography in which he makes the distressing statement that he has "read a book a day since he was seven years old." Oh to be able to say that! I am not going to list a whole bunch of old novels and say that you can't be a writer without having read them all; this is not English Lit 101 at college. But I am going to mention a few novels that have helped me to know what good writing is and have shown me techniques which were within my ability to comprehend and to assimilate. The only old classic that I urge you to read is *Madame Bovary*. Though written in 1856, it seems very modern and immediate. I suggest that you read it not so that you can say you've read it, but because you will learn so much from it about characterization, conflict, and storytelling. For the same reasons I think you should read *The Adventures of Huckleberry Finn*.

Although a long short story, I recommend Jack London's "To Build a Fire" for his lean style. Peter Matthiessen's *At Play in the Fields of the Lord* is a superb adventure story, and more. Read *A Handful of Dust* by Evelyn Waugh for elegance of style and deftly drawn characters; *Serenade* by James M. Cain for exotic suspense; *Shibumi* for intrigue and atmosphere as only Trevanian can do it; *The Eye of the Needle* by Ken Follett for suspense. Read Somerset Maughams's *Of Human Bondage* for the brilliant study of an obsessive love affair. ("It makes more of an impact," Sinclair Lewis told me, "when you know that Mildred was a man.") Read Michener's *Hawaii* for a great sprawling saga; Budd Schulberg's *The Disenchanted* for his portrait of the twilight of F. Scott Fitzgerald. Read F. Scott Fitzgerald's *Tender Is the Night* for his superb use of the English language; Turgenev's *First Love* for one of the most beautiful love stories ever written; A.B. Guthrie's *The Big Sky*, for a superb adventure story of the West. Read *Lonesome Dove* by Larry McMurtry because of its surprises and characterizations; *Gorky Park* by Martin Cruz Smith for its stark suspense; *For Whom the Bell Tolls* for Hemingway adventure at its best. Read Steinbeck's *East of Eden*, an uneven but ultimately rewarding novel; *Daddy* by Loup Durand, a 1989 thriller with a truly chilling Nazi villain; read the early Elmore Leonard books for the tough, realistic dialogue. Mary Webb's touching *This Precious Bane*. *Gone With the Wind* for memorable characters and panorama. *Lolita* for Nabokov's incredible way with language. Irwin Shaw's exciting story of characters at war, *The Young Lions*. James Clavell's riveting account of prisoners of war *King Rat*. Thomas Harris' *Red Dragon*, one of the finest psychological thrillers about a serial killer. D.H. Lawrence's *Lady Chatterly's Lover*, still the ultimate novel of sexual love.

The thing all the above have in common is great characterizations, storytelling, and readability. I know I shall curse myself for having left out a dozen wonderful books and authors. When asked what three novels he would recommend to a creative writing class Faulkner replied: *Anna Karenina, Anna Karenina, Anna Karenina*.

And don't be discouraged; you can't read 'em all! But at least read deeply into the genre in which you yourself are hoping to publish.

IRVING STONE

The late writer wrote some of the best-selling fictionalized biographies of all time. (Alex Haley has said: "Nobody can write about events that happened 200 years ago that isn't more fiction than fact.") The author of *Lust for Life* and *Sailor on Horseback* came and spoke to the Conference in 1987.

I'm a failed playwright. I'm a failed short story writer. I was a second-class mystery writer. I had three failures in my life and along comes Vincent van Gogh and his life. And all of a sudden my failures turn into great, great virtues and values. From my playwriting, I learned how to stage scenes under a proscenium with you not in the audience but up on the stage as a central character. From my detective stories I learned how to weave suspense. From the short stories I learned how to foreshorten. And I taught myself how to research.

What you want most is to write something of lasting value, something that has universal appeal. Why do I appeal to people from all over the world with whom I would seem to have nothing in common? It's because I go after the universal.

I have never had an agent. I peddled my manuscripts in New York to publisher after publisher.

We here can convey to you all the mechanics of writing, all the techniques of writing. But there is no way than anyone here, good as we are, and we're pretty good, can teach you the *art* of writing.

I fumbled and I stumbled for the definition of art for years, and only found it a year ago when UCLA asked me to give their Honors Collegium lecture: Art is a singing in the bloodstream, an exaltation of the nervous system, a flare in the heart, and a glow of human values in the mind.

There must be lilting style which embraces and gladdens the eye, the balm of humor which bubbles indigenously from character and situation, the reprise of plot and suspense so that every line is interlocked with every other, the dramatizing of the master scenes under a proscenium so that the reader is on stage in the midst of the action as a principal. It means putting the reader in a state of grace, enthralled with the flow of printed words which become a living reality, in which the fortunate turner of pages has his horizons pushed back by the explosions of new ideas, deeper concepts, broader understandings of human fate. So you can see all around the curve of the planet Earth and our universe as well.

The plunging into the human, both conscious and unconscious, so that we can understand motivation, personal relationships, the flarings of anger, defeat, and despair, as well as the exaltations of love and creative accomplishment. And at the same time, the unfolding of a moving story which captures universal appeal.

Art is the custodian who jealously guards the wisdom of the past and weighs it against the present.

The Selling of the Short Story

B ethel Laurence has been both a student and lecturer at the Conference. Her short stories have appeared in many magazines
including *Redbook*, *Good Housekeeping*, and *Ellery Queen*, and her fiction
has been published in the prestigious *Best American Short Stories*. Now
she shares her expertise with us.

We writers of short stories face the dilemma of wanting to sell, yet
wanting to resist the demands and specifications of the market place.
Oh, it will work out, we think, because—let's face it—we all have the
same dream: To make our work so magnificent that awestruck editors
will accept the unacceptable.

"*I must have it!*" we can hear them cry.

Isn't it a lovely dream?

We go on dreaming it.

Until more stories come back.

Somewhere there begins a turning point, a time to rethink. This
is the time to pick up each of your stories and read it as though you
have never seen it before. And when the reading is over you first ask
yourself:

What type of story is this?

The current *Novel & Short Story Writer's Market* lists the following
categories: Religious/inspirational, confession, teen, science fiction,
fantasy, translations, senior citizen/retirement, regional, horror, psy-
chic/supernatural/occult, humor/satire, gay/lesbian, erotica, adventure, mainstream, ethnic, romance, experimental, sports, contemporary, ethnic, feminist, historical, prose poem, preschool, serialized/
excerpted novel, spiritual, suspense/western, mystery, juvenile, and
Canadian.

Which type of story is yours?

Examine it. Put the stethoscope of your intelligence to the body of the work and ask yourself: What condition is this story in? Is it strong enough to go out in the world and compete? To find its proper place? And by the way, what *is* its proper place? Thus evolves some of the most challenging work you will ever face. You begin to look at your stories in a totally different light; you begin to look at printed stories in a totally different light: These little devils have managed to get themselves published. Now how on earth did they do it?

What secrets do they hold?

Plenty. These stories come from writers who know what that editor wants. Well, then, how can you learn what that editor wants?

There are ways.

First, are you keeping track of all the seminars and writing conferences in your area? Are you saving your money for a conference which may not be in your area, but that features an editor who it would be to your advantage to meet? And remember, even if you don't actually meet this editor at the conference, when you mail your manuscript you will be able to include a personal note saying what a pleasure it was to hear him or her speak. This is an admittance pass, something you would not ordinarily have.

Futhermore, you will be hearing, straight from the horse's mouth, the requirements of this particular editor. A warning: There may be one point that requires your interpretation. This might come when the editor tells you that what is needed most is something fresh.

I had an experience along these lines once when I decided to write a romance novel; I listened carefully to an editor from a large romance house state her desires: "Above all, be fresh," she insisted. "We are looking for new concepts, innovative ideas." I went home and, after reading approximately *two hundred romances*, wrote and submitted one in which I strayed a bit from the romance formula. An insulting letter arrived from the editor in which she said that my work sounded as though I had never read a romance. I sighed, tucked away my manuscript, and gave away my two hundred romances.

Well, it *had* been fresh.

Eventually I was able to calm down and understand: Had I really been concentrating when I read all those romances I would have seen *unbroken* patterns, then noted variations *within* those patterns — *within* — and I would have known then that these variations are what the editor meant by "freshness."

Think of what I could have saved myself.

Most markets, I realized then, do have their boundaries. They require freshness and variations, yes — but within these boundaries.

And it then becomes the writer's job to discover where the lines are drawn.

In the case of magazine stories, there is one sure way to find out what an editor wants. The answer is right before you: *Study the magazine*. The magazine won't merely tell you, but show you what this editor wants.

These magazines are the writers' textbooks, the writers' bibles, because the editor's desires are all there on the pages, ready to be decoded.

Every editor I have ever spoken to has said that far too many unsolicited stories sound as though the writer has not read the magazine. Some say that submissions give the impression that the writer has acquired a list and is systematically going from top to bottom of this list. In other words, that the writer is totally unfamiliar with the markets.

At any new writers' group, I would put more stress on marketing. In an advanced class or group I would have each person state before reading what market that work is intended for and some part of each session would be devoted to marketing. I would assign one person to analyze one magazine at each meeting—a magazine, of course, that is homogenous with the aims of the group.

The same thing can be done individually. *Novel & Short Story Writer's Market* lists most magazines with their addresses, preferable time, if any, to submit, and requirements. It is *not*, however, a substitute for reading the magazine; it is simply a guide. Most commercial magazines can be found at local libraries and many literary magazines are available at college/university libraries and college book stores. If you can afford it, subscribe to a few most likely to be right for you and remember that single issues are available.

You will find annual collections of literary stories in both hard cover and paperback. These are: *Best American Short Stories*, *O. Henry*, *Pushcart Prize*, and *Hot Type*. Other anthologies appear, though not annually.

There are also guidelines. Most magazines have these, stating their particular requirements, which, for an S.A.S.E. (you probably know by now that that is a self-addressed stamped envelope) they will mail to you.

But don't stop with guidelines: *Read the stories*. You are *not* reading to *copy*. You are not reading to *contrive*. For instance, you do not calculate: "Well, children and dogs seem to work well, so I'll throw in a child and a dog." The point is to be original, to develop your own concepts. *Nothing succeeds like originality*. But here you are simply learning the boundaries, the editors' preferences, the types of stories, in short, what these magazines are all about.

Read each story once for pleasure and first impressions. Then read it again, and get down to business. You'll find that there is a big difference between reading for enjoyment and reading to analyze a market. To analyze, you formulate a list of questions such as:

Is this story from a male or female point of view?

What is the theme of the story?

Who are the characters?

What is the problem?

Is this problem resolved happily? Hopefully? Or not at all?

What kind of background?

How deeply, how *realistically*, does the story delve into the characters and into their problems?

How subtly?

Don't skimp. Make your list long and probing and keep developing it as you go. You'll find surprises. For instance, from my own recent experience: There is a literary market that I was eager to sell. After reading four copies I discovered that every story was in a rural setting. So I, writing always from an urban point of view, was able to eliminate this market, thereby saving months of time—plus a few fingernails from being chewed.

Will there ever be an urban story there? Oh, probably. But with so many literary magazines to choose from, why should I play the exceptions? Exceptions are just that. Once in a while you take a chance. Once in a while you go to Vegas.

"They all look alike to me!"

Are you familiar with this cliché? Well, isn't that the way we often feel about groups of magazines? The women's, for instance. Isn't it common to lump them all together, to assume that their voices are all the same? Nothing could be further from the truth. Study them. See how different they are. Would you send the same story to *Good Housekeeping* that you would to *Mademoiselle*? If you would, you'd better go back and study some more.

Pick up a copy of *Woman's World*, which publishes 104 stories a year (by far the most of any magazine). Study its individualities, apply all your questions. Then pick up more copies. More. Do you understand what they want? Wouldn't it be nice to be one of the 104?

And the men's magazines—have you lumped them all together, too? Well, I have. And the reason I know so well what not to do is that I, personally, have committed the entire repertoire of writers' errors.

There *are* stories, however, that can be changed. In response to one story that I submitted to women's magazines, I received letters stating that they found the work impressive but because of sexual connotations were unable to print it. The sale meant a great deal to me so instead of having the male character make sexual threats to the woman, I changed them to threats of death. This story turned out to be a heaven-sent Dream Story: It was anthologized and received offers from television, stage, and movies. And all because I thought to make that one easy change.

So you see, there are some stories that can be reconceived, molded, while others are much less pliable.

And there are some stories, Lord help us, that cannot be made to fit a single publication on this planet Earth.

These stories have defective parts or parts that don't mesh well together. For instance, a friend of mine wrote a story with a heart-warming plot suitable for *Good Housekeeping*. One character in it, however, swore and was involved in ethnic problems. It is a story whose parts don't mesh, and no matter how well it is written it is dubious that it can find a market. *Good Housekeeping* will not accept the serious ethnic problems; literary magazines will not accept the *Good Housekeeping* plot.

Eventually you'll be able to spot these discrepancies. You will also be able to tell the difference between a literary and a commercial story and a few hybrids in between. If you've been taught rules and points of plotting you'll see that these rules are usually far more applicable to commercial than to literary stories, which tend to swing much freer of restrictions. The greatest demand of literary magazines is just plain good writing and they allow you more room to experiment, to stand up and holler, and in general to be more your own person.

Back to your market studies: Before you are through with the analyses you should be able to spot certain errors that have felled you previously. When you have slowly ingested your possible markets you will find that this effort has had a four-pronged benefit:

1. You will know the markets and their requirements.

2. You will recognize your own stories for what they are.

3. You will therefore know where these stories fit or do not fit.

4. But the fourth result is the most dramatic of all: Having committed these first three things to your writing memory, you will see your work gradually evolving. Automatically you will begin to fashion your stories differently, to create concepts within a category, eliminating or adding in appropriate places.

This adapting of concepts will not be forced or contrived, but simply natural, your unconscious subtly guiding you along different paths.

And sometimes you will smile indulgently at a former effort and say, Why on earth did I ever do that?

In the end you will save yourself time, money, and blows to the heart. The unnecessary ones.

Now let's assume that you have a story completed. Study it with your stranger's, I-never-saw-this-before-in-my-life eye. What do you *honestly* see? Never be embarrassed to say, "This is poor." The most famous writers have all turned out something poor. After all, why should writers be less infallible than the rest of the world?

Ask yourself: Do I need to return to the typewriter? To forestall any premature births?

In *Novel & Short Story Writer's Market* Amy Kaufman the editor of *Stories* comments, "Most writers submit half-finished work—they haven't taken themselves seriously enough." (This from a person who receives approximately eight thousand submissions a year.)

Think: What will make this work more finished?

Start with the beginning: Does it catch and hold interest? After all, this is your story's first impression, its "Hello, this is who I am." Remember the old lines, *"Will you walk into my parlour?"/said a spider to a fly?* Well, you are the spider, enticing people in.

Laura Vitale, fiction editor of *Penthouse*, stresses the importance of beginnings. "You only need to take one bite," Laura states, "to know if it's a good sandwich."

Is that first bite going to make someone want to complete your sandwich?

Now move to the body of the piece. Adrian LeBlanc, fiction editor of *Seventeen*, says that she sees a great many short stories that are good, but not quite there yet—which backs up Amy Kaufman's "half-finished work." Adrian mentions that other common problems she finds are: "Stories overwritten. Parts with no relevance to story. Repetition." She suggests that you read your work aloud, an excellent way to pick up irrelevancies and repetitions. They seem to *stick out* more than in reading to yourself and sometimes you will find your voice will actually falter as it comes across them.

Stanley Lindberg, editor of *The Georgia Review*, says that he would like to see an improvement in technical quality. Common errors, he notes, are "shifts in point of view, change of tone, heading in one direction and then turning in another. You lose trust in a writer," he notes, "when these inconsistencies occur."

This manuscript that you have been working on—is its editing, typing, and physical form also of value? Every editor interviewed commented on the importance of a clean, correct-looking manuscript. Every editor stated that manuscripts are not always clean and correct-looking.

If you don't know the proper manuscript form, check it out. Greg Michalson, managing editor of *The Missouri Review*, states that he finds glaring grammatical errors and misspellings even on the first page. If you can't spell, use your dictionary, use your friends—use your head! Would you go out, seeking to make a good impression, dirty and torn, inappropriately dressed? Even if you would, your manuscript can't!

Jon Tribble, editor of *Indiana Review*, stresses the importance of appearance. He says, "A little care helps a great bit" and adds that it is not uncommon to receive worn, even stained pages, and that he has also received stories with rejection slips from other magazines and cover letters addressed to editors of other magazines.

You finally have this well-edited, well-typed manuscript, you have chosen your market in advance and are ready to submit. At this point it is not advisable to consider agents. Most agents simply do not care to handle short stories. For one thing, there is very little money in them and they are hard to sell. If you are working on a novel that is simply sensational, they may handle your short stories as a favor, but on the whole it is best forgotten.

Another thing best forgotten is submitting a collection of stories to publishers before several of the stories have been published. Again, the odds are strong against this.

So we are back now to your single story which you are prepared to mail *flat*, accompanied, *always*, by a S.A.S.E.

We now come to the cover letter.

Most, though not all, editors find this note advisable. Jon Tribble states that "It is a polite formality that makes a much more human process of submitting."

Write a *brief, simple* note, about five lines, but certainly under a page, stating *pertinent* literary facts, such as you would want written about yourself at the end of your story. List sales, if any, but no more than four. The sales, too, should be pertinent to your target market.

Some local or minor sales can be eliminated—not that there *are* any minor sales to us—but if the editor has to stop and think, What is it? it's probably better left unlisted. You might simply state, "I have sold to local publications." Or: "I have sold to children's magazines," and so forth, summing up everything not connected to the market at hand. If you have no sales don't bother to apologize or explain; and don't worry about it because, after all, your manuscript is your actual spokesperson.

What do you say if you have nothing to say?

You write something to this effect:

I'm enclosing my story for consideration in your publication. Thank you for taking the time to consider it.

Do not—*ever*—attempt to tell what the story is about in the letter. This, again, is the job of the story. Don't jeopardize its position or destroy its freshness.

Do not—ever—tell the editor in the letter that "this story really happened." He doesn't give a darn. Unless, of course, you are writing nonfiction.

We now come to the much-discussed problem of single or multiple submissions. This, I believe, is ultimately a personal decision. Some, though not many, editors say that they are not opposed to multiple submissions *provided they are labeled as such*; but most magazines simply do not want them. It's easy to see why; and also easy to see why the writer might want them.

The problem lies with the time element. A vicious circle has been created as more and more writers send more and more manuscripts: "Oh well, what have I got to lose?" they say. But we do have something to lose; we flood the market and topple the slush piles and bleary the eyes of the readers with too often inappropriate submissions. Then our beautiful, absolutely-right manuscript gets buried in a pile and sometimes this bleary-eyed reader goes right past it.

An editor at *Good Housekeeping* told me they get more than 25,000 manuscripts a year. Imagine dealing with that. Small literary magazines receive up to eight thousand and most read during only a part of the year. When I first submitted stories I would regularly receive notes, suggestions, or a handwritten "Sorry" at the bottom of a rejection slip. Editors would often explain how they thought the story could be improved. But we've done ourselves out of this help by the sheer numbers of stories, so many of them inappropriate. Now help occurs much less often; there simply isn't time.

And in the editor's office, manuscripts pile up. Months go by. The writer multiple submits. The piles grow higher. And higher.

That is why multiple-submission is a personal decision. You gain time, but you risk annoying or losing a valuable market. It is a Catch-22.

There is good news, too. C. Michael Curtis, senior editor at *The Atlantic*, comments that he is seeing more high quality fiction than he has seen in previous years. In general there is enthusiasm and warm welcome for the emerging writer. Dolores Weinberg, co-editor of the literary magazine *Other Voices*, which requires that stories be about relationships, says, "I like to discover new, talented writers. I want to be the one to publish them first."

Each editor interviewed has mentioned the large number of new writers that his or her magazine has presented. Stanley Lindberg notes that he has published at least sixty. "I publish the story," he adds, "not the name and reputation of the author."

Greg Michalson says, "'The big thing that writers forget is that most manuscript readers are writers themselves and are really interested in doing right by the writer." He concludes, "If I were deciding between two manuscripts, all things being equal, I would choose the unpublished writer over the published one every time."

Those are beautiful words.

And Gordon Lish, editor of *The Quarterly*, has said, "The new, young writers . . . are far more interesting than many people who have been publishing stories for years and may have achieved great things in the past but haven't kept themselves as energetically in touch with English sentences as they once did."

So, get to it!

K E Y N O T E R

IRWIN SHAW

"What would be your greatest goal in life?" someone in the audience at the Miramar Hotel asked the author of *Evening in Byzantium, Lucy Crown, Night Work, The Young Lions, Rich Man, Poor Man* and uncountable other books and short stories.

"Standing here talking about myself and my writing," Irwin Shaw replied deadpan.

Several times during the talk Shaw quoted his eighty-five-year-old mother. She evidently told him that he should write, not give talks. But the audience didn't agree.

"My mother says I ski too fast, shouldn't play singles in tennis, and should stop drinking," he said. "And she tells me I'm working too hard. I'm not working, I'm writing."

"What was your reaction to the TV presentation of your book *Rich Man, Poor Man?*" was another question.

"Gratitude," came the instantaneous reply. And then Shaw elaborated a bit on how handy the monetary returns from the television show had been for taxes and problems like that. "It was well produced, and I found myself sitting there enjoying it. When I saw the film of *The Young Lions*, I was embarrassed. And I wouldn't go to see some of the other films they've made of my books because I heard they were so bad."

He told the story of asking his eight-year-old son one day in their home in Switzerland what he wanted to be when he grew up. "A writer," came the reply. "Why a writer?" Shaw asked. "So I can ski all winter and play tennis all summer."

He quoted Ernest Hemingway's formula for being a good writer: an unhappy childhood. "My own formula is a happy childhood, but an impoverished youth." Then he added, "Avoiding hunger is an excellent provoker of genius."

On the same general theme he cautioned, "Do not despise money. Poverty itself does not make you a great stylist. With money you can take your own time to perfect your work. Why do I allow my books to be used on television or in the movies? The truth is, I need the money. I tell people, if you don't like the movie, go read the book. The book remains."

He spoke of facing that typewriter every morning, keeping a tight schedule when possible, writing from eight o'clock to one every day. "The challenge is enormous. There's always the fear that you've lost it, or maybe never had it," he said. "There are too many flashes in the pan who have had one good book and then nothing. Endurance plus continuing education are two important ingredients for the writer. I *force* myself to write. As writers you must cling to the belief—however ill-founded—that you have talent. Turn a deaf ear to criticism."

Shaw said that he rewrites constantly. He usually doesn't show a draft of his work to anyone until he feels it is ready; then he shows it to his publisher. After that he might show it to close friends. Then he does a revision. He said that he was halfway through *Lucy Crown* and wanted to give up on it, but he showed it to a friend. The friend said to finish it, so he did. "It took two and a half years to write *Nightwork*," he said of his current best seller, "but it looks like a puff of whipped cream."

"What do you read?" was one of the questions from the audience. "Anything," he replied. "and everything. I'm a great reader of the *Encyclopaedia Britannica*."

The Publishing Business: Marketing the Manuscript

Sir, no man but a blockhead ever wrote except for money.
— Samuel Johnson
Instead of marvelling with Johnson, how anything but profit should incite men to literary labour, I am rather surprised that mere emolument should induce them to labour so well.
— Thomas Green

The senior editor of a famous New York publishing house was addressing the Conference in 1982 when a member of the audience complained that she had mailed his firm a manuscript many months ago and still hadn't heard anything.

"I don't recall the title," said the editor uncomfortably. "Was it a mystery?"

"No," said the writer.

"A romance, perhaps?"

Again no.

"A historical novel then?"

"Not," replied the writer bitterly, "when I sent it in."

To me this encounter sums up the wary, impersonal, adversarial attitude that exists today between author and publisher. What really goes on in that strange world?

Frances Halpern, for many years an invaluable cornerstone at the Conference, is the author of *Writer's Guide to Publishing in the West* and a contributor to *The Complete Guide to Writing Nonfiction*. Her column "Bookmarks" appears in the Sunday edition of the *Daily News* of Los Angeles and she hosts a lively, informative radio talk-show which focuses on writing and publishing. Once a student at the Santa Barbara Writers' Conference, she now conducts the "Take Your Words to Market: The Business of Publishing" workshop at the Conference. Here's what she has to say about marketing fiction:

Dear literary toilers, you've been advised and admonished, cajoled and encouraged about the gentle art of writing fiction. Craft and plot, characters and conflict, focus and structure all stirred into the mix. You've been writing to share what you know and feel and care about.

You've been writing to entertain, to touch others, and yes, to earn money. At last, the passion for storytelling fulfilled, you have a finished manuscript in hand.

And now the focus changes. The time has come to analyze the marketplace. Who publishes fiction? What kind of fiction have you written? A commercial, glitzy blockbuster, a generational saga? Are you dreaming movie or television series? Is your manuscript a mainstream historical novel or a story about modern relationships? Do you write for children or young adults? Is your book a painstakingly crafted literary effort reflecting your inner vision and philosophy, or a fictionalized autobiography? Is it category or genre fiction you've written? (Genre is simply a publishers' word used to define westerns, mysteries, adventure, horror, romance, gothic, science fiction.)

The subcategories in this fiction can be defined specifically. For example, no writer simply writes a "romance novel." There are many forms of the romance novel including Regencies, historicals, and romantic adventure; this is an enormous market. The mystery category also has many faces. You can write fictional versions of real crimes, spy/adventure, horror thrillers, or use as a vehicle the urbane or hard-boiled private-eye protagonist. Science fiction and westerns are also pigeonholed into subcategories by publishers.

In the past, popular genre fiction (which sells so well today) garnered very little respect from the literary establishment. They were not taken seriously or properly reviewed. It was the novelist whose book could not be categorized who was lionized. Sometimes starving, often hard-drinking, eccentric, irresponsible, solitary, selfish, true only to the art of writing; this was the popular perception of the real writer. No one leading a "normal" life—housewife, businessman, student—was expected to create serious fiction. Nonfiction was (and in some circles still is) labeled a lesser occupation. Many authors say they write articles and how-to books to put bread on the table but insist their passion will always be fiction. "The greatest achievement for us is to see our bylines in a fine literary magazine or of course on the jacket of a novel." A newspaper journalist, in the business for years, remembered that his colleagues in the newsroom constantly told each other, "Don't get big ideas, we're not writers, we're just reporters!"

Well, whatever we call ourselves novelists, freelancers, journalists, we are independent entrepreneurs, forced to wear many hats, and generally unprepared to cope with the complex publishing industry. The pressure on writers is tremendous. We conjure up the idea. We struggle to put the written word onto a lined pad, into the typewriter, or word-processor. We shape the writing into a finished manuscript (lovely white paper, double-spaced, lots of margin) and then we are supposed to take it to market. Ah, but who and what is our market? How do we reach the agents and publishers, the distributors and booksellers who can deliver our creation to the ultimate audience— the reading public? At this point you must assess with a critical eye what you have written. Your completed manuscript may represent years of toil and you are not going to be foolish enough to ship the work into the marketplace without preliminary businesslike research.

Before we describe the process of getting published, we should face up to one terrible truth. Most manuscripts are rejected because they are poorly written, disorganized, clichéd or totally uninteresting. Sometimes a beautiful work or good commercial literature is also rejected. Often these manuscripts are lost in the pack of really bad stuff cluttering publishers' mail rooms and never reach the desks of agents and editors. "Our careers depend upon the books we publish," is the cry of all editors. "We don't get brownie points or salary increases for rejecting manuscripts." Editors need good manuscripts they can turn into profitable books. Your assignment is to meet that need.

Market your work intelligently and with the same passion you created it. Completing a wonderful novel is a labor of love (as is completing a bad one). Getting it published is an extraordinary feat. But learning about the industry is easy.

1. Join professional writers' organizations. Many of them have associate memberships for new writers. Your reward will be interacting with professionals, and newsletters full of information about agents and editors, contracts and copyright law and all manner of resources for writers.

2. Subscribe to magazines for writers and invest in *Publishers Weekly* (share the expense with a writing colleague). *PW* provides an insight into the daily activities of publishing professionals. If you are really serious about being an author, you read *Publishers Weekly*. And read the local newspaper to keep up-to-date about literary events in your community.

3. Loiter in your local bookstore, a good place to learn about publishing and also to meet the publisher's reps (the people who sell books to the bookstore) and usually know what's going on.

4. Get friendly with the library and librarians. They too are aware of which books are doing well and what people are grabbing off the shelves to read.

5. Attend conferences and seminars in order to gaze upon and meet agents and editors in the flesh. Along with writing well, an agent can be the key to publication. Your game is to find out which

agents might be interested in your work. Contacts are crucial. Editors and agents are individuals with personal tastes. Be informed about them. Make notes, make a card file. Don't be afraid to use the telephone and the post office. Call or write to agents and publishers and ask for guidelines and information on how they want manuscripts submitted. They will tell you that the first step is to submit a brief query describing the work. Enclose an SASE with all correspondence. Sending out unsolicited manuscripts is an exercise in futility.

6. Study the small publishing houses. Many of them actively seek quality fiction which they have the time and resources to distribute properly. They supply the independent and specialty bookshops, and the same print run and sales which a large publisher considers a failure could be a publishing success at the smaller publisher.

7. If you write short stories, keep submitting to the literary magazines. Editors and agents do read them. One agent, an unusual zealot in search of new voices, is said to subscribe to seventy-five literary magazines!

What does go on in the publishing process? The story of how each book gets published is often more fascinating than the book itself. Generally here's what happens. A writer gets smart/lucky/knows the right people/gets discovered in "slush." A carefully chosen agent (see page 288) agrees to represent the novel. A competent, experienced agent has many contacts among editors and knows within reason exactly what editors and publishing houses are looking for. A finished manuscript is given to one or more editors. Multiple submissions are finding more acceptance and if the agent feels the book has big potential, a bidding situation obviously ups the price of the advance.

Now we have an editor who is crazy about the manuscript. In some cases, that editor has the power to purchase the work. More often, the editor has to consult with others at the publishing house. Publishers differ from one another in their method of choosing books. At some houses editors gather informally to discuss new manuscripts. Others defer to the decision of a chief editor or the publisher. Some will have a formally appointed board of editors who meet weekly. Your manuscript will be copied and passed around to be read. A memo on the merits of the book and a profit-and-loss statement will be submitted for discussion. The editor who brought the manuscript to the house will speak in behalf of the project. And then it is the luck of the draw or in the lap of the Gods. Does the publisher want/need a book on its list like yours? Are you an author with a future? Perhaps a potential best-selling author? Is there a chance they can sell enough copies to earn a profit?

What can the author anticipate if the publisher decides to go with the manuscript? A contract is drawn up, and remember, the publisher's lawyers wrote that contract with (understandably) their client's best interests at heart. Most first authors will sign anything put in front of them. An agent will assess the contract and eliminate or add clauses in behalf of the author and, depending on a variety of circumstances, will get the best deal possible. Incidentally, good agents don't always go for the most money, but will with the consent of their clients accept an offer from the publisher who in their opinion will do the best job of manufacturing and merchandising the book.

A brand new novelist, being presented for the first time, will have to sit still for a very small advance. Occasionally of course (and it makes headlines) big advances are offered in the hundreds of thousands. West coast agent Sandra Dijkstra negotiated a megabuck deal for *The Joy Luck Club*, a first novel by thirty-seven-year-old Amy Tan (who came to the Conference in 1990). However, more realistically, be prepared for figures in the neighborhood of well under ten thousand dollars, and usually five thousand. Print runs are usually about four to five thousand books. If something terrific happens and the book receives rave reviews, gets noticed in the press, sells by word-of-mouth, the publisher will get excited, print more books and crank up the sales and advertising departments. If the book has been issued in hardcover, subsidiary rights people will try for a paperback sale, book club, foreign sales, audio-cassette deal. Royalties (paid twice a year) generally begin at 10 percent of the retail price of the book and escalate depending on sales and other factors. If the hardcover book costs $20, author gets $2 for each book sold. No royalties are paid on copies the publisher distributes to reviewers, etc.

Paperback publishing exploded in recent years and continues to change and evolve. One of the decisions agents, authors, and editors make constantly is whether to publish in hardcover or paperback. Most authors want the hardcover book. It's prestigious and looks great on the shelves. However, in 1989, Nobel Laureate Saul Bellow made history when he chose to have his short novel, *A Theft*, published by Penguin as a $6.95 paperback. Generally, money, the market, and the book's category govern the final call on this complex question. The newly published mass-market author can expect about a 6 percent royalty, but a much larger print run than hardcover novels.

The fiction world has changed considerably and in spite of the grousing about how terrible the publishing business is now, and the misty-eyed recalling of the "good old days," conditions are favorable for getting a first novel published (and occasionally even a big advance). Having said this, there is a caveat. Publishers are inconsistent gamblers who admit they pour too many books into the marketplace: At last count somewhere between 50,000 and 60,000 titles a year! The audience is also inconsistent and easily distracted. Although the two major bookstore chains, B. Dalton and Waldenbooks, sold approximately two billion dollars worth of merchandise last year, with a population of 240 million the figures break down to an investment in books of a little over eight dollars a person!

The good news is that more writers are getting a chance at being published. The unhappy fact is that most of them will not be well-published. That is, the books will not find a market, will not sell well, and will earn very little money for the author. Why are publishing houses turning out more merchandise than they can properly sell? By their own admission, they can't clearly predict which title will establish a new author, be a bestseller, or just not make it. As one publisher explained, "We are like lovers. We see a manuscript that captures our fancy and think, let's do it, despite the fact that seven out of ten books lose money and one in ten supports the whole system!"

The distribution and publicizing of books (in spite of the computer age) remains a very large problem. You've all heard authors scream about the tour which could have been such fun, except there were no books delivered to the stores! An audience of writers concerned with distribution asked a distinguished publishers panel at a meeting of the American Booksellers Association how they planned a campaign for a new novel. The editor-in-chief of a large, prestigious publishing house answered, "Oh, we throw it out there and hope it sticks to the wall!" What exactly does that mean? They cannot explain why one book which has been given a royal send-off with a big advertising budget fails and another title they've paid no attention to soars to best-sellerdom by word of mouth.

And so Cinderella and Horatio Alger live. An aspiring writer in his early twenties sits down and dashes off a rite-of-passage novel; another writes a literary masterpiece. Both books are successful. There's a bandwagon effect. Other very young writers get their manuscripts accepted. Publishers give them large advances. The public likes and buys the books. The media is fascinated by these young writers and gives them lots of publicity. Movie deals are made.

People in their sixties and seventies also get a crack at the dream. They get lucky with manuscripts, which in some cases they have worked on for years (interrupted by family responsibilities) and find agents to represent them and editors who love their novels. At our conference not long ago Harriet Doerr told us how she left college at twenty, married, raised a family, returned to school fifty years later! Her novel, *Stones for Ibarra* published when she was seventy-three, won prestigious awards, was made into a television series and established her career.

Today's successful authors cannot be categorized (as their books are). They are of every age group, from all over the country, and with educational backgrounds ranging from none to graduate degrees. They have produced work at kitchen tables surrounded by toddlers, at odd hours while scratching for a living, on grants at writers' retreats, or in posh offices aided by research assistants. The prolific best-selling author Fern Michaels did not go to college. She was a New Jersey housewife with a dream. She wrote a romance novel with a colleague which they submitted unsolicited to a large paperback house. "Timing and luck was on our side," she remembers. Her 1989 bestseller *Texas Fury* had two million, four hundred thousand copies in print! Judith Merkle Riley, a California college professor and historian, sent a query about her novel set in 14th century England to a New York agent she chose after studying agent lists. *A Vision of Light* was beautifully published and is now out in paperback. Duane Unkefer walked away from his advertising job and spent three years subsisting in one room writing *Gray Eagles*. After a huge advance, it was published in hardcover and mass-market paperback in the United States and Canada. Unkefer is now working on a multi-book deal for a New York publisher.

If you wish to join their ranks you must be informed, continue to make contacts, and be lucky. Publishing is a complex, contradictory business where arbitrary decisions based on gut reactions are made by people who really love books. Nevertheless, it is an industry which will close ranks and fortify the walls against writers who through ignorance or indifference do not respect its rules and traditions.

Keep in mind that the competition is fierce and writers are not an endangered species. Apparently they never were. More than 400 years ago Martin Luther, the fellow who nailed those demands to the church door, opined, "The multitude of books is a great evil. There is no measure or limit to this fever of writing; everyone must be an author, some for vanity to acquire celebrity and raise a name, others for the sake of lucre or gain." Whatever your reason for wanting to be published (vanity, celebrity, money), you do not stick your manuscript on the end of an arrow and shoot it out hoping it will hit the right agent or editor. Unsolicited manuscripts by the thousands pile up in editors' offices. They can't deal with them. They are generally returned unread, but there are exceptions. Carol Houck Smith, vice president/editor at W.W. Norton, a New York house that publishes quality fiction, says she or an assistant will look at everything that comes in. "Sometimes it takes only thirty seconds to decide whether the manuscript is well-written or right for us," she adds. Smith knows exactly what she wants, "Voice and energy, strong writing, idiosyncratic and quirky personal experiences." Send fifty pages, consecutive chapters please, and a one-page cover letter describing the concept of the novel. Do not include a synopsis.

How and why is a manuscript selected for publication? How does the process happen? A number of editors from publishing houses all over the country have addressed this question in personal interviews, in response to written questionnaires and at conferences. They perceive of themselves as wide open, willing to listen and cooperate with writers. Some of them actually are. They say they spend their waking hours in holy pilgrimage seeking the fresh story, the beautifully written word, and the commercial property to put between two pieces of plain or fancy cardboard, call it a book, and ship it to market.

Editors have special interests and can be categorized just like books. Some editors are crazy about historical novels, others love westerns, or are experts on mysteries. Acquiring editors seek out manuscripts and negotiate contracts. Other editors clean up grammatical errors, clarify syntax, and in some cases rewrite enough to make a marginal book coherent or a good book great. At some publishing houses, editors handle both jobs. There is more pressure now on editors to move books through the system quickly. Corporate ownership and "bottom-line economics" has definitely influenced the publishing process. With more and more editors devoting their time to acquisitions, publishers are using freelancers to edit manuscripts.

Fran Fisher, who edits for major New York publishers in her West Coast office, has basic advice for new writers. "Don't three-hole punch and bind manuscripts. It's a waste of time, aggravates editors and marks you as an amateur. Don't renumber pages at each chapter. If your first chapter ends on page fifteen, the next chapter begins on page sixteen. And please, edit out all those, 'she said meekly,' 'he said pompusly,' sentence interrupters and get rid of those thousands of adjectives." Fisher also begs novelists to do careful research. Having a sailing vessel call in at an island that hadn't been discovered at the time of the book's setting can worry an editor into wondering what else is wrong with the manuscript.

Editors are constantly asked about why manuscripts are rejected. Here are some of their thoughts. If a basically interesting manuscript needs a lot of editing, it might be turned down because the publisher doesn't want to spend the time and money to fix it. The solution is to teach yourself to edit critically or find someone who can. Publishers also plead with writers to distinguish between private fantasies and worthwhile literature. Many editors admit they become depresssed when they have to reject a manuscript because they understand the emotional commitment writers put into their work. Some insist that any good book will be snapped up and published. But other editors say there are a variety of reasons for rejection that have nothing to do with the quality of the work.

Confusing? Definitely. One publisher describes the industry as more complex than life.

And finally, an editor told an audience of novelists, "I am in the business of passion. It's a lousy business, but a wonderful profession." And most editors echo one of their colleagues who said, "The dream of every publisher is to wake up each morning hoping maybe that book I've been waiting for all my life will come into the office today."

And every writer fervently works to create a compelling, passionate tale which will fulfill that dreamy expectation.

The Be-getting of an Agent

M any unpublished writers who come to the Conference don't think they need to learn to write better; they just need an agent.

More from Frances Halpern:

The three major questions writers always ask about agents are: "When do I need one? How do I get one? Where do I find a good one?

To "get" an agent you have to do the same thing necessary to "get" published. Write a publishable manuscript; if you want that manuscript read by an editor at a viable publishing house, you'll probably have to find an agent willing to represent it. In recent years more and more publishers are adopting a policy of sending back unsolicited manuscripts unopened. This reflects publishers' calculations over the last two decades that of the thousands of manuscripts received "over the transom" only a handful had literary value or commercial possibilities.

Before the when, how and where questions are answered you should know that these mysterious, shadowy creatures called, or who call themselves, agents come in all sizes, degrees of competence, and experience. Some charge reading and critiquing fees. Many do not. New agents say charging fees gives them a chance to get established, and established agencies say the fees provide an opportunity to take a look at new writers in a very crowded field. There are still people in the publishing community who condemn the practice.

Be wary of "agents" with little or no experience or publishing contacts who show up at a writers' conference and try to sign up naive writers for money up front. Literary agents, unlike agents who represent film and television writers, do not have to be licensed and are answerable only to their own consciences. And be particularly suspicious of agents who place those seductive "seeking new authors" ads in magazines and newspapers. Almost invariably they tell writers "the manuscript shows great promise but needs fixing" and for (fill in the amount) they do some critiquing and then send the writer back to the drawing board. Check on these people and ask them to send a list of writers they represent, who published them, and when. Legitimate agents are proud of their client lists and more than happy to publicize them. There are also established agents who set up manuscript critiquing businesses which have very little to do with their agencies. The manuscripts are parcelled out to hungry young college students or aspiring editors who may or may not recognize publishable literature. Many writers have coughed up substantial sums to these agencies for generally superficial critiques resulting in the writer being poorer (wiser?), and without representation.

Most agents do not have time to be editors. Their days are filled with contacting editors and negotiating contracts. There are a few who have the ability, education, and interest in working with an author on the manuscript until it is ready for submission. Rare birds these; find one if you can.

Now, let's answer the questions. *When do you need an agent?* Your search begins at the same time your novel begins. Just as you thought about and planned and researched before the opening sentences of your book were committed to paper or processed into the computer, you think about and study the agents in advance. By the time your work is finished you will need an agent. Be ready to zero in on at least five who might be interested in your manuscript. Most agents do not handle short stories — too time-consuming, too little money. They do however, read certain literary journals and often contact writers of work they admire.

How do you get an agent? First, you have to know where to find them. That's the easy part. (See the resources at end of this chapter.) But, you have already done the research while writing the book and you've targeted certain agencies. You've also learned how to write a smashing book proposal and the first three chapters of your novel are polished and really ready to go. An agent's livelihood depends on finding publishable material and (believe it or not) they are always looking. Trouble is, they thrash about constantly in a sea of manuscripts and their method of looking is to rely on recommendations and meeting writers personally (often at conferences) or responding to a fascinating query. Your assignment is to attend every writing conference or seminar you can get to which features agent panels.

You introduce yourself, if possible. You do not tell agents the story of your life or the premise of your novel. You do indicate that you've listened carefully to what they had to say and that you will take the liberty of sending a query and outline to their offices. On occasion, if you and the agent have found each other compatible a manuscript might change hands.

Just remember there is no incentive for an agent to get involved in an author's solely ego-motivated effort to break into print. On the other hand, nothing arouses agent interest more than a writer who responds to the appetites of the reading public or can supply the particular need of the marketplace and a publisher's lists. Writers, of course, must follow inner voices, but it is imperative that there be something in the work that will grab readers amidst the clamor of thousands of new titles published each year.

When you have to contact agents cold, the query letter and a brief summary of the novel is your calling card. Keep the original manuscript. Submit quality copies and enclose a self-addressed stamped envelope. Multiple submissions to a limited number of carefully chosen agents is okay. However, you will of course, address each proposal to a name. Never "Dear Agent!" And don't fuss about hearing from more than one. You'll be in the enviable position of having to choose. Allow at least one month and follow up with a note or phone call inquiring about your work.

The final question: *How to find a "good" agent?* One writer's gourmet feast can be another's deadly poison. Therefore, an agent who is good for thee might be very wrong for me. It's a serendipitous business. A little like finding the right "significant other." Obviously, every writer's fantasy is to be signed on by an agent with clout who can negotiate a big money deal at the best publishing house. And every year, a handful of first-time novelists actually experience this heady adventure. The good agent understands and believes in the writer/client's work and knows which editor is hankering for just what they've written. A good agent sells dreams, matching up your dream of getting the book published with an editor's dream of finding that special manuscript.

Let's assume you have found an agent willing, nay eager, to represent you. The deal will be consummated with a written contract or a simple handshake. Agents generally receive either 10 or 15 percent of the proceeds of sales and royalties. The good agent looks after your business interests; becomes your record keeper and collection service; chases after royalty payments; works with the publisher on subsidiary rights sales (audio, film, television, foreign, serializations). An agent is a salesperson, hired on consignment to represent you in the literary marketplace. Your apples, the agent's pushcart.

The good agent crawls over every word in the publisher's contract before you sign the document and consoles you when you are feeling crazy and cranky about the process.

Incidentally, there is a fourth question writers ask and that's about lawyers. There are literary-lawyer agents. However, a lawyer who knows nothing about the publishing business generally develops symptoms of cardiac arrest when given a publishing contract to read. Publishing negotiations are better left to experienced agents or literary legal beagles.

So back to square one. All writers agree that looking for an agent is like searching for the Holy Grail. Begin your campaign by reading *Literary Agents: How to Get and Work With the Right One For You* by Michael Larsen, and *How To Be Your Own Literary Agent* by Richard Curtis. Then check out the resources listed below. And happy hunting.

Literary Market Place — This annual directory of the American book publishing industry, which can be found in most libraries and on the desks of all literary people, has the most comprehensive list of agents.

Writer's Market — The chapter on literary agents describes the world of the agent accurately and answers questions writers should be asking. The detailed list of hundreds of agents includes information about how each of them operate.

Literary Agents: A Writer's Guide — Published by Poets & Writers, 72 Spring Street, New York NY 10012.

Literary Agents of North America — Author Aid Associates, 201 W. 54th Street, New York, NY 10019.

Writer's Guild of America — WGA East, 555 West 57th Street, New York, NY 10019. WGA West, 8955 Beverly Blvd., Los Angeles, CA 90048. Provides lists of agents who are signatories of WGA and can represent film and television writers as well as literary properties.

K E Y N O T E R

RAY BRADBURY

People always ask writers where they get their ideas. Here's Bradbury's answers:

How I get ideas? A friend called me to say he'd read in the encyclopedia about a remarkable happening one hundred years ago. When the locomotives on the Trans Egyptian Railroad ran out of fuel, they burned creosoted mummies removed from nearby crypts. I was inspired to write a poem entitled *The Nefertiti-Tut Express*. Then I recycled the idea into a screenplay and sent one copy to Alfred Hitchcock and the other to Mel Brooks.

I continue to experiment with word association. I began this in my teens, made a list of words—trapdoor, night, wind, locusts—and as years passed, I said, there is some reason I thought about these words. They keep coming back. Cinnamon is a favorite word: "cinnamon sands of Mars sweep across the landscape."

Before you're born, you're taking it all in. Five years ago, I went back to my home town of Waukegan. This barber told me that when I was three years old, I used to gather dandelions because the family used to make dandelion wine. I had been thinking this was only a memory—the wine sitting on the window shelf in the bottles, the golden sunshine streaming in, and I had written a novel about it at age twenty-five out of memory—*Dandelion Wine*. I was so relieved to learn from the barber that we actually went out and gathered dandelions and did it.

That's what we do, we dredge it up bit by bit, out of the rain barrel, the kind that used to sit outside my grandmother's house. And that's what we writers do, we go to the rain barrel and collect all the rains that fell, the clouds, the rainbows, and we dip into it, wash our hair with it. The more I dipped, the more it filled, huh?

Then in summertime, we run barefoot through the grass, take off our shoes, feel the clover and feel the stem of the clover under our feet, and it's a Braille process you're doing with your foot. The more you do this, the more you run through the grass, you run through the attic, find all the photos of the lost people, some dead, some alive. I didn't know I was writing a novel, *Dandelion Wine*. I trust the subconscious. There it was, huh?

Publicizing Fiction

*I*t seems every published writer I know has a horror story about his publisher's lack of attention to his book once it has reached publication. Once again, here is our marketing expert, Frances Halpern:

The two terrible frustrations authors experience are the manuscript unpublished and the published book unheralded. It's difficult to decide which is more traumatic to the writer—constant rejection of a work submitted or, after the euphoria of acceptance, the frantic, failed attempt to reach the audience and sell the book. A happily published book gets reviewed, moves out of the publisher's warehouse into the bookstore (or wherever books are sold), and then out again into the hands of readers. We all know the stories of the desperate author running from bookstore to bookstore unable to find a copy of the title anywhere. And so we asked Annette Swanberg, an author and independent publicist with offices in Los Angeles, to share her expertise and thoughts on publicizing fiction. Swanberg handles local and regional publicity for major publishing houses and in addition represents individual authors from all over the country.

First, a brief explanation of what a book publicist is. Most publishing houses have publicity departments staffed by people who plan campaigns for their authors. Immediately following the celebration in honor of selling the manuscript, you want to know who these folks are and whether/how they plan to promote your book. Publicists (in-house and independents) promote books and authors by soliciting television, radio, newspaper, and magazine interviews. They may also arrange bookstore promotions, speaking engagements at literary lunches or to any organization interested in hearing authors, and they coordinate the ubiquitous book tour. A particular responsibility of the publicist is to create a handsome press packet which includes the author's biography, photo, background material on the book, rave reviews (if available), and suggested questions to ask the author. The savvy publicist then mails it to carefully selected talk-show hosts, talent bookers, and feature editors at newspapers and magazines.

Publicists are not in the business of helping aspiring authors get published. That's the agent's job. Nor do publicists involve themselves in book distribution, a publisher's task.

Long before your book is finally published you should be aware of the publicity department's plans for promotion. How much money is the publisher investing? If you're lucky and shrewd, you might be able to get an advertising budget written into the book contract. However, if your publisher does not intend to promote the book (generally the case) or if the publicity department has not done the job you hoped it would, then it is time, if you can afford it, to consult with an independent book publicist.

A publicist for over ten years, Swanberg has represented major bestselling authors and many first-time novelists. The following is a memo she prepared in which she shares her practical experience on publicizing fiction.

The ultimate goal in any kind of advertising campaign is to reach people who want to know about a good novel. And publicity is not by any means the only, or in many cases, the most important channel by which to reach the potential book purchaser. Word of mouth can make a best seller. May I repeat that for emphasis. Word of mouth can make a best seller! Increasingly, in this age of hype and the belief that Andy Warhol was right about everyone being entitled to at least fifteen minutes of fame, too many authors think that unless they've appeared on a number of national talk shows, their novels will die. They see the novelist-celebrity (a Jackie Collins, a Tom Wolfe) basking in the limelight and are deluded into believing that this is the only road to success.

What are the alternatives to glitter and glitz publicity? Novelists should be reminded that the marketing and sales departments at publishing houses usually employ a wide range of highly effective techniques to excite their own sales forces, and also the distributors, wholesalers, and booksellers. These efforts, unlike those of the more highly visible publicity deparments, often go unnoticed and unappreciated by authors. Advance reading copies or galleys (the uncorrected typeset version of a book) are sent to sales representatives, key wholesale buyers, and bookstore personnel in order to build the word of mouth about a particular novel. An important point here, and one too often overlooked, is that those of us in the book business love to read books and the surest way to build momentum for a particular title is to urge others to read it. And with the right urging, we often succeed.

There will undoubtedly be a sales conference about your book and what you the author should do is offer to consult with your editor in advance of the meeting. Do you have, or can you develop a video-tape, graphics or special handout about yourself or the subject of your book that will encourage the sales force to climb on your bandwagon? You inquire tactfully about the marketing department's plans to pro-mote your title. Will there be point-of-purchase bookmarks, bookstore posters, special mailings, print advertising? A publisher who believes strongly in a first novel may decide to put its marketing resources into print advertising. They may opt for an ad in *The New York Times* book section which costs a great deal of money rather than invest in a pub-licity campaign. Depending on the circumstances, this might be a very wise expenditure of usually limited funds. If the publisher decides on an all-out publicity approach, the author must be prepared to endure some crazy travel schedules and be charming and articulate at all hours of the day or night in the process of selling the book. Most writers are willing victims.

A publicity campaign for fiction is a challenge. Interviews on radio and television or with newspaper or magazine editors frankly are diffi-cult to obtain. Many media people don't like to interview authors of fiction because they fear there won't be enough fireworks to keep the audience tuned in or they worry about giving away the book's plot. And most media people find it easier to interview nonfiction or celeb-rity authors rather than do some homework to find out what's inter-esting about a fiction writer.

How do we overcome the media bias against novelists? We re-search every angle. We phone our media contacts and attempt to convince them that our novelist-client is lively, quotable, and person-able. We do not book tongue-tied or painfully shy authors on talk shows. It would do them an injustice and impair our credibility as competent publicists. Authors with an unusual or interesting back-ground or area of expertise can be more easily marketed to the media. For example, a writer of crime thrillers who is a former secret service agent will have a better chance of getting publicity than one who is merely a very talented writer. A novel with a good nonfiction "hook" is a candidate for the talk and interview circuit. If the subject of your novel coincidentally deals with a current big news story or on-going political, health, or environmental problem everyone is talking about, your publicist may book you onto some very effective national shows.

To sum up . . . it is not easy to schedule interviews for novelists (particularly a first-timer). But it's not impossible either. Perhaps the author had some great adventures while researching the novel or a little digging uncovers intriguing tidbits about the writer's life. Anything about the book or its creator which will engage the interest of media people and finally their audiences is grist for the publicists' mill.

The self-promoting author

Let's face it. You're a writer who can't afford your own personal Annette Swanberg. Your publisher is moving the novel through the production process and you have been told, emphatically, "There will be no promotion money." But you worked so hard writing the manuscript and getting it published, you are determined to have your novel find its market. Perhaps this is your first published novel and you have not been designated this year's Cinderella or Horatio Alger. You are somewhere down there in the mid-list category getting the average author treatment. No reflection on your writing ability. You're going to be ignored and you thought publishers were in business to sell books. Yes, they are. But they have peculiar ways of showing it. When your book comes out, you are probably going to be the only one interested in beating the drums. Oh, your title will be listed in the publisher's catalog and shown around by the sales reps. Obviously, that isn't enough. Unless you are already writing your next opus, plan some time for marketing.

You are going to do exactly what professional publicists do only not on quite so grand a scale. You switch from fiction to investigative reporter and discover the process of taking a book to market as long before publication date as possible.

Whether you have written a mainstream, literary or category novel, can we hope you have joined and participated in a number of national and local writers organizations? That you have been poring over their newsletters, studying *Publishers Weekly* magazine, Don Poynter's *Self-Publishing Manual,* and *Literary Market Place* so that you are knowledgable about the business of publishing?

With some understanding of the circuitous route a book can travel from printing press to bookseller's shelves, you begin to ponder on who is your audience. Naturally, the most significant way to create demand for a title is to deliver the goods, have an appealing book the public will want to read. And now, on with the campaign.

Are you a bookstore/library loiterer? Have you browsed regularly at a number of independent and chain booksellers, made friends with the owners and staff, purchased books and cards and magazines? You don't want to show up a total stranger and announce you are a new author looking for favors. Because you are going to ask these booksellers most graciously, whether you can host an autograph party, pay for some refreshments and get your friends and family into the store.

You will have postcards, flyers (perhaps a copy of your book cover), and press releases printed. Mail the cards to every contact you've ever made. Distribute the flyers to as many bookstores as possible. Send the press releases about your book signing to the columnists and events sections of the local newspapers. Don't blather on. Simply say, (your name) of (where you live) will be signing (name of book), a novel about (brief description) at (name of bookstore and locale). Add one or two lines about yourself. No more. And include a phone number so that you can be reached for further information.

Continue to call in at bookstores and tactfully ask whether the book is selling and being restocked. Chat with the manager when things are quiet and find out how the microfiche works, which wholesalers and distributors carry your book, who your publisher's sales rep is.

Offer to speak at writing conferences, libraries, college writing classes, service organizations, any group that might be interested in you as a writer and the content of your book. You should purchase enough books from your publisher (at a deep discount) so that they will be available for sale to groups you address. Or if you prefer, sign out as many as you might need from your favorite bookstore. The manager, grateful for whatever you've sold, will simply return the remaining books to the shelves.

For possible radio and television appearances and articles about you in the local newspapers and magazines, get up-to-date media lists of the hosts and producers and editors. Send this to your publisher's publicity department and urge them to mail review copies of your book to the people on the list or directly to you so that you can deliver them personally. The whole exercise is to alert the local media that you exist and what might follow are articles about you and an opportunity to get the word out about the novel.

And finally, still in the role of investigative reporter, you research the awards and honors available to published authors. They are legion and in every category. What could be more rewarding than to call attention to your novel by winning a prestigious prize? Private and government foundations, publishers, writer's associations, corporations and newspapers are among the groups who bestow money and honors on authors every year. Your publisher may not know about some of these awards. Alert them and hope they judge your title worthy of entering the competition. There are books published about contests, awards, and grants specifically established for writers.

In conclusion, it is understood that a sensitive or shy author might feel, "No way, I cannot involve myself in this process. I'll just hope for the best and wait patiently for those twice-a-year royalty checks and get on with my next book." But at least you are now aware of the marketing and hype, the publicity and advertising, which may or may not make this merchandise, your novel, into a critical or commercial success.

IRVING STONE

Storytelling is as old as men. What they didn't know they made up. There is no difference between fiction and fact.

First of all what do I mean by human stories? It is a story that has universal appeal. It is a universal man or woman. What does that mean?

It means that if you are a writer of books it is your duty to write stories about all ages, all peoples, all cultures, religions, all colors, all creeds, so that if you read a hundred of these — let's say they are biographical novels, since that is my cup of tea — you will have lived the entire life of man since man became man. And that is a tremendous experience.

In a biography you have three persons involved: You have the hero or heroine, you have the author in the middle, and you have the reader. And these three persons will go down parallel tracks, but they will almost never merge so that you can read this intellectually but not emotionally.

In a biographical novel there is only one person involved. How do we do that? Because my job, as I perceive it, is to go wherever my story is laid. Because I the author must become the main character. I must live inside his skin with his bones and his blood and his spirit and his brains. I have to read every letter he ever wrote or received. Every note he ever put into a diary or journal. Every action that man or that woman ever took I must know about, and after I know about it, I must absorb it. So that *I* am the one doing this act or feeling this feeling or thinking this thought, or creating whatever is being created.

The reason I want to do this is because by the time the readers get to page two or three, I want them to forget their name, their calling, their occupation, the fact that it's 1987 and we're here in Santa Barbara and I want the reader — I must have the reader — to become Vincent van Gogh or Mary Todd Lincoln or Sigmund Freud. The reason being that I don't want you to read intellectually, but emotionally. That you become that character going through all of his defeats, all the despairs, all the depressions, all of the annihilation, but at the same time all of the exaltations, and all of the victories, and all of the gratifications, and all of the creativity.

I think this is the reason for any success that I have: I keep demanding to find things. Other people say, "Well, this isn't important" or "We don't know how to do that" or "We're not interested in this." I have a thousand *whys* below the surface *why*, and I am determined that I should have everything in my hero or my heroine's life so that I can absorb it, become the person, and enable the reader to become that persona and live that life.

We keep a complete weather report for all the years of our book even if it's thirty or forty years. It took us days and weeks and months to make sure that when we staged something on a day, we knew what the weather was. And that's how we make these books.

THIRTY-ONE

In Conclusion

D eciding to be a writer and actually *becoming* a writer are two
different stages. Charles Champlin told the Conference of a
friend of his who once asked Robert Frost when he decided to be a
poet. "My dear," he answered, "when did you decide to become a
beautiful woman?"

On the same subject Arnold Bennett said:

There will come a day, if you persist, when your pen will move
nimbly and you will feel elated, and exclaim to yourself: "*Now* I
know that I can write."

I wanted to be a writer at a very young age, but becoming a writer
took a series of important painful stages. It came to me one day after
about three years of hard work. One morning I just said to hell with
Fitzgerald, Faulkner, and Hemingway and the way they said it, I'm
going to say it my way, tell my story just as it bubbles up out of me,
from deep down in the truth of me. I hope it comes to you sooner. At
a recent Conference Ray Bradbury said: "It should come from deep
inside you—you should go to the typewriter every morning and throw
up—then clean it up every afternoon. I want the truth to come out. I
want that great stuff from your gut to come out. I don't want you to
intellectualize—*don't think!*—I have had a sign on my typewriter for
twenty years that says 'Don't think—do it!' "

When I was sixteen Stewart Edward White, whom I mentioned in
the introduction of this book, lived across the canyon from us in what
was then thinly populated, rural Hillsborough, California. He was the
Ernest Hemingway of his day, big game hunter, explorer, one of the
first millionaire writers with his thirty-some adventure novels (and
daring books into metaphysics). One day I showed him a story I had

written for my school's literary magazine. I watched him read it anxiously. We were in his studio surrounded by a taxidermed pride of lions, a leaping leopard that had clawed him almost to death, and a full-sized giraffe. He was sort of a god to me.

When he finished the last page he merely thrust out his hand and said: "Welcome to the club!"

Then he added: "But if you can be anything else in this life, *be* it. Writing is hard."

I like what Sidney Sheldon quoted in an earlier chapter: "A blank piece of paper is God's way of telling us how hard it is to be God."

E. L. Doctorow has said:

"Writing a novel is like driving a car at night. You can see only as far as your headlights, but you can make the whole trip that way."

When Sinclair Lewis told one of his Yale English teachers that he wanted to be a writer, the man said: "But you will starve!"

"I don't care," said Lewis.

"Then you will succeed," said the teacher.

Like Lewis — and me — you will probably disregard any advice to quit writing. And more power and luck to you.

Truman Capote said: "Finishing a book is just like you took a child out in the back yard and shot it."

But this book is coming to an end.

On the final day of our Conferences I like to read a passage from James Michener's *Fires of Spring* that never fails to move me. It doesn't have much to do with writing specifically, but it does have a lot to do with life, and, really, aren't they the same?

For this is the journey that men make: to find themselves.

If they fail in this, it doesn't matter much what else they find.

Money, position, fame, many loves, revenge are all of little consequence, and when the tickets are collected at the end of the ride they are tossed into the bin marked FAILURE.

But if a man happens to find himself — if he knows what he can be depended upon to do, the limits of his courage, the positions from which he will no longer retreat, the degree to which he can surrender his inner life to some woman, the secret reservoirs of his determination, the extent of his dedication, the depth of his feeling for beauty, his honest and unpostured goals — then he has found a mansion which he can inhabit with dignity all the days of his life.

NOW IT'S UP TO YOU

So, what are you waiting for? Get to work on that story or novel!

And whenever you get really down and discouraged, read and

reread these lines from the diary of a guy named John Steinbeck as he struggled, like you, with his daily writing on a novel.

No one else knows my lack of ability the way I do . . . Sometimes, I seem to do a good little piece of work, but when it is done it slides into mediocrity.

Got her done. And I'm afraid she's a little dull.

My many weaknesses are beginning to show their heads.

My work is no good, I think — I'm desperately upset about it . . . I'm slipping. I've been slipping all my life.

Young man wants to talk, wants to be a writer. What could I tell him? Not a writer myself yet.

I am sure of one thing — it isn't the great book I had hoped it would be. It's just a run-of-the-mill book. And the awful thing is that it is absolutely the best I can do.

Steinbeck wrote this book we're talking about in five months, beginning in May and ending in late October 1938, writing in longhand and producing 2,000 words a day, the equivalent of seven double-spaced typed pages, an enormous output for any writer, and ultimately a daily *tour de force*. But at the same time he was flagellating himself like this also:

Vacillating and miserable . . . I'm so lazy, so damned lazy.

Where has my discipline gone? Have I lost control?

My laziness is overwhelming.

This novel would be his ninth work of fiction in ten years, and he would be thirty-seven years old at its publication. It was called *The Grapes of Wrath.*

So what are *you* complaining about? Hit those keys, that computer, or that yellow pad. Don't be a writer who talks at conferences and parties about the great short stories and novels he's *going* to write. *Write 'em!* As Hemingway wrote to Fitzgerald in 1927: "However am now going to write a swell novel—will not talk about it on acct. the greater ease of talking about it than writing it and consequent danger of doing same."

When I was starting in to write, my older brother used to read my stuff, shake his head, and say: "If I only wrote I could write so much better than you."

And he was probably right, because he had a rare gift with words, but we'll never know because he never got around to writing; it was safer that way. Why take a chance of the product's turning out badly? Why risk rejection, criticism, and even scorn?

Erica Jong went for years not finishing anything: "Because, of course, when you finish something you can be judged . . . I had poems which were rewritten so many times I suspect it was just a way of avoiding sending them out."

The old-time humorist, George Ade, had a mother who used to tell the world: "Everyone says they can write better than George does—but George *does!*"

Yea, verily, I say unto you, go forth and doeth as George doeth!

K E Y N O T E R

IRVING STONE

Let us give the very last words to this enormously popular writer who in 1987 addressed the Santa Barbara Writers' Conference thus:

What is a writer? A writer is a seer, a prophet, an alchemist, creating wisdom where none existed before. The writer is an entertainer, but hopefully not a court jester. The writer is a bringer of order out of chaos. And the writer is a creator of new religions, new governments, new mentalities, new cultures and social patterns. The writer is a midwife giving birth to new civilizations and an undertaker burying the old ones. The writer is an archeologist uncovering layers of the past, and a sculptor giving form to the unmolded and uncoalesced materials of life. The writer is a destroyer, putting to the sword and fire old shibboleths, ancient fears, tribal myths, falsehoods that have paraded as truths for thousands of years. A writer is a warrior fighting to possess human minds and a composer attempting to capture the music of life for a tone-deaf world. The writer is a poet, trying to compress the complexity and confusion of a spent life into exit lines that scan and perhaps even rhyme. The writer is an explorer, penetrating impassable jungles, traversing mountain ranges, which start at the peak of Mount Everest, searching for regions where man can live in dignity. A writer is a philosopher, attempting to extract the meaning of life from the passing hurricane. And the writer is an interpreter, reducing to simple language the ultimate designs of God, the devil, and fate. The writer is a mirror in which all humankind can see themselves reflected all too clearly. A writer is a seducer, attempting to break young people to pleasure, and an encyclopedia which knows everything and understands nothing. A writer is a sieve, allowing all thoughts and ideas to pour through him or her. A writer is a doctor, prescribing pills whose contents have not been tested, for patients whose ills cannot be fathomed. And the writer is a catalyst, bringing together people and visions who would otherwise not have bowed to each other while passing on the street. A writer is an aging athlete required to break the four-minute mile every morning. And the writer is a deep-sea diver who comes up with priceless treasures from the deep until the day when someone or something fouls the oxygen line. The writer is a scientist working without equipment in a dark room or a giant redwood forest trying to find new meanings of life. The writer is a psychiatrist going behind the insanity of the modern world to chart the trails whereby we have reached the sanitarium and the paths out of it. And finally the writer is a dinosaur, extinct for thousands of years yet believing because he has a shinbone and a piece of jaw he is still a monumental creature.

The End

Other Books of Interest

Annual Market Books

Children's Writer's & Illustrator's Market, edited by Lisa Carpenter (paper) $17.95
Guide to Literary Agents & Art/Photo Reps, edited by Robin Gee $15.95
Humor & Cartoon Markets, edited by Bob Staake (paper) $16.95
Novel & Short Story Writer's Market, edited by Robin Gee (paper) $19.95
Photographer's Market, edited by Sam Marshall $21.95
Poet's Market, by Judson Jerome $19.95
Songwriter's Market, edited by Brian Rushing $19.95
Writer's Market, edited by Mark Kissling $25.95

General Writing Books

Beginning Writer's Answer Book, edited by Kirk Polking (paper) $13.95
Discovering the Writer Within, by Bruce Ballenger & Barry Lane $17.95
Freeing Your Creativity, by Marshall Cook $17.95
Getting the Words Right: How to Rewrite, Edit and Revise, by Theodore A. Rees Cheney (paper) $12.95
How to Write a Book Proposal, by Michael Larsen (paper) $10.95
Just Open a Vein, edited by William Brohaugh $15.95
Knowing Where to Look: The Ultimate Guide to Research, by Lois Horowitz (paper) $16.95
Make Your Words Work, by Gary Provost $17.95
Pinckert's Practical Grammar, by Robert C. Pinckert (paper) $11.95
12 Keys to Writing Books That Sell, by Kathleen Krull (paper) $12.95
The 28 Biggest Writing Blunders, by William Noble $12.95
The 29 Most Common Writing Mistakes & How to Avoid Them, by Judy Delton (paper) $9.95
The Wordwatcher's Guide to Good Writing & Grammar, by Morton S. Freeman (paper) $15.95
Word Processing Secrets for Writers, by Michael A. Banks & Ansen Dibell (paper) $14.95
The Writer's Book of Checklists, by Scott Edelstein $16.95
The Writer's Digest Guide to Manuscript Formats, by Buchman & Groves $18.95
The Writer's Essential Desk Reference, edited by Glenda Neff $19.95

Fiction Writing

The Art & Craft of Novel Writing, by Oakley Hall $17.95
Best Stories from New Writers, edited by Linda Sanders $5.99
Characters & Viewpoint, by Orson Scott Card $13.95
Cosmic Critiques: How & Why 10 Science Fiction Stories Work, edited by Asimov & Greenberg (paper) $12.95
Creating Characters: How to Build Story People, by Dwight V. Swain $16.95
Creating Short Fiction, by Damon Knight (paper) $10.95
Dialogue, by Lewis Turco $13.95
The Fiction Writer's Silent Partner, by Martin Roth $19.95
Handbook of Short Story Writing: Vol. I, by Dickson and Smythe (paper) $10.95
Handbook of Short Story Writing: Vol. II, edited by Jean Fredette (paper) $12.95
How to Write & Sell Your First Novel, by Collier & Leighton (paper) $12.95
Manuscript Submission, by Scott Edelstein $13.95
Mastering Fiction Writing, by Kit Reed $18.95
Plot, by Ansen Dibell $13.95
Spider Spin Me a Web: Lawrence Block on Writing Fiction, by Lawrence Block $16.95
Theme & Strategy, by Ronald B. Tobias $13.95
The 38 Most Common Writing Mistakes, by Jack M. Bickham $12.95
Writer's Digest Handbook of Novel Writing, $18.95
Writing the Novel: From Plot to Print, by Lawrence Block (paper) $11.95

Special Interest Writing Books

Armed & Dangerous: A Writer's Guide to Weapons, by Michael Newton (paper) $14.95
The Children's Picture Book: How to Write It, How to Sell It, by Ellen E.M. Roberts (paper) $19.95
Comedy Writing Secrets, by Mel Helitzer (paper) $15.95
Creating Poetry, by John Drury $18.95

Deadly Doses: A Writer's Guide to Poisons, by Serita Deborah Stevens with Anne Klarner (paper) $16.95

Families Writing, by Peter Stillman (paper) $12.95

A Guide to Travel Writing & Photography, by Ann & Carl Purcell (paper) $22.95

Hillary Waugh's Guide to Mysteries & Mystery Writing, by Hillary Waugh $19.95

How to Pitch & Sell Your TV Script, by David Silver $17.95

How to Write Action/Adventure Novels, by Michael Newton $4.99

How to Write & Sell True Crime, by Gary Provost $17.95

How to Write Horror Fiction, by William F. Nolan $15.95

How to Write Mysteries, by Shannon OCork $13.95

How to Write Romances, by Phyllis Taylor Pianka $15.95

How to Write Science Fiction & Fantasy, by Orson Scott Card $13.95

How to Write Tales of Horror, Fantasy & Science Fiction, edited by J.N. Williamson (paper) $12.95

How to Write the Story of Your Life, by Frank P. Thomas (paper) $11.95

How to Write Western Novels, by Matt Braun $1.00

Mystery Writer's Handbook, by The Mystery Writers of America (paper) $11.95

The Poet's Handbook, by Judson Jerome (paper) $11.95

Successful Scriptwriting, by Jurgen Wolff & Kerry Cox (paper) $14.95

The Writer's Complete Crime Reference Book, by Martin Roth $19.95

Writing for Children & Teenagers, 3rd Edition, by Lee Wyndham & Arnold Madison (paper) $12.95

Writing Mysteries: A Handbook by the Mystery Writers of America, Edited by Sue Grafton, $18.95

Writing the Modern Mystery, by Barbara Norville (paper) $12.95

The Writing Business

A Beginner's Guide to Getting Published, edited by Kirk Polking (paper) $11.95

Business & Legal Forms for Authors & Self-Publishers, by Tad Crawford (paper) $4.99

The Complete Guide to Self-Publishing, by Tom & Marilyn Ross (paper) $16.95

How You Can Make $25,000 a Year Writing, by Nancy Edmonds Hanson (paper) $14.95

This Business of Writing, by Gregg Levoy $19.95

Writer's Guide to Self-Promotion & Publicity, by Elane Feldman $16.95

Writing A to Z, edited by Kirk Polking $22.95

To order directly from the publisher, include $3.00 postage and handling for 1 book and $1.00 for each additional book. Allow 30 days for delivery.

Writer's Digest Books
1507 Dana Avenue, Cincinnati, Ohio 45207
Credit card orders call TOLL-FREE
1-800-289-0963
Prices subject to change without notice.

Write to this same address for information on *Writer's Digest* magazine, *Story* magazine, Writer's Digest Book Club, Writer's Digest School, and Writer's Digest Criticism Service.